'9L

SATHER CLASSICAL LECTURES

VOLUME EIGHT

1932

THE MYCENAEAN ORIGIN

OF

GREEK MYTHOLOGY

THE MYCENAEAN ORIGIN

OF

GREEK MYTHOLOGY

BY

MARTIN P. NILSSON

PROFESSOR OF CLASSICAL ARCHAEOLOGY AND
ANCIENT HISTORY IN THE UNIVERSITY OF LUND,
SATHER PROFESSOR OF CLASSICAL LITERATURE
IN THE UNIVERSITY OF CALIFORNIA
1930-31

UNIVERSITY OF CALIFORNIA PRESS
BERKELEY, CALIFORNIA
1932

Printed in the United States of America
by Joseph W. Flinn, University Printer

CONTENTS

CHAPTER I

HOW OLD IS GREEK MYTHOLOGY?

The question: *How old is Greek mythology?* may at first sight seem idle, for Greek mythology is obviously of many different ages. For example, many genealogies and eponymous heroes created for political purposes are late, such inventions having been made through the whole historical age of Greece; yet most of them are earlier than the very late myths like the campaigns of Dionysus, or the great mass of the metamorphoses, especially the catasterisms, which were invented in the Hellenistic age. The great tragic poets reshaped the myths and left their imprint upon them, so that the forms in which the myths are commonly known nowadays often have been given them by tragedy. Similarly, before the tragic poets, the choric lyric poets reshaped them. The cyclical epics also are thought to have exercised a profound influence upon the remodeling of the myths. In Homer we find many well-known myths, often in forms differing, however, from those in which they are related later. Finally, it cannot be doubted that myths existed before Homer.

Our question concerns, however, not the reshaping and remodeling of myths, which often consists only of an imitation of current patterns, but the real creation of myths, especially the creation of the great cycles of myths. From this standpoint, the Hellenistic and many earlier myths may be put to

one side. The tragic poets hardly invent new myths
but do reshape old ones, often in a very thorough
fashion, and the same is to be said of the choric
lyric poets. For the glory and fame of ancient
poets depended not, like that of modern poets, on
their invention of something quite new and original,
but rather on their presentation of the old traditional
material in new and original fashion.

Consequently our question concerns the old stock
of mythology after all secondary inventions have
been discarded and is really not so idle as may appear
at first glance. In fact various attempts have been
made to give an answer, although the question has
not been put so simply and straightforwardly as it
is here, but has been enveloped in inquiries and
reasonings having other purposes. The point, however, which I wish to emphasize is the importance
of the principles which underlie our research and
determine our procedure.

I pass over comparative mythology very lightly,
because it began to lose favor in my youth, thirty
years ago or more, and nowadays is very little
reckoned with in scientific discussion. But I should
like to draw attention to one point of some interest
in this connection. Comparative mythology was
so called because it compared Greek myths with
those of other Aryan peoples and by this means
tried to discover the original myths and religion of
the Aryan people from whom the peoples of Europe
and some peoples of Asia are descended, just as
comparative philology discovered by similar means
that the languages of these peoples were derived
from the language once spoken by the old Aryans.

The underlying supposition was clearly that the Greek myths were pre-Greek in the sense that the Greeks had taken them over from the Aryans and brought them with them when they immigrated into Greece. Comparative mythology overlooked, however, the very important distinction between divine and heroic mythology and thought erroneously that the heroic myths were derived from the same source as the myths concerning the gods. This source it found in the phenomena of nature. If the view of comparative mythology were right, these lectures would really be pointless, for then it must needs be admitted that Greek mythology existed not only in the pre-Homeric age but also before the Greeks immigrated into Greece. But since the seventies of the last century the whole problem has been extraordinarily deepened and complicated. We have learned to distinguish between religion and mythology and we have learned to know a new epoch of Greece which cannot be considered as wholly prehistoric in the usual sense of the word— the Mycenaean age.

Max Müller and his followers condemned Euhemerism, but this theory has come to the fore again in recent years. In my opinion the reaction is just but goes too far. Certain English scholars take mythology as reproducing actual historical facts, just as the logographers did when they brought the myths into a historical system. They do not, of course, overlook the fabulous elements of the myths but think that the mythical persons and such exploits as are not of a fabulous character are good history, and they go so far as to accept without question the

mythical genealogies and the mythical chronology.
I am unable to do this. I know and appreciate the
tenacity of folk memory, but I know also how
popular tradition is preserved—and confused and
remodeled. The remodeling affects especially the
chronological relations of the personages, which are
changed freely.[1] In so far as epical tradition is
concerned, the right analogy is not the traditions
which have an historical aspect but the Nibelungenlied and the Beowulf and similar epical traditions
which I shall characterize later. We know how
badly historical connections fared in them, how
history was confused and mixed up with fabulous
elements. If good historical tradition is to be preserved, an undisturbed life both in regard to settling
and to civilization is an absolute condition, but the
downfall of the Mycenaean civilization was a most
stormy and turbulent age, and its turmoils, which
mixed up the Greek tribes and changed their places
of settlement, mixed up and confused their traditions,
too. The historical aspect of Greek mythology and
especially the mythical chronology are products of
the systematizing of the myths by the poets of
cyclical epics and still more the product of rationali-
zation and historification by the logographers.[2]

[1] See my article "Ueber die Glaubwürdigkeit der Volksüberlieferung
bes. in Bezug auf die alte Geschichte" in the Italian periodical *Scientia*,
1930, pp. 319 *et seq.*

[2] The lectures of one of my predecessors in the Sather professorship,
Professor Myres, came into my hands through the kindness of the author
after my lectures had already been written down. Professor Myres
thinks that heroic genealogy makes up a fairly reliable chronological
scheme. My different standpoint I hope to justify in the following
pages. I have tried to take justly into account the circumstances of
time, of popular tradition, and of the transmission of epic poetry.

A very different standpoint is taken by German scholars, whose preoccupation is a historical treatment of the myths; in opposition to the theories of comparative mythology, this school is called the historical school. The answer given by this school is not so simple as that proposed by nature mythology. I must therefore try to clear up the underlying principles to the best of my ability, although the numerous works of the school often are contradictory in details and it is very difficult to do full justice in a short analysis of principles.

The historical school acknowledges that elements of myths existed in an early period, before the development of epic poetry, but supposes that these rather simple elements were brought into connection with one another and composed so·as to form more complex myths through the agency of poetry. From this process a very deep-going reshaping and even creation of myths resulted. The poetry to which this creative expanding of mythology is ascribed is the epic poetry; viz., the Homeric and post-Homeric epics, the cyclical epics, and many lost epics of which we have only a scanty and fragmentary knowledge. Further, it is reasonably inferred that epics existed also before Homer and were used in composing the extant Homeric poems.

The historical school assumes not only a remodeling and reshaping of myths but indeed a creation of cycles of myths—and that is what concerns us here—for it is supposed that the mythical cycles came into being through the union of various simple mythical elements. If this process were ascribed to the Mycenaean age, I should have little to say

6 HOW OLD IS GREEK MYTHOLOGY?

against it; but as it is ascribed to the Homeric and the immediately preceding and following periods, I must disagree. I shall use a few examples to illustrate the methods of the historical school and the discrepancies to which they lead.

Several years ago Professor Friedländer tried to trace the development of the Heracles cycle.[3] According to his theory, the fundamental fact is the belief of the Tirynthians in their helpful hero. From the Peloponnese, Heracles emigrated to the island of Rhodes and here new adventures were added to those which had been brought from the Peloponnese. Thus the cycle of the twelve adventures was developed and formed on Rhodes.

The most comprehensive and significant example, however, is Professor Bethe's attempt to explain the origin and development of the Trojan cycle.[4] He finds the old kernels of this cycle in the duels between heroes who, according to him, were originally localized on the mainland of Greece. These simple and unconnected myths were brought to Aeolia by the different tribes to which the heroes belonged when these tribes immigrated to northwest Asia Minor shortly before or in the seventh century B. C. The Aeolians brought their Achilles, the Locrians their Aias, the Arcadians Aeneas, and the Troes, who originally were a tribe living in the mother country, the name of the Troes (Trojans), etc. The various myths of the various immigrant tribes met and were fused in Aeolia and were attached to

[3] P. Friedländer, "Herakles," *Philologische Untersuchungen*, H. XIX (1907).

[4] E. Bethe, *Homer*, I–III (1914–27; Vol. II, ed. 2, with only slight additions, 1929).

the ruins of the city of Ilion. In this manner the Trojan cycle was created. The destruction of the sixth city of Troy is ascribed to barbarians immigrating from the north. If this view of the development of Homeric poetry were right, it would of course imply not a reshaping but an actual creation of myths, for the fundamental idea of the Trojan cycle would be due to the epic poets of the seventh century B. C. Although space forbids my entering upon a criticism, I cannot but point to the improbability involved in assuming three different waves of immigration into Aeolia about which tradition is absolutely silent. They are invented only in order to suit a hypothesis which is very artificial and has not succeeded in gaining approval.

Another great scholar, Professor Wilamowitz, differs from Professor Bethe in the analysis of the poems but takes the same point of view in regard to the development of the myths. In a recent paper[5] he states briefly that Phthiotians and Magnesians who emigrated from Thessaly to Aeolia brought Achilles with them; that the house of Agamemnon originated at Cyme and in Lesbos, whilst his appearing as king on the mainland of Greece is due to epic poetry; and that Ionians, in whose towns descendants of Glaucus and Sarpedon were rulers, introduced these heroes into the epos. But, and in this he differs essentially from Professor Bethe, who takes the Trojan war to be an invention of the seventh century B. C., he gives voice to the opinion that the historical fact underlying the

[5] U. v. Wilamowitz-Moellendorff, "Die griechische Heldensage, II," *Sitzungsberichte der preussischen Akademie der Wissenschaften*, 1925, p. 241.

Homeric story of the Trojan war was an old one, a
vain attempt of the Greeks to gain a foothold in the
Scamander Valley.

The underlying presumption is an echo of the
tribal mythology of K. O. Müller, the founder of the
historical school. The leading idea is that the myths
were transferred to other regions with the wanderings
of the tribes and that, as the tribes met and mixed,
their myths met and were fused. If this leading
principle were applied to Teutonic epics, we must
needs date the Scandinavian invasion of England
two or three centuries earlier than it actually took
place, for Beowulf tells only of Danes, Swedes, and
Geatas, nothing of the English. And we must needs
assume an immigration of Teutonic tribes from the
Continent to Scandinavia before the ninth or tenth
century A. D. in order to explain the fact that the
myth of Sigurd appears in the Edda songs. I omit
the Russian *bylinas* and their wanderings. I cannot
but think that in regard to the wanderings of myths
and songs, conditions in Greece were not altogether
dissimilar to those in other countries. Consequently
I cannot but suppose that even in Greece myths and
songs wandered independently of the wanderings of
the tribes. As soon as we know anything of the
minstrels, we find that they are wandering people.
The localizations of cults and heroes must be regarded
with a critical eye and must not be used as arguments
unless their reliability is tested, for they are often
due to the influence of epics. The localizations of
Agamemnon are illuminating examples to which I
shall recur in another place.[6]

[6] Below pp. 148 *et seq.*

All that we know of other epics tends to show that the fundamental principle, the doctrine that the wanderings and the amalgamating of the myths depend on the wanderings and the amalgamating of the tribes, is erroneous. With this presumption another is connected which, according to my view, is the fundamental error of the method; namely, that two things are identified which must be distinguished—the development of the myths and the development of epic poetry. Moreover, epic poetry is taken into account only to the extent to which it can be reached through an analysis of the extant poems and fragments. It has very often been said that a lost epos of Heracles created the cycle of Heracles, and this may seem not improbable in this case where we do not have the epos but are free to reconstruct it according to our fancy. The attempt to carry through the same idea in regard to the Trojan cycle proved to be a failure and showed the frailty of the principle, for in this case we have the epos and can use it as a control. To take another instance, Professor Wilamowitz contends that the bravery of Diomedes is the oldest song of the Iliad and an imitation of the Thebais.[7] If this is true, it is extremely remarkable that the Theban myths in Homer and Hesiod differ so markedly from the common version.[8] The unavoidable conclusion would be that the Thebais, supposed to be earlier than Homer, has not been able to impress its version either upon Homer or upon Hesiod. Wild shoots of the myth have lived in spite of epical cultivation.

[7] U. v. Wilamowitz-Moellendorff, *Die Ilias und Homer* (1916), p. 339.

[8] *Il.* xxiii, v. 676 *et seq.*; Hesiod, *Erga*, v. 161 *et seq.*

The fundamental but hardly expressed principle underlying the work of the historical school is that a mythological cycle is created and developed through the agency of and contemporaneously with the development of epic poetry; and furthermore, only that epic poetry is taken into account of which we have some knowledge through literary sources. But this principle does not stand the test. The opposite alternative also must be considered; namely, that a cycle of myths existed in its chief outlines and was the store from which the Homeric poets drew, of course not without remodeling the material, in composing their chants. If this view is accepted, the epic poets followed the same line as the choric lyric and the tragic poets, who took over and utilized the old store of myths, remodeling them, sometimes profoundly. This is the case with epic poetry in countries where our knowledge of its development is fuller than is our knowledge of the development of the Greek epics. Neither of the two alternatives is strictly demonstrable, but it ought to be evident that both are to be taken into consideration.

The view of the development of mythology which I have tried to characterize here is, however, closely bound up with the methods of Homeric research prevailing among the scholars who have adopted it; namely, with the literary analysis of the poems. In England and America this method is now little heeded, and Homeric research follows different lines. I think in fact that full justice has hardly been done to this method and the many works produced by its adherents. In spite of the apparent discrepancies in their results, they have brought about a pro-

founder apprehension of Homer and Homeric prob-
lems and have obtained important results. But
literary analysis is not the last word in the Homeric
question. To shut our eyes to a further development
than that which can be traced through literary
analysis leads us astray, if the earlier development is
regarded as irrelevant because it is hard to unravel.
Such a standpoint is unjustifiable, but it is in fact
taken up by those who ascribe the development of
the mythical cycles to the Homeric and post-Homeric
periods, neglecting what may have happened in an
earlier age of which no literary records are preserved.
The Homeric question must be widened so as to be
the epic question. The proverb says: *vixere etiam
ante Agamemnona fortes viri;* I think: *vixere etiam
ante Homerum poetae.* Homeric poetry is an issue
of countless generations. That is recognized,
generally speaking, but we must try to work out in
earnest the implications of this thesis.

The gap is apparent if the two following questions
are put side by side: *How far can literary analysis
be carried back?* and *How old are the oldest elements in
Homeric poetry which can be dated with certainty?*

Literary analysis discovers earlier poems which the
Homeric poets utilized and partly took over in
composing their poems. Not even the most zealous
unitarians deny that such poems may have existed.
Nobody will of course believe that these earlier
poems were written down, so that they could have
been preserved for a long time. But if they were
preserved by the memory of the minstrels and
handed down by oral tradition, it is difficult to
imagine that they survived more than two or at most

three generations. However, I have nothing against
granting them a life of four or five generations,
although that they survived so long seems extremely
unlikely. The unavoidable conclusion is that the
earliest poems incorporated in the Homeric poems
and utilized in their composition cannot be more
than a century or a little more older than the Homeric
poems themselves. That is the limit which literary
analysis cannot transgress.

Archaeology affords means of dating certain
elements appearing in Homeric poetry. The latest
of these elements belong to the Orientalizing period;
here we are concerned with the oldest. These go
back to the Mycenaean age and moreover, what is
most remarkable, many of them to its earliest phase.[9]
At this point a few hints concerning this important
subject must suffice. Homeric arms have given rise
to a vast literature, and Nestor's cup is often mentioned; yet the body shield was already superseded
by the small shield in late Mycenaean times—the
attempts to vindicate it for later periods are proved
by archaeology to be futile. Nestor's cup was found
in the fourth shaft-grave at Mycenae, one of the
earlier group. To this another most remarkable
observation is to be added; namely, that these
Mycenaean elements appear not only in the earliest
and earlier parts of the Homeric poems but in the
latest and later parts also. For example, the boars'
tusk helmet which we had been unable to understand
until aided by the Mycenaean finds is described in
one of the very latest parts, the lay of Dolon.

[9] H. L. Lorimer, "Defensive Armour in Homer," *Liverpool Annals
of Archaeology and Anthropology*, XV (1928), pp. 89 *et seq.*; and "Homer's
Use of the Past," *Journal of Hellenic Studies*, XLIX (1929), pp. 145 *et seq.*

Archaeology is, however, not the sole means of dating some elements of Homeric poetry; there are also references to conditions of history and civilization which may serve the same end. When we meet the Phoenicians as masters of the sea and traders who bring the most appreciated and valuable articles to Greece, we recognize of course the end of the Geometric and the beginning of the Orientalizing period. On the other hand, Homer hardly mentions the Dorians although at his time they had already long inhabited the Peloponnese. The king of Mycenae is the overlord of the Greeks, and the other heroes are his vassals. Mycenae rich in gold is the foremost city of Greece and its king the mightiest monarch of Greece. The attempt to derogate these facts[10] is vain, for it is inconceivable that an Ionian minstrel of the seventh century B. C. should have happened on the idea of ascribing such a position to the town and the king of Mycenae, which at that time was in fact a rotten borough. Nor has Agamemnon any real existence except in the Trojan cycle, although the contrary often is asserted.[11] Attempts to deny these facts can only lead us into error and to the erection of frail hypotheses. Here we ought also to speak of the really kingly power of Agamemnon, but as this is not so evident I shall recur to it in a later place.

In regard to these elements in Homer, derived from widely differing times and civilizations, scholars have divided themselves into two parties engaging in a tug of war. One party tries to put as much as possible in a time as late as possible; namely, into

[10] Bethe, *loc. cit.*; cp. below p. 45.
[11] *Vide* below, pp. 46 *et seq.*

the developed Geometric and the Orientalizing periods, and to treat the elements which it is impossible to fit into this scheme as irrelevant survivals. The other party treats the elements which undoubtedly belong to a late age as irrelevant additions and takes Homer on the whole to be Mycenaean. It appears that neither of these two methods is the right one. We have to concede without circumlocutions that Homer contains elements from very differing periods and to try to comprehend and explain this state of things, not to obliterate it and get rid of it through artificial interpretations.

The gap between the earliest and the latest elements in Homer comes nearer to a whole millenium than to a half-millenium. Literary analysis of the extant poems can reach only the time immediately preceding the latest elements and so can cover only a very small part of this gap, say a century or at most a little more. Some scholars who think that we cannot attain a well founded opinion of the stages preceding the literary evidence have confined themselves to literary analysis. The unitarians by principle are still less interested in the preceding stages. But this voluntary restriction makes them shut their eyes to more far-reaching vistas and vitiates the fundamental problem. The epic question has been unduly limited to the Homeric question. The extant Homeric poems are, however, the final achievement of a lengthy development— *fuere etiam ante Homerum poetae;* the epic question, i.e., the problem of the origin and development of Greek epics from their beginnings, cannot be put on one side.

It can be understood why some scholars have done so, for they are of the opinion that all means are wanting for attacking a problem which goes so far back into an unknown age. That is not literally true; for there is a method which may be utilized. Since, however, it is neither strictly philological nor strictly historical but is comparative in a general sense, it is viewed with undue diffidence by many who know it only from the outside.

Many years ago Professor Steinthal tried to introduce a comparative study of epics, but his attempt had no decided success, chiefly because he was hampered by the romantic presumption of collective popular poetry. A comprehensive study of this vast subject has never been taken up, only hints and minor attempts have been made. Professor von Pöhlmann drew attention to living epic poetry and pointed to the failure of Homeric research in not taking this into account,[12] but in vain. Professor Drerup gave a survey of various popular epics[13] but seems to have been forgotten, perhaps because these materials were not utilized by him in their true bearing upon Greek epics. English works are one-sided, and that is true not only of Professor Andrew

[12] R. v. Pöhlmann, "Zur geschichtlichen Beurteilung Homers," *Sybel's historische Zeitschrift*, LXXIII (1894), pp. 385 *et seq.*; reprinted in his "Gesammelte Abhandlungen," *Aus Altertum und Gegenwart*, I., pp. 56 *et seq.* What he says, p. 59, is true to this day: "Es ist ein wesentlicher Mangel der modernen Homer-Forschung, dass sie dieses gerade für die geschichtliche Seite der homerischen Frage so überaus wichtige Material bei weitem noch nicht in dem Umfang herangezogen und verwertet hat, in welchem es uns jetzt vorliegt."

[13] E. Drerup, "Homerische Poetik," I., *Das Homerproblem in der Gegenwart* (1921), pp. 27 *et seq.* Cp. the brief survey by John Meier, *Werden und Leben des Volksepos* (1909).

Lang's more cursory comparison of Homeric epics
with the *chansons de geste*[14] but also of Professor
Chadwick's important book, in which he institutes a
detailed comparison between Greek and Teutonic
epics.[15] It is self-evident that a comparison ought
to be instituted on the largest possible basis, and
that everything which is accidental and not essential
ought to be discarded.[16]

It is impossible here to give an account of the
numerous instances of popular epics. I simply
enumerate them. We have, in the first place,
Teutonic epics in their branches: old German,
Anglo-Saxon, and Scandinavian epics. Their off-
shoots are, at least in part, Finnish-Esthonian,
Russian, and even old French epics (*bylinas* and
chansons de geste). In Serbia popular epics are still
living; in Asia we find epics among several tribes, the
Kara-Kirgizes and the Abakan Tartars in Siberia
and the Atchinese on Sumatra. The historical
incidents underlying Greek mediaeval epics (Digenis
Akritas) are too little known. From a comparative
study of these epics the following statements may
be deduced. Epics do not originate in collective
popular poetry but are the creation of a heroic age,
a fact which Professor Wundt stated and Professor
Chadwick developed at length. They originate in
an aristocratic or even feudal society, praising the
deeds of living men and describing contemporary
events, but mythical traits and folk-tale elements

[14] A. Lang, *Homer and his Age* (1906), pp. 297 *et seq.*

[15] H. M. Chadwick, *The Heroic Age* (1912).

[16] I hope to be able to give a fuller exposition of this subject in a
forthcoming book with the title *Homer and Mycenae*, the basis of which
is a series of lectures delivered in the University of London in 1929.

may be attributed even to living men. The exaggerated praise of heroes and the still undeveloped intellectualism of the age, from the very beginning, open the doors for the supernatural. Epic poetry is composed not by the people in general but by certain gifted individuals, who live as minstrels and often as court minstrels in the *entourage* of some great man. But there is no intellectual cleavage between persons of higher and of lower standing; the lower classes share the warlike spirit and the admiration of valorous deeds and take up epics enthusiastically.

This is the original stage, which usually is short-lived. It is impossible to confine the subsequent development within a scheme, as Professor Chadwick has attempted, but two alternatives are to be considered. The heroic age may continue; epics chant ever fresh materials which change according to circumstances. Or the heroic age may come to an end and the people settle down to a less eventful life. But the interest in great deeds and the zeal for epic poetry do not die out immediately. Epic poetry is preserved but it sings now of the deeds of a past age and shows a tendency to limit itself to one cycle or to very few cycles of adventures, from which the minstrels choose their subjects, although fresh songs are invented, additions made, and changes devised. Under such conditions epics may be still more popular than before and may spread among the common people but they are in a certain sense stagnant.

This state of things may be interrupted by a new heroic age and by new epics dealing with contemporary men and events, but the stagnant conditions may also continue until epics are abandoned for other kinds of literature or obliterated by a higher culture. The epics may also wander far abroad and be received by people who lead a monotonous life on a low cultural plane but love poetry and preserve the epic chants. Of course epic poetry will undergo many and varied changes under such varying conditions.

Epic poetry is a floating mass confined within certain limits. This it is essential to know and to understand, and to this end the art and technique of composition must be considered; they seem to be similar everywhere. The art of singing is always exercised by certain gifted persons; but talents vary, and the most gifted become craftsmen, minstrels who chant in the courts or to the people according to circumstances. Everyone learns through hearing, consequently family tradition is important. Families, even schools, of minstrels appear.

The art of singing and of composing epic poetry is learned, and hence a question of fundamental importance is, how this art is learned. First, it is to be stated that every one learns through hearing; but that a poem is never learned and repeated word by word, even if a minstrel takes over and repeats a chant, as occurs frequently. In fact the forms of a poem are just as many as its recitals. The variability differs considerably, however, according to time, individuals, and other conditions.

For that which is learned is essentially not single poems, even though a successful chant may be learned and repeated by others, but is the epical technique, the poetical art by which the material is formed; the subject may be taken from the usual store or a new one may be chosen. Every chant is in its form more or less an improvisation, so that the minstrels may claim divine inspiration as Phemius does in the Odyssey. Such an art of singing is possible because the minstrel through lengthy practice possesses a language which puts words and phrases on his lips.

In the epical language of all peoples occurs a store of stock expressions, constantly recurring phrases, half and whole verses and even verse complexes; and repetitions are characteristic of the epic style. E.g., when a message is delivered it is repeated word for word. Of the 27,853 verses in Homer, 2,118 verses occur two or more times making a total of 5,162 repeated verses, or one-fifth of Homer. Furthermore, typical descriptions are characteristic of all epics. Though they are not repeated in identical words, they are substantially identical. These are the elements which the epical technique delivers ready for use to the minstrel forming his chant. What is said of the Kara Kirgiz minstrels is applicable to all: The singer has a large store of poetical parts ready, and his art consists in coordinating these parts according to the course of events and connecting them by the aid of new-made verses. A skilled poet is able to improvise a poem on every subject.[17]

If we consider the effect of this traditional technique, we understand why epics which sing of by-

[17] W. Radloff, "Die Sprachen der nördlichen Türkstämme," V, *Der Dialekt der Kara-Kirgizen* (1885), p. xvi.

gone days always archaize both in contents and in language. The stock expressions and typical descriptions preserve the old elements, even if they are no longer understood, and introduce them into even the latest chants. The old background of events is kept because the singer is conscious of chanting the past and not his own time, but with the naïveté characteristic of his cultural stage the minstrel mixes up the old elements with new taken from his own time.

These general statements agree completely with what Greek epics themselves, especially the Odyssey, say as to the art and manner of the recital of Greek mistrels, and we may surmise with certainty that it was not otherwise in the pre-Homeric age. The fact that the stock expressions often are philologically very old-fashioned and that their meaning was no longer understood by the minstrels themselves proves a great antiquity in the epical technique and in the epics themselves. If this high degree of antiquity of epical tradition is considered earnestly, a natural explanation ensues of the fact that Homer contains elements which differ in age by more than half a millenium, in fact by nearly a whole millenium. This long lapse of time is not amazing though it may seem so; Russian epics vegetated nearly a millenium, preserving reminiscences of the empire of Kieff and the age of the Vikings.

To this view that the origins of Greek epics must be carried back into the Mycenaean age a serious objection may be made. For the Mycenaean civilization is essentially Minoan, and it is an acknowledged fact that the Minoan civilization sprang from a non-Greek and not Aryan people at all. Consequently Sir Arthur Evans himself and many scholars take the Mycenaeans to be Minoans who have established themselves on the mainland of Greece and subjugated the indigenous population. He admits the view that epics go back into the Mycenaean age and supposes consequently that they were at first chanted in the Minoan language and afterwards, in a bilingual society, transferred into Greek.[18] A similar process took place elsewhere, but the result was in reality new epics, and such a process would of course invalidate the above reasoning concerning the preservation of old elements through the epical technique.

Like epics, mythology, too, would consequently originate among the Minoan people. But this seems to be disproved through the fact that almost all mythical names are clearly Greek; those which are certainly Minoan are extremely few. One would of course expect a considerable number of Minoan mythical names if the epos descended from the Minoans. In spite of the great authority of the scholar I have mentioned, I am firmly convinced that the Mycenaeans were immigrated Greeks who took over the Minoan civilization. It would take too long to set forth my reasons and I refer the reader to previous writings in which I have dwelt upon this question.[19] This view is prevailing nowadays. Younger archaeologists are prone to throw back the commencement of the Greek immigration

[18] A. J. Evans, *Journal of Hellenic Studies*, XXXII (1912), pp. 387 *et seq.*

[19] In my *Minoan-Mycenaean Religion*, pp. 11 *et seq.*

to the end of the Early Helladic age or earlier, whilst I find it probable that it began at the end of the following Middle Helladic age. Thus I take it for granted that the Mycenaeans were Greeks, and I hope that the following exposition will corroborate this view.

Epics praise heroes and originate in a heroic age. They belong to a social milieu in which certain persons become prominent through power, wealth, or deeds, and desire to be praised and chanted. Such an age was the Mycenaean age; for although opinions differ, it was admittedly an age of great wanderings of tribes and peoples, and its wealth and power are proved by the treasures of the shaft-graves of Mycenae, and of the bee-hive tombs at Dendra, Vaphio, etc., not to mention the bee-hive tombs themselves, the palaces, and the mighty walls of the cities. To this age the oldest elements in Homer go back, and I hesitate not the least in stating that in this age Greek epics originated. The minstrels chanted their songs at first to the princes and their retainers, but the people, who shared this admiration for valorous deeds, took over the epics and preserved them.

The stormy Mycenaean age came to an end and the subsequent transitional period between the Mycenaean and the Geometric ages is the poorest and darkest in all Greek history and pre-history. Conditions were poor and straitened; people were attached to the soil; and Greece was split up into a great number of cantons without much inter-communication, as the marked local varieties of Geometric ceramics prove as contrasted with the uniformity of Mycenaean pottery. Moreover, the

Phoenicians became masters of the sea. It seems unthinkable that epics originated in such a time, but epics which already existed may very well have been preserved, stagnant and vegetating, just as they were, e.g., in Russia or Finland. The subjects were limited to one or two cycles, to the Trojan and perhaps even the Theban cycle. Why these were preferred to others is just as difficult to say as why the unimportant skirmish of Roncevaux was put into the foreground of French epics. How epics were transmitted we have already seen. The elements were at hand and they were repeatedly composed anew and mixed up with new elements.

In the ninth and the following centuries a fresh life cropped up in Greece; wealth commenced to increase; the Greeks began again to sail the sea and to make expeditions on a large scale; the period of colonization began, which in a certain sense is another heroic age; but aristocracy preserved still its social and political privileges. Thus the ground was prepared for a renascence of epics, but the old tradition was so vigorous that the old cycle was kept and the new elements incorporated with it. The really new creation is the Odyssey, which does not deny the stamp of the age of colonization which it glorifies. The salient point was, however, the appearance of a great poet, whom I should like to call Homer. He infused new life and vigor into epic poetry, putting the psychology of his heroes into the foreground and planning a comprehensive composition under this aspect.

I may seem to have given an only too dogmatic exposition of my opinions of the Homeric question

instead of entering upon the subject of the Mycenaean origin of Greek mythology. But this exposition could not be passed over, because some scholars
neglect the previous stages of Homeric poetry, and
others adhere to the opinion that before the time
which on an average may be called the Homeric
age only single and disconnected myths existed and
that these myth elements were composed into cycles
of myths by the poets whose chief representative is
Homer. If this were right, my thesis that the cycles
of myths go back into the Mycenaean age would
evidently be wrong.

In opposition to this view I have tried to prove
two things: The first is that the development of
epics lasted much longer and that epics go back
into an early period of the Mycenaean age, a fact
which is proved by the Mycenaean elements im-
bedded in the epos. It is clear that this first point
must be still more valid for mythology than for
archaeological objects or for elements of civilization
and social life, because both the latter are much
more liable to be altered and changed through assimi-
lation to the conditions prevailing at the time when
the poems were composed. Thus we have a great
general probability that the myths occurring in
Homer go back into the Mycenaean age, though
nothing is proved in detail for specific myths.

Secondly, it appears that the background of the
Greek epos, i.e., the Trojan cycle in its chief features,
the power of Mycenae, and the kingship of Mycenae,
cannot possibly have come into existence through
the joining together of minor chants and myths,
but that it existed beforehand, being the cycle

from which the minstrels took their subjects. A cycle of events with certain chief personages invariably appears in all the epic poetry of which we have a more definite knowledge than we have of Greek epics as the background from which episodes are taken and to which episodes are joined; it is a premiss of epics, not their ultimate result. I refer to the tale of the Nibelungen in German epics, to that of Roland in old French epics, to the narratives of Vladimir the Great and his men in the *bylinas*, of Marko Kraljevitch and the battle on the Throstle Field in Servian epics, of the Islamic prince Manas and the heathen prince Joloi in the Kara Kirgiz epics, etc. In the same manner the background of the Homeric epos—the story of the war of Troy between the Trojans and the Greek heroes under Agamemnon's leadership, or, in other words, the chief features of the Trojan cycle—must be the primary fact and originate in the Mycenaean age. From this the minstrels chose and to this they added episodes. It is of course in detail uncertain and questionable what is of ancient origin and what is added later; here we are concerned with the fundamental idea, which we call the Trojan cycle, and we have tried to prove that this idea originated in the same age as the epos, the Mycenaean age.

I have drawn attention to the fact that the minstrels limited their choice to one or two cycles of myths. Other myths may have been chanted at an earlier age and have gone out of fashion. It may not be inferred that other cycles did not exist or were quite forgotten. We have to take account not only of epics but also of plain tales told in prose and preserving a great number of myths which lyric and tragic poets made famous in a later age. Such prose epics are not unparalleled. The cycle of the Nartes, heroes of the Ossetes and other peoples of the Caucasus, is told in prose.[20]

It can be demonstrated that numerous other myths and cycles of myths go back into the Mycenaean age. I begin by referring to an acute philological observation which proves that a number of mythical heroes must go back to an age much earlier than that of Homer. Professor Kretschmer drew attention to the fundamental difference between two series of heroic names.[21] The names of the older series have the ending *-eus* and are generally abbreviated forms; the names of the sons of these mythical personages are on the contrary chiefly common compound names; e.g., Peleus, Achilleus, as compared with Neoptolemus; Odysseus—Telemachus; Atreus—Agamemnon, Menelaus; Tydeus—Diomedes; Neleus—Nestor; Oeneus—Meleager, etc. The names of the older series are often difficult to explain etymologically; those of the younger series are clear and explicable. It is evident that the heroes whose names belong to the series ending in *-eus* go back to earlier times than the heroes with common names, and to this philological fact corresponds the mythological fact that the latter are said to be sons and descendants of the former. But the latter are quite current in Homeric poetry; their ancestors must consequently go back to much earlier, pre-Homeric times. That this time is the Mycenaean

[20] G. Dumézil, *Légendes sur les Nartes* (1930).

[21] P. Kretschmer, in the periodical *Glotta*, X (1920), pp. 305 *et seq.*

age is of course not demonstrable through philology solely, but the span of time necessary for the development of this difference must be supposed so great that these heroes are thrown back some centuries and very probably into the Mycenaean age. And if the names are so old, the myths attached to them must also be so to a certain extent.

It may be rightly objected that hereby only the great antiquity of isolated myths is demonstrated, but it can also be proved that the great mythical cycles are very much older than Homer, that, in fact, they go back to the Mycenaean age. I have briefly given the proof of this in earlier writings[22] and a detailed discussion will be the chief content of my subsequent lectures; here I dwell only on the question of principles. We know that mythology was the guide which led to the discovery of the Mycenaean and Minoan sites; it conducted Mr. Schliemann to Troy and Mycenae and Sir Arthur Evans to Cnossus. In these cases myths served as a heuristic means and the success of the investigations thus induced proved a connection between mythological centers and Mycenaean centers. My proof is nothing but a consequent application of this principle, a thorough-going comparison of the cities to which mythological cycles are attached with the cities where finds from the Mycenaean age have been made. If the correlation is constant; i.e., if we find that the cities to which the mythological cycles are attached were the centers of the Mycenaean

[22] See my article, "Der mykenische Ursprung der griechischen Mythologie," 'Αντιδωρον, Festschrift für J. Wackernagel (1924), pp. 137, et seq. and my History of Greek Religion, pp. 38 et seq.

civilization also, this constant correlation cannot be considered as accidental; it will prove the connection between the mythological cycles and the Mycenaean civilization; i.e., that the mythological cycles in their chief outlines go back into the Mycenaean age.

The proof however goes much further. For a close inspection shows that the mythical importance of a site closely corresponds to its importance in Mycenaean civilization. The mythical importance of a city is, to use a mathematical term, a function of its importance in Mycenaean civilization. This close and constant correspondence precludes any thought of casual coincidence. There are additional proofs also, elements inherent in certain myths which are of Mycenaean origin, but as these are less frequent and sometimes doubtful, they must be discussed separately.

To the application and elaboration of this principle of the close relationship between mythology and Mycenaean sites the following exposition will be devoted. But I am well aware of the difficulties and pitfalls of the detailed discussion and therefore it will be to the purpose to add some methodological remarks.

In regard to the Mycenaean remains, it may be objected that they are known only incompletely and that they have not been methodically explored all over Greece.[23] That is true, for every year new

[23] A good but very summary review of the prehistoric sites and find-places is given by Dr. Fimmen in his book, *Die kretisch-mykenische Kultur* (1921). The second edition (1924) is merely a reprint with very slight additions. In particular, a better map is needed than the rather poor one which has been added; moreover, the Mycenaean sites ought

discoveries are made. In time their distribution will certainly be much better known than now, but on the other hand it seems not likely that the picture will be changed essentially. The primacy of Argolis and next to it of Boeotia will remain. And so much is already known concerning other provinces that it is hardly to be expected that new discoveries will greatly change their relative importance. The map of Mycenaean sites and civilization will be completed, not turned upside down nor even substantially altered. Certain irregularities exist which will be treated in due course.[24]

In regard to mythology, certain points ought to be emphasized. We have noted that myths were remodeled in late and even in very late times. The science of mythography sets forth the development of the myths as far as it can be traced with the aid of literary and monumental evidence. As mythographic research is concerned with the historical period of the development of the myths, we have here only to accept its results, when it proves that certain forms of myths are developed or added in historical times. Far-reaching deductions concerning the development of the myths have often been connected with the reconstructions of lost epics or of those preserved only in fragments, but these reconstructions are very hypothetical and conflicting and must be regarded with a certain diffidence. The

to be sharply distinguished from the pre-Mycenaean sites. A summary of the reports on excavations and finds with very rich illustrative material is given by the late Professor O. Montelius in his work, *La Grèce préclassique*, I, II:2 (1924–28). It is to be regretted that this posthumous work has not been brought up to date.

[24] Cp. below pp. 128 and 182.

form in which a myth appears in Homer is often
treated with a certain disesteem; nevertheless it
must be considered thoroughly because it is the oldest
recorded form, although of course not always the
oldest form which has existed.

Further, a distinction is to be made between
myths of different kinds and especially between
divine and heroic mythology. The divine mythology
consists of myths concerning the gods, and cult
myths. I cannot dwell here upon this important
distinction; we are little concerned with divine
mythology and only casually with cult myths.
Nor are we concerned with the many minor and
isolated myths which crop up everywhere. For every
town had its heroes or made them, and eponymous
heroes were created freely. We are chiefly concerned
with the cycles of heroic mythology and our aim is
to test to what extent their distribution and varying
importance correspond to the Mycenaean remains.

Well marked differences appear even in heroic
mythology, since it incorporated very different
elements, beginning with folk-tales and ending with
incidents having a rather historical appearance.
Motifs of the folk-tale are, e.g., prominent in the
myths of Perseus and of Achilles, whilst on the
contrary the Pylian myths seem very little mythical,
but rather almost historical. This is intelligible in
view of the lengthy development of myths and of
epics. The Pylian cycle is a late creation referring
to the deeds of princes who were very little mytholo-
gized, whilst Perseus and Achilles are older and more
popular heroes. The Oedipus myth is in its kernel a
folk-tale, but the War of the Seven is an historical

myth and the same seems to be true of the Minyans of Orchomenus.

I am quite aware of the difficulty of the subject and I am prepared to be met with objections. It will perhaps be said that I resuscitate the old and justly condemned method of eliciting history from myths. There are certainly historical facts underlying heroic myths to a certain extent, but mythology can never be converted into history, and we can never attain a knowledge of these historical facts if there is not an independent historical tradition as there is, e.g., in the case of the Nibelungenlied. For myths are always myths and largely fiction; the underlying facts have been reshaped and confused by fiction. For Greek myths no historical tradition exists which can serve as a control. There is only archaeology, and control by archaeology does not suffice for proving historical events but serves at most to present the cultural milieu. This cultural background, however, carries weight. If details in my reasoning may be contradicted or proved to be erroneous, this does not ruin the whole. The historical background of Greek heroic mythology is amply proved by its close correspondence to the geographical distribution of Mycenaean civilization.

That the thesis of the Mycenaean origin of Greek mythology has not been set forth and recognized earlier is due to some peculiar circumstances. Although numerous works of art and various sculptural or pictorial representations from the Mycenaean age have been discovered, mythical scenes seemed to be wanting in these works. They have been eagerly sought for, but those representations which until lately were claimed to have mythical contents are very doubtful. One is the so-called Scylla of a Cretan seal impression depicting a man in a boat who seems to fight with a marine monster rising up from the sea. The monster is not like Scylla and it is very doubtful whether a mythical incident is here represented.[25] The second instance is a gold ring from a find near Tiryns, the engravings on which represent a ship and two couples, each consisting of a man and a woman. The scene is called the abduction of Helen, but this interpretation has never been taken in earnest; it is quite arbitrary; the scene may as well be a scene of salutation or of congée. It belongs probably to the scenes of daily life which sometimes occur in Mycenaean art.[26] I prefer to pass over the famous treasure from Thisbe in silence.[27]

In the light of these facts one must needs reason as follows: the Minoan art, which had no mythical but only cultual representations, was taken over wholly and without change by the Mycenaeans. It is practically certain that Minoan artists worked for the Mycenaean sires; as mythical representations were absent from their art, Mycenaean myths were not depicted although they were related. Even elsewhere Mycenaean characteristics were ousted by Minoan art and appear only rarely and hesitatingly. It seems, however, somewhat astonishing that the

[25] British School at Athens, *Annual*, IX, p. 58, fig. 36; the latest treatment by S. Marinatos, Μινωική καὶ Ὁμηρικὴ Σκύλλα in Δελτίον ἀρχαιολογικόν, X, pp. 51 *et seq.*

[26] See e.g. my *Minoan-Mycenaean Religion*, p. 44, n. 3.

[27] A. J. Evans, "The Ring of Nestor, etc.", *Journal of Hellenic Studies*, XL (1925), pp. 1 *et seq.* The genuineness of this most amazing find is vigorously contested; I have given some objections in my *Minoan-Mycenaean Religion*, pp. 304 *et seq.*

Mycenaeans had a rich supply of myths but did not
depict them in spite of their high standard of art,
although such a fact would not be inconceivable.
The same thing occurs in Geometric art, which loves
to depict men, women, horses, and ships but does
not represent mythical scenes—though there are
one or two exceptions belonging to its late phase.
But the Geometric period is the Homeric age, which
had plenty of myths.

Quite recently, however, a new discovery has put
it beyond doubt that myths were represented occasionally even in Mycenaean art. Among the very
rich and beautiful contents of the bee-hive tomb at
Dendra, near old Mideia, which was excavated in
1926 by Professor Persson, were eight plaques of
blue glass, evidently made in a mold, for they are
identical. They show a woman sitting on the back
of a big bull.[28] The representation is very similar to
that of the well-known metope from Selinus, and if
it had belonged to classical times everybody would
have immediately recognized Europa on the back of
the bull. I am unable to see why we should not
accept this identification, even if the object is
Mycenaean.

Among the same finds there are also another glass
plaque and fragments of two others which represent
a big standing lion and before it a man.[29] From the
back of the lion a head seems to grow up; the lion's
tail is very long. The plaques are in a bad state of
preservation so that details are uncertain, but it

[28] A. W. Persson, *Kungagraven i Dendra* (1928), p. 123; cp. below
p. 38, n. 6.

[29] *Loc. cit.*, p. 125.

cannot reasonably be doubted that this is another
mythical representation, the Chimaera and Bellerophon. It may seem astonishing that of the two
myths illustrated the scenes of both are laid in
foreign countries—I shall recur to this topic later.[30]
A third representation referring to a Greek myth is
that of two centaurs, each with a dagger in his hand,
on a steatite gem found by Dr. Blegen in a Late
Mycenaean tomb during his excavations at the
Argive Heraeum.[31] Here I wish only to stress the
fact that Mycenaean representations of Greek myths
actually have come to light. If it is proved that the
myths of Europa, of Bellerophon, and of the Centaurs go back into the Mycenaean age, the view
will be still more justified that the great mythical
cycles also which are attached to the Mycenaean
centers go back into the Mycenaean age.

[30] Below pp. 53 *et seq.*

[31] Dr. Blegen has kindly shown me a design of this gem, which will
be published in his forthcoming work, *Prosymna*, and has given me his
permission to mention it.

CHAPTER II

MYCENAEAN CENTERS AND MYTHO-
LOGICAL CENTERS

Having in the first chapter laid down the principles
and premisses according to which we have to proceed,
we now enter upon our main subject, a detailed
comparison between the centers of Mycenaean
civilization and the centers of mythological cycles,
and their relative importance. The chief facts of
Mycenaean archaeology being well known and easily
accessible, this side of our task will need fewer words.
It will suffice to recall the main features of the more
important finds and sites, for according to our principles there is little place for a discussion of details.
What is essential is to comprehend the whole body
and the importance of the Mycenaean relics found
in certain places. There exist good surveys of this
age.[1] For our purpose Dr. Fimmen's book is most
helpful with its condensed list of Mycenaean find-
places and of the authorities on the subject.[2] I
add solely such things as are of special importance
or were discovered after its publication.

[1] H. R. Hall, *Aegaean Archaeology* (1914); *The Civilization of Greece
in the Bronze Age* (1928). G. Glotz, *The Aegaean Civilization* (1925).
Cambridge Ancient History, II, chap. 16, "Crete and Mycenae" (by
A. J. B. Wace).

[2] See p. 28, n. 23.

The mythological side will need more space and more discussion, for in spite of the many handbooks on mythology,[3] the mythological materials are not so readily at hand as is the archaeological information. They need to a certain extent to be worked up. It will be necessary to discuss what parts of the myths may with more or less probability be referred to the Mycenaean age and to consider the evidence for this reference, evidence which is often of a rather difficult kind and sometimes, certainly, questionable.

1. ARGOLIS

I commence of course with Argolis, for this province held the primacy both in Mycenaean civilization and in Greek mythology. It is the richest in Mycenaean remains as well as in myths. Its capital was Mycenae, and that this city should give its name to the age and the civilization with which we have to deal is justified by discoveries which have been surpassed nowhere;[4] for in this connection we do not speak of Crete and the Minoan civilization. Mycenae was the proudest and wealthiest town of Mycenaean Greece. The architectural remains are imposing: the city wall with the Lion Gate, the only monumental sculpture from prehistoric times,

[3] The standard work on Greek Mythology is the fourth edition of L. Preller's *Griechische Mythologie*, edited by C. Robert. The volumes treating heroic mythology are a quite new and most substantial and learned work with the separate title: *Die griechische Heldensage* (1920–26); only the indexes are still wanting. The best English handbook on the subject is H. J. Rose, *A Handbook of Greek Mythology* (1928).

[4] The important results of the recent excavations of the English School are published in the *Annual* of the British School at Athens, XXV (1921–23).

the unfortunately very ruinous remains of the great palace, the nine bee-hive tombs which in number and size surpass those found on any other site. The so-called tomb of Atreus is the largest and stateliest dome erected before the building of the Pantheon in Rome nearly a millenium and a half later. The famous shaft-graves yielded the finds through which the Mycenaean civilization was first discovered; their richness is still unsurpassed. There are also numerous chamber tombs; Professor Tsoundas excavated some of them long ago and the English School in Athens explored recently the extensive cemetery of Kalkani.[5] Their great number proves that Mycenae was populous and their contents, that its inhabitants were prosperous.

Tiryns seems almost to rival Mycenae because of its mighty walls with their galleries and the well preserved remains of the palace, although it is a distinctly smaller town, and what has been found there of other remains and objects is not so important as the finds at Mycenae. There is, however, an extensive lower town and a well built bee-hive tomb. Quite recently an extensive work was discovered through which a river southeast of Tiryns was diverted in order to protect the lower town from being flooded.

The third Mycenaean fortress in Argolis is Midea. Its imposing walls enclose an area larger than that of any Mycenaean site except Gla; it is still unexplored, but in the neighborhood hardly a mile to the south at the village of Dendra, Professor Persson had the

[5] The report on these excavations is forthcoming in the periodical *Archaeologia*.

luck to discover a collapsed but untouched bee-hive
tomb and several chamber tombs. The finds are
famous and rival in value those of Mycenae.[6]

It is proved by archaeological facts that on the site
where the famous temple of Hera, the Heraeum,
stood later, there once was another Mycenaean city.
There are traces of Mycenaean walls and houses;
Mycenaean sherds and idols are found;[7] there is a
bee-hive tomb in the neighborhood, and, finally,
rich chamber tombs from all periods of the Mycenaean age were recently excavated by American
archaeologists.[8]

The remains from Argos, the capital of Argolis in
historical times, are less significant. On a low hill
called Aspis, Mycenaean sherds were found and on
Deiras, the ridge which unites this hill with the
imposing acropolis, the Larissa, some chamber
tombs were excavated. On the Larissa some remains
of Mycenaean walls were discovered recently.[9]

There are also several minor sites in Argolis; e.g.,
in the neighborhood of Corinth, Nauplia, and Asine,
where a Swedish expedition has unearthed a small

[6] A. W. Persson, *Kungagraven i Dendra* (1928), is a popular survey
in Swedish. The final publication of these most important finds is
forthcoming in the *Acta* of the R. Society of Letters of Lund.

[7] *Tiryns*, Vol. I (1912), pp. 114 *et seq.*; cp. my *Minoan-Mycenaean
Religion*, pp. 410 *et seq.*

[8] Preliminary reports in the *American Journal of Archaeology*, XXIX
(1925), pp. 413 *et seq.*, XXXI (1927), p. 105, and in the *Journal of
Hellenic Studies*, XLVI (1926), pp. 226 *et seq.*; XLVII (1927), pp. 237
et seq.; XLVIII (1928), p. 184.

[9] For the recent finds on the Larissa see Vollgraff in Mnemosyne,
LVI (1928), pp. 313 *et seq.*, and in *Mededeelingen der K. Akad. van
Wetenschappen, Letterkunde*, Vol. LXVI (1928), Ser. B, No. 4.

Mycenaean town and found a series of chamber tombs.[10]

This brief recalling of the outstanding archaeological facts will be sufficient for our purpose. Turning to the myths, we commence with the capital in the Mycenaean age, Mycenae. There are two series of strikingly different tombs, the shaft-graves and the bee-hive tombs, both testifying to great wealth and power. It has been said that this difference in funeral customs is accounted for in the mythical narratives telling of two royal houses at Mycenae, one of which succeeded the other, the Perseidae and the Atreidae. The earlier series of tombs, the shaft-graves, have been said to be those of the Perseidae and the later, the bee-hive tombs, to have been erected by the later dynasty, the Atreidae; but this parallelism can hardly be held reliable. It is more specious than founded on facts and had better be left out of account.[11] We turn to the myths themselves.

[10] Concerning the sites near Corinth, see Blegen, *American Journal of Archaeology*, XXIV (1920), pp. 1 *et seq*. A preliminary report of the excavations at Asine is published in the *Bulletin of the R. Society of Letters of Lund*, 1924–25, but this does not include the still more important finds of the campaign in 1926, especially the results of the excavation of the Lower Town, in which the sanctuary described in my *Minoan-Mycenaean Religion*, pp. XX *et seq*., was discovered. A supplementary excavation having been made in this year (1930), the final publication is in preparation.

[11] Consequently I need not discuss the recent theory of Sir Arthur Evans reversing the old view referred to in the text. He thinks that the bodies and objects found in the shaft-graves were transferred thither from the bee-hive tombs, and adds vivacious polemics against the dating of the bee-hive tombs proposed by Mr. Wace (A. J. Evans, *The Shaft-Graves and Bee-Hive Tombs of Mycenae and their Interrelation*, 1929).

The most prominent hero of Mycenae in the earlier mythical generation is Perseus. The kernel of his myth is the slaying of the monster Gorgo, and is perhaps the best instance of a folk-tale received into Greek heroic mythology.[12] To this kernel his birth story had already been added in Mycenaean times, but the episode taking place on the island of Seriphus seems to be of a rather late date and may be passed over here. The myth of Perseus is unusually crowded with folk-tale motifs and this is in some measure a proof of a high antiquity. Folk-tales are told in all countries everywhere and they are not localized by other peoples. In Greece, however, they were localized because of the innate tendency of heroic mythology to localize its heroes, and because the folk-tale was preserved only when it was received into the heroic mythology.

It is generally recognized that Perseus belongs to Mycenae. He is said to be the founder of the city. An etymological explanation was invented later.[13] That the founding of the city had to be fitted with some pains into the series of his adventures seems to make it probable that his connection with the city of Mycenae depended on old tradition. There was a heroön said to be that of Perseus on the road from Mycenae to Argos, but that may be late, as was certainly the altar on Seriphus.[14] There is better evidence for his cult at Mycenae. An inscription in archaic letters found between the

[12] E. S. Hartland, *The Legend of Perseus*, I–III (1894–96).

[13] Paus. ii. 16, 3. See p. 123, n. 46.

[14] Paus. ii. 18, 1.

Lion Gate and the so-called tomb of Clytaemestra
speaks of some officials connected with Perseus to
whom judicial functions are attributed in certain
cases.[15] This proves that these officials were an
old and venerable corporation. Professor Robert
assumes that it was sent from Argos to provide for
the cult of Perseus, following the destruction of
Mycenae by the Argives some time after the Persian
war. If this is right, the cult was so old and venerable
that the Argives felt themselves bound not to
discontinue it. The inscription seems, however,
to be too early to permit such an interpretation.
In regard to the date of the cult, we can only infer
that it existed in the archaic age, a fact which proves
that Perseus' connection with Mycenae is of old
date. During the Roman age it was a matter of
course.[16]

The genealogies are of little or no value, being
invented in order to fit Perseus into the common
pseudo-historical scheme. I gave voice above to
the opinion that the story of his birth was already
in Mycenaean times joined with the folk-tale of
his slaying of the Gorgon. This cannot be proved
by the story of the subterranean bronze thalamus
in which his mother was enclosed and where she
was sought by Zeus in the shape of a golden rain.
For even if a bee-hive tomb decorated with bronze

[15] *Inscr. Graec.*, IV. No. 493, which mentions ἰαρομνάμονες τὸς ἐς
Περσέ. Judicial functions are attributed to them when there is no
δαμοργία. Cp. Wilamowitz, *Aristoteles und Athen*, II., p. 48, n. 26.

[16] During the Roman age the honors of Heracles and Perseus were
decreed for citizens of merit (*Inscr. Graec.*, iv., No. 606, cp. No. 586).
The noble family of T. Statilius Lamprias attached its genealogy to
Perseus and the Dioscuri (*ibid.* Nos. 590 and 940).

ornaments is rightly recognized in the description
of this subterranean thalamus, it has been justly
remarked that such a story may have been invented
only after the bee-hive tombs had fallen into disuse.
Some of them may have been accessible for a long
time after being opened by plunderers.

There is, however, a more certain indication to the
same effect: the name of Perseus' mother Danaë
signifies nothing but "the Danaan maiden."[17]   In
the beginning the Danaan maiden had of course
no father, or if she had one he was evidently a
Danaan man, a Danaüs, just as Chryses is the father
of Chryseis, the maiden from Chryse.   Acrisius
was introduced later and made the father of Danaë
in order to attach the genealogy of Perseus to
Argos, the historical capital of Argolis.   Danaoi
is a tribal name, already obsolete in Homer, and the
same name is recognized in Egyptian inscriptions
from the times of Echenaton and Ramses III: it is
Mycenaean and was out of daily use in the Homeric
age.   The consequence is that such a name as "the
Danaan maiden" cannot have been imposed upon
the mother of Perseus except in Mycenaean times
and that the birth story therefore had already been
created in this age.   This result leads to the conclusion that the birth story was joined in this age with
the tale of his slaying of the Gorgo.   Thus the Perseus
myth is in its essential parts of Mycenaean origin.

The second kingly house of Mycenae is that of
the Atreidae, whose cruel deeds and misfortunes
have been celebrated in so many famous tragedies.

[17] So Ed. Meyer also, *Forschungen zur alten Geschichte*, I (1892), p. 73.
Cp. below p. 65.

This house and especially its chief representative
in Homer, Agamemnon, seem to be firmly localized
at Mycenae, but even this has been denied. Professor Wilamowitz has said that the artificial make-
up of the name of Atreus is apparent;[18] i.e., he is
of the opinion that this name is formed from the
family name attributed to Agamemnon, the Atreides.
This seems hardly to be a happy idea. We have
seen that names ending in -eus make up an older
series of mythical names and go back to a great
antiquity.[19] Of course a name may have been
formed later with this ending, but in this case
one would expect the stem of the name to be clear,
as it is, e.g., in the name of Eurystheus' herald
Copreus, "the Dung-man." This is not true of
the name Atreus. Or if Atreides is the primary
form from which an eponymous hero Atreus was
abstracted, as Minyas was abstracted from the
Minyans, it would be in fact a tribal name, and this
is very unlikely. On the other hand, if Atreides is
a true gentilicial name, the name of an ancestor
Atreus is its basis, and this seems to be by far the
most probable view. Atreus is certainly an old
mythical personage and no late invention.

This opinion is corroborated by the famous
passage describing the scepter of Agamemnon,[20] in
which the genealogy of the house of the Atreidae is
given. The scepter carried by Agamemnon is said
to have been wrought by Hephaestus and given to
Zeus; Zeus gave it to Hermes, Hermes to Pelops,

---

[18] "Agamemnon führt einen Vatersnamen, dessen künstliche Mache
klar ist," Wilamowitz, "Die griech. Heldensage, II," *Sitzungsberichte
der preuss. Akad. der Wissenschaften*, 1925, p. 242.

[19] See above p. 26.   [20] *Il.* ii. vv. 101 *et seq.*

Pelops to Atreus, Atreus at his death to Thyestes, and Thyestes left it to Agamemnon to carry, and so to rule over all Argos and many islands. Even those scholars who embrace the opinion that Homer's description of the kingship reflects the conditions of the early historical age recognize in this passage a relict of a much older age, in which the king was invested with a really kingly power; it can but be the Mycenaean age.[21]   But the genealogy is so closely linked up with this description of the kingly power that the former cannot be separated from the latter. Both go back into the Mycenaean age.

The most questionable and at the same time a superfluous figure of the genealogy is the father of Atreus, Pelops.   The house being called after Atreus, Pelops appears to have been put at the head of the genealogy secondarily.   He is recognized to be nothing but the eponymous hero of the Pelopes, the vanished tribe which gave its name to the Peloponnese.[22]   The form is that of a number of Greek tribal names ending in -ops, plur. -opes. That is the reason why at an early date he was made the ancestor of the kingly house which ruled the peninsula or at least the most important part of it. Other myths connected with Pelops are late.   He plays an important part in the myths of Olympia, which are post-Mycenaean,[23] and his connections with Asia Minor are certainly also of late date. Pelops himself is by his name proved to be of Greek origin.

[21] See my paper, "Das homerische Königtum" in *Sitzungsberichte der preuss. Akad. der Wissenschaften*, 1927, p. 27; cp. below pp. 240 *et seq.*
[22] By Ph. Buttmann, *Mythologus*, II (1829), p. 170.
[23] See below pp. 91 *et seq.*

Of the many cruel deeds attributed to the house of the Atreidae there is no word in this passage nor was there any place for them. In the Iliad, Clytae-mestra is barely named as the wife of Agamemnon, but in the Odyssey her seduction by Aegisthus and the murder of Agamemnon are fully related. It is impossible to pronounce any well founded judg-ment on the age of this tragic myth, but it is the oldest of the family tragedies of the Atreidae, and it was followed by other myths of a similar nature attached to this house. The story of the Atreidae and the story of the Labdacidae are similar, being of a highly tragic nature, but there is a marked difference between them: on one side unwittingly committed guilt and internecine feuds, on the other, cunning cruelty and deceptive ruse.

One would think that at any rate Agamemnon's localization at Mycenae is firm and well attested, but even this has been denied. When Professor Bethe says[24] that in the Iliad Agamemnon is only twice or thrice called king of Mycenae and in other passages is said to be from Argos,[25] and from this pretended discrepancy concludes that he was origi-nally not king of Mycenae but a war king, a com-mander-in-chief of the Greek troops, he is using a logic by which it would be possible to argue that the king of Prussia was not at the same time emperor of Germany. I confess that I cannot imagine a war king without a city and country of his own.[26]

[24] E. Bethe, *Homer*, III (1927), pp. 11 and 50; P. Cauer, *Grund-fragen der Homerkritik*, ed. 3 (1923), pp. 274 *et seq*.

[25] E.g. *Il.* ii. v. 108.

[26] Cp. my above-quoted (p. 44, n. 21) paper, p. 27.

There are other more specious arguments to the
same effect. The best one is the oft repeated contention that Agamemnon originally was a god.
I do not enter upon the question of principles.[27]
Some time ago scholars preferred to regard Greek
heroes as faded gods. This theory has lost much of
its attractiveness, although there are certainly such
heroes even if there are not so many as was imagined.
But for Agamemnon's godhead no good evidence
exists, as has been proved in a searching analysis.[28]
The idea is founded upon an expression in the
enigmatical poem of Lycophron,[29] but here the
expression is partly a copy of the Hellenistic cult
of the rulers, partly a synecdoche; Agamemnon is
used for Zeus and vice versa. The scholiast com-
menting on the passage or his source was guilty of
the conclusion that Agamemnon was venerated as
Zeus Agamemnon and gave him a temple, too,
whose emplacement he deduced from a following
verse[30] to be a deme in Laconia which elsewhere is
unknown, Lapersai. The temple is not mentioned
elsewhere, but there was a memorial of Agamemnon
in the temple of Alexandra at Amyclae.[31] This Zeus

[27] For this view I quote only H. Usener, "Der Stoff des griech.
Epos," *Sitzungsberichte der Akad. der Wissenschaften in Wien*, CXXXVII
(1897), III, pp. 5 et seq., reprinted in his *Kleine Schriften* IV (1913),
pp. 203 et seq.

[28] I. Harrie, "Zeus Agamemnon," *Archiv für Religionswissenschaft*,
XXIII (1925), pp. 359 et seq.

[29] Lykophron, *Alexandra*, vv. 1123 et seq., ἐμὸς δ' ἀκοίτης, δμωῖδος
νύμφης ἄναξ, Ζεὺς Σπαρτιάταις αἱμύλοις κληθήσεται τιμὰς μεγίστας Οἰβάλου
ἰέκνοις λαχών. Inversely Agamemnon is named instead of Zeus, v. 335,
ὁ δ' ἀμφὶ τύμβῳ τἀγαμέμνονος δαμείς; i. e., Priamus who was killed on the
altar of Zeus Herkeios.

[30] *Ibid.*, v. 1369 (Agamemnon) Ζηνὶ τῷ Λαπερσίῳ ὁμώνυμος Ζεύς.

[31] Paus. iii. 19, 5.

Agamemnon was of course welcome to the Euhem-
erist authors and their followers, the ecclesiastical
writers. Thus there is no wonder that he appears
in Clemens Alexandrinus and Athenagoras. The
source is said to be a certain Staphylus from Nau-
cratis who has written about different Greek provinces, of course a Hellenistic author.

Still worse is the second testimony. Pausanias
relates that the inhabitants of Chaeronea venerated
Agamemnon's scepter, of which Homer speaks,
but states that they called it a spear and that it
had been found together with some golden objects
on the boundary between Chaeronea and Panopeus.[32]
I cannot see why this information should be rejected.
Why is it improbable that people had discovered
an old tomb containing gold objects and a spear
or staff which they took the fancy to venerate?
But apart from this the inhabitants of Chaeronea
called it a spear, not a scepter, and the title *Agamemnon's scepter* is clearly nothing but the usual attri-
bution of old and curious things to Homeric heroes.
Moreover, if Agamemnon's scepter was venerated,
this in no wise proves that Agamemnon himself
was a god.

Other so-called testimony quoted to the same
effect is most futile.[33] It is related that Agamemnon
dug wells at Aulis and in other places of Greece,
that he was honored in baths at Clazomenae, and
that the inhabitants of Smyrna called a bath by

[32] Paus. ix. 40, 11, who states that it was a δόρυ.

[33] I refer to the only attested cult, at Tarentum, in a note, because
it is evidently secondary. The cult applied more justly to the descendants of Atreus and Agamemnon and other heroes; cp. my *Griechische
Feste* (1906), p. 457, n. 8.

his name.[34] In the same way warm springs, even
baths, were attributed to another hero, Heracles.
It is hardly necessary to state that this is no proof
of the existence of a cult. A god Agamemnon
never existed except in the fancy of the interpreters
of Lycophron.

Others do not believe in the old god Agamemnon
but contend that the hero Agamemnon originally
belongs to Asia Minor; his family is said to have
survived on Lesbos and at Cyme. Only Homer
brought him to Greece, for Perseus was the hero
of Mycenae.[35] To begin with, I cannot see why a
town cannot have two heroes or more; most of them
have. In regard to the descendants of Agamemnon
in Asia Minor, the testimony is as follows. A
passage in Pollux[36] speaks about those who invented
the process of coining money, mentioning Pheidon
and Demodike from Cyme, wife of the Phrygian
king, Midas, and daughter of a King Agamemnon of
Cyme. That the kingly house of Cyme claimed
descent from Agamemnon because one of its members
bore his name is not a very striking inference, and
if they did ennoble their pedigree by attaching to it
one of the famous heroes of Greek mythology, so
also did others, for example, the kingly house of
Lydia. For my part I am inclined to draw quite
another conclusion; namely, that in the end of the
eighth century B. C.[37] Agamemnon was still used

[34] See Usener, *op. cit.*, p. 6 or 203 resp. with notes.

[35] Wilamowitz in the paper quoted, p. 43, n. 18, p. 242.

[36] Pollux, ix. 83.

[37] For the Midas in question ought to be the last king of Phrygia,
whose empire was crushed and who was killed by the Cimmerian invasion
in the very beginning of the 7th century B. C.

as a human name, for names of heroes were not given
to men before the Hellenistic age. It follows that
Agamemnon was not venerated as a hero at that
time and still less was he believed to be a god.

On Lesbos there was a town, Penthile,[38] and to
this belongs probably the noble family of the Pen-
thelidae. Aristoteles relates that the members of
this family were wont to go about at Mytilene
striking people with clubs but were overcome by
Megacles and his friends.[39] Further, it is related
in several differing versions that Orestes or his
descendants emigrated to Asia Minor.[40] The tradition here relevant says that the son of Orestes and
Erigone, Penthilus, or his grandson Gras, went to
Lesbos and founded cities there. This Penthilus
is of course taken to be the ancestor of the Pen-
thelidae, but their claim to descent from Agamemnon
is no better founded than the descent from Heracles
claimed by the Mermnades in Lydia or by the
royal house of Macedonia. Penthilus is a late
invention akin to Megapenthes, the bastard son
of Menelaus, or the son of Proetus who exchanged
Tiryns for Argos with Perseus; his name hints at
the calamities of the house of the Atreidae. The
fact that a noble family of Lesbos was called Pen-
thelidae[41] facilitated a connection with heroic genealogy, such as noble families loved. Their name was
certainly derived from that of the town.

[38] Steph. Byz. s. v. Πενθίλη.   [39] Aristot., Polit., v. 10, p. 1311 b.

[40] Pindar, Nem., xi. 44, says of a victorious athlete from Tenedos
that his ancestors emigrated from Amyclae with Orestes; for other
testimony see Robert, Griech. Heldensage, pp. 1340 et seq.

[41] The names are not quite identical, differing in the second vowel.
Steph. Byz., however, calls the town Πενθίλη and its inhabitants Πενθελεῖς.

There are no valid grounds either for the godhead of Agamemnon or for the theory that he belonged originally to Asia Minor; he exists only as a mythical personage, and the attempt to sever him from Mycenae is vain. The arguments adduced to prove the contrary are as fallacious and vain as arguments are wont to be when somebody tries to give reasons for a preconceived opinion.

Corresponding to the paramount importance of Mycenae in the Mycenaean age, two of the most famous cycles of Greek myths are attached to this town, that of Perseus and that of the Atreidae. It would have been necessary only to point to this fact, not to enter upon a discussion of the myths, if doubt had not been cast upon the connection of Agamemnon and his house with Mycenae. His position as overlord of the Greek princes is another heritage from the Mycenaean age, due to the wealth and power of his city; I shall recur to this topic in my last chapter.[42] Finally, it is to be observed that it is quite incomprehensible how the wealth of myths attached to Mycenae came into existence if they were created in historical times, when Mycenae was a very small and unimportant town; but it is perfectly comprehensible if the origins of the cycles go back into the time of the glory of Mycenae, the Mycenaean age. They were popular from of old and were taken up by literature and developed by means of new accretions and inventions, for many details of the cycles are evidently of later date.

In regard to Tiryns, things are not quite so clear as in the case of Mycenae and need more discussion.

[42] Below pp. 240 *et seq.*

The foremost hero of Tiryns is of course Heracles, for the Heracles who performs his labors on the injunction of his suzerain, Eurystheus, the king of Mycenae, is at home at Tiryns. But, as I propose to treat the Heracles cycle in a separate chapter, I only note the fact here, emphasizing its bearing on our judgment as to the mythological importance of Tiryns, and proceed to another hero whose connection with Tiryns seems more questionable.

Bellerophon is always said to be a Corinthian by birth, the son of Glaucus, and the grandson of the wily Sisyphus. At Corinth he had a sacred precinct, a cypress grove on the road to the harbor town Kenchreai,[43] and Athena Chalinitis, who had a temple at Corinth, was said to have this epithet because she had tamed Pegasus, placed a bit in his mouth, and given him to Bellerophon.[44] More important than this tradition is the fact that Pegasus appears on the coins of Corinth and of the neighboring town of Sicyon from the earliest time of coinage. In the sixth century B. C., Corinth and Sicyon laid claim to Bellerophon.

Homer, who narrates his story at length,[45] says that he was the son of Glaucus and the grandson of Sisyphus, but states that he came from Ephyre in the interior of horse-breeding Argos. The current identification of Ephyre with Corinth is questionable.[46] Further, Homer has no mention of Pegasus, and Aristarchus may be right in concluding that he

[43] Paus. ii. 2, 4.

[44] Paus. ii. 4, 1.

[45] *Il.* vi. vv. 152 *et seq.*

[46] E. Bethe, *Thebanische Heldenlieder* (1891), pp. 182 *et seq.*

did not know this feature of the myth.[47]   Hesiod has
it, just as he has many other innovations.

Genealogies are not to be trusted very much in
proving the old localization of a myth.   A more
reliable indication is provided by the locality of the
chief myth of a cycle; i.e., that part of the myth
which must be considered to be the old kernel,
especially if there is no apparent reason why this
myth should be localized in a certain place.   Such
a localization depends presumably upon old, good
tradition.   Genealogies cannot be admitted without
being tested, for they were often invented in order
to transfer a hero from one place to another and to
bring him into connections which for some reason
it was desired to establish.   So Corinth, and probably
Sicyon also, laid claim to Bellerophon and succeeded
in appropriating him for themselves.

The kernel of the cycle of Bellerophon is a series
of adventures, the killing of the Chimaera, the battles
with the Solymi and with the Amazons, and finally
the ambush which Iobates laid for him; but, as in
many other such cycles, this chain of adventures
is preceded by a story which seeks to explain why
the hero was driven out to stand these hardships.
Here we have the old motif known from the biblical
story of Joseph and the wife of Potiphar.   Potiphar
is called Proetus and his wife is called Anteia by
Homer, Stheneboia by later authors.   Proetus is
unanimously said to be king of Tiryns; the Cyclopes
built its mighty walls for him.   Homer says that
Proetus drove Bellerophon out from the people of
the Argives because Bellerophon, though subject

[47] *Schol. Il. A*, vi. 183, and *T*, vi. 192.

to him, was a better man than he.[48] This is the regular epical opinion concerning a king's jealousy of a brave vassal; it may have been introduced surreptitiously or it may have preserved an earlier tradition; in the next lines the Potiphar motif is substituted for it.

The scene of this introductory myth is laid at the court of Tiryns, and as there appears no reason whatever why it should have taken place precisely at Tiryns, which in a later age was highly unimportant, I venture to refer this localization to the heyday of Tiryns. This reference to the Mycenaean age receives perhaps a certain corroboration from Homer's hint at a vassalship of Bellerophon, such as was unknown in historical times and even in the Homeric age, if by the Homeric age we understand that age in which the poems were ultimately composed.

The series of adventures which make up the kernel of the myth take place in far-off Lycia. The Amazons are at home in Asia Minor, whatever fact or people may be underlying the myth. The Solymi are always located in the neighborhood of Lycia, although it cannot be proved that references in later authors are independent of Homer. Professor Malten proved in a substantial paper[49] that the Chimaera and the winged horse are of Oriental origin; he thinks that Bellerophon is a Lycian hero

[48] Il. vi., vv. 157 *et seq.* The words ἐκ δήμου ἔλασσεν --- 'Αργείων are of course not to be taken as a contradiction of the localization of Proetus at Tiryns; similarly Agamemnon sometimes is called king of Mycenae and sometimes king of the Argives.

[49] L. Malten, "Bellerophon," *Jahrbuch des deutschen archäolog. Instituts*, XL (1925), pp. 121 *et seq.*

who was taken over by the Greeks during their
wanderings and wars on the eastern shores of the
Mediterranean in the Mycenaean age. If this
kernel of the cycle dates from the Mycenaean age, it
may seem strange that its setting is far-off Lycia,
and that may perhaps be adduced as an argument
against this dating. Happily a Mycenaean representation, the glass plaque from Dendra,[50] shows that
the adventure with the Chimaera was known in the
Mycenaean age.

If we consider things closely, it is not to be wondered at that a Mycenaean myth has its setting
in Lycia. It is contended that the Bellerophon
myth was introduced into Homer by the Ionians.[51]
It is, however, to be observed that there is a wide
tract of land between Ionia and Lycia inhabited
by Dorians and Carians, and the question is relevant,
why have not the Ionians introduced their own
myths? The answer is that they had none. Ionia
is singularly devoid of myths except for foundation
legends of the Ionian cities. Here is a remarkable
fact which ought to be well observed and which
requires an explanation.

This fact agrees with certain outstanding omissions
in Homeric geography.[52] The islands situated in the
neighborhood of Troy, Lesbos, Tenedos, Lemnos,
and Samothrace, are mentioned, but not the rich
Ionian islands, Chios and Samos. On the contrary
the Dorian islands Cos and Rhodes are mentioned,

[50] See above pp. 33 et seq.

[51] Wilamowitz, Die Ilias und Homer (1916), p. 305.

[52] I do not take the Catalogue of the Ships into account, since it is
to be judged on its own merits.

Cos in connection with a myth of Heracles[53] and
Rhodes in a passage considered to be a later addition,
in which is described at length how the Rhodian
hero Tlepolemus was killed by Sarpedon.[54] It is
really curious that the Ionian minstrels had nothing
from their own country to put into their poems.
This fact is notable, for it agrees in a surprising
manner with the well-known but too little appreciated fact that Mycenaean remains are almost
entirely lacking in Ionia. Mycenaean vases and
sherds were found at Troy, at Phocaea, and at
Miletus, a single tomb was discovered at the Heraeum
of Samos,[55] and a bee-hive tomb was discovered at
Colophon.[56] That is all, and nobody will doubt that
if there were Mycenaean tombs their contents would
have appeared in the hands of the dealers. This was
the case on Rhodes, which, on the contrary, is full of
Mycenaean tombs and finds. It is a remarkable
coincidence that a Rhodian hero has found a
place in Homer, and I am not disposed to think it
accidental.

The curious facts and connections put forward here
are further stressed by a consideration of the peoples
allied with the Trojans.[57] If we take the relevant
passages into consideration, omitting the Catalogue,
it appears that the range is strictly limited to northwestern Asia Minor and the neighboring parts of

[53] *Il.* xiv. v. 255; xv. v. 28.

[54] *Il.* v. vv. 628 *et seq.*

[55] *Comptes rendus de l'académie des inscriptions et belles lettres*, 1921,
p. 122. *Gnomon*, III, 1927, p. 189.

[56] *Art and Archaeology*, xiv (1922), p. 259.

[57] Cp. the interesting survey by W. Leaf, *Troy* (1912), pp. 269 *et seq.*

Europe.[58] Most prominent are the Thracians of
Europe, with one exception to which I recur below,
even if the Doloneia is left out of account. Next to
them come the Paeones, a more western Thracian
tribe. For the description of the death of the two
Paeonian heroes is more full than that of the death
of the two Paphlagonian heroes. With the Paphla-
gonians we cross to Asia Minor. Less important is
the mention of the Halizones and of the Mysi; each

[58] I give herewith a survey. Thrace and the Thracians are mentioned fairly often. The death of Peirous from Ainus is described at
some length (*Il.* iv. vv. 517 *et seq.*); another Thracian chief is mentioned
(v. 462) and killed by Aias (vi. 7). Especially in the Doloneia the
Thracians play a prominent part. A leader of the Kikones is killed
(xvii. 73). The Trojan allies are enumerated in this book (x. vv. 428-
434). Following this list we inquire what their parts are in the Iliad.
The Paeones dwelt at the river of Axius in Macedonia. A Paeonian
hero, Pyraichmes, is killed by Patroclus (xvi. 285 *et seq.*) and another,
Asteropaeus, by Achilles; the latter description especially (xxi. 140 *et
seq.*) is rather full; he is mentioned in several other passages and with
him (xvii. 348 *et seq.*) Apisaon. The Paphlagones are not mentioned in
the quoted enumeration, but their chief, Pylaimenes, is killed by Menelaus (v. 577), and his son, Harpalion, by Meriones (xiii. 656 *et seq.*).
The Caucones lived to the west of the Paphlagones; except in the enumeration they are mentioned only in passing (xx. 329). The chief of
the Halizones, Odius, is killed by Agamemnon (v. 39); their town,
according to the Catalogue (ii. 856), was Alybe, but their habitat is
unknown. A Mysian hero is killed by Aias (xiv. 511). It is told that
Priamus received gifts from them (xxiv. 278); and their country is mentioned (xiii. 5), so that it seems to belong to Europe. The Mysi are
a part of the Moesian tribe which emigrated to Asia Minor. Phrygia is
said to be the neighboring country to the empire of Priamus (xxiv. 545);
his queen was a Phrygian princess. Apollo appears to Hector in the
figure of her brother Asius who lived on the shores of Sangarius (xvi. 715
et seq.). The Maeones were a tribe living in Lydia. Their country
is mentioned in passing (iii. 401; and xviii. 291), and the people are
mentioned in the quoted enumeration. A Maeonian woman is said to
be skilled in dyeing (iv. 142); and Iphition who was born at Hyde near
Mount Tmolus is killed by Achilles (xx. 385 *et seq.*), and in this connection
the Gygaean lake and the rivers of Hyllus and Hermus are mentioned.

people has the death of a hero briefly mentioned.
The Caucones are mentioned twice in passing.
No Phrygian hero takes part in the war, but the
country appears in the background as the mighty
empire it was, in the description of Priam's visit
and in the fact that Hecabe was a Phrygian princess.
The Maeones, who belonged to Lydia and lived
south of the Mysians, are mentioned only in passing,
and some knowledge of the country is displayed in
another passage. The Carians occur only in the
enumeration of the Trojan allies in the Doloneia.

This is a very consistent limitation to the neighboring peoples north and east of Troy, and it is most
natural in view of the situation of Troy. It is obvious
and reasonable that the Homeric poets took the
conditions of their own age into account in describing
the allies of Troy, of whom old myths had not much
to tell. I have dwelt more fully upon this in order
to emphasize the astonishing fact that none of the
Trojan allies plays such a prominent part as the
people hitherto not mentioned, the Lycians who lived
in the far-off south of Asia Minor.

The passages where Lycia and the Lycians are
mentioned are too numerous to be enumerated, and
I need only point to the prominent part played by
the Lycian heroes Sarpedon, Glaucus, and Pandarus
in various songs of the Iliad.[59] But in the fourth
book it is said that Pandarus came from the town
of Zeleia and the river Aesepus,[60] which flows from
Mount Ida to the sea,[61] and these indications are

[59] Especially in v, xi, and xvi.
[60] Il. iv. vv. 105 and 91.
[61] Il. xi. v. 21.

reproduced in the Catalogue.[62] This contradicts
the Lycian localization of Pandarus, but scholars
have generally held the opinion that the habitat
of the Lycians was erroneously transferred to the
Troas and the shores of Aesepus. Professor Wilamowitz and Dr. Finsler on the contrary have put forward the view that the Lycians were originally at
home there and that their name was transferred to
the Termiles,[63] as the native inhabitants of Lycia
called themselves. There is no apparent reason for
such a transference and the mythological expression
which usually is given to such a change is wanting.
It would of course imply that Sarpedon and Glaucus
also were at home in the Troas, but the above-
mentioned scholars have not been inclined to draw
this conclusion. The old opinion is certainly right.
The Homeric poets, who did not know the south of
Asia Minor, transplanted Pandarus to the Troas,
naturally placing the allies of the Trojans in the
neighborhood of Troy.

Moreover, the same thing seems to have happened
in the case of the Cilicians. Andromache is said
to be the daughter of Eëtion, ruler of the Cilicians
and king of Thebes beneath Mount Plakos, a town
which was taken by Achilles.[64] Evidently this
Thebes is not far from Troy, but the existence of
Cilicians elsewhere than in southeastern Asia Minor

---

[62] Il. ii. vv. 824 et seq.

[63] Wilamowitz, *Hermes*, XXXVIII (1903), p. 585; Finsler, *Homer*
(ed. 3; 1924), p. 17.

[64] *Il.* vi. vv. 395 et seq.; cp. i. vv. 366 et seq. and xxii. vv. 479 et
seq. E. Bethe, *Neue Jahrbücher für klass. Altertumswissenschaft*, VII
(1901), p. 671, proposed the hypothesis that this Thebe is the Thessalian
town with that name. This view was supported by O. Kern, *ibid.*, XIII
(1904), p. 16, and by P. Cauer, *Grundfragen der Homerkritik* (ed. 3, 1921),

is unknown. I can but think that the poet had vaguely heard about the Cilicians but did not know their habitat and made them, off-hand, inhabitants of Thebes beneath Mount Plakos.

Be this as it may, the enigmatical fact remains that the most prominent adversaries of the Greeks next to the Trojans themselves are a people in the far-off south of Asia Minor. And this fact is connected with the other, that the myth of Bellerophon, of which the Mycenaean date is attested by a Mycenaean work of art, is localized in Lycia. Here the observation comes into play that the middle part of the western coast of Asia Minor, Ionia, is almost devoid of Mycenaean remains. On the other hand, Rhodes has both myths and Mycenaean remains, and a Rhodian hero appears in the Iliad, though many scholars think that the passage is an interpolation.

There is, however, a very obvious explanation of these facts, one which, moreover, corroborates the Mycenaean origin of the myth and the Mycenaean background of epics. I have pointed to the scarcity of Mycenaean remains in Ionia.[65] Archaeology proves that the western coast of Asia Minor was colonized by the Greeks only at the very end of the Mycenaean age. Prior to this time the wandering Greek tribes followed the highway toward the east, enticed by the great and rich civilization of Syria

p. 261. It was also developed by F. Staehlin, *Das Hypoplakische Thebe, eine Sagenverschiebung bei Homer* (Programm, München, 1907), but it fails to account for the inhabitants being Cilicians, and is most unlikely. It is a remarkable fact that the names of the cities which are by Homer attributed to the Cilicians, Thebes and Lyrnessus, recur in Pamphylia (Steph. Byz. *s. v.* Θήβη and Σάρδησσος; cp. P. Kretschmer, *Glotta*, XIII (1924), p. 209 *et seq.*)

[65] In my *Minoan-Mycenaean Religion*, p. 27, and above p. 53.

and Egypt. In doing so they followed the lure of
wealth and civilization just as other barbarous
peoples have followed it, e.g., the Teutonic tribes
when they flooded the Roman empire. These
wanderings have left their traces in the early colonization of Cyprus and its numerous Mycenaean
remains. Here the statement in the Iliad may be
noticed, that Agamemnon received a valuable gift,
a richly decorated cuirass, from the Cyprian king
Cinyras.[66] Mycenaean finds are fairly numerous
also on the coast of Syria. Greek tribes appeared
in the Delta about 1200 B. C. Dr. Forrer's great
Achaean kingdom with possessions on the southern
coast of Asia Minor coincides remarkably with this
movement of the Greek tribes.

The road which the Greeks followed went along the
southern shore of Asia Minor. They colonized the
islands of Rhodes and Cyprus and seem to have had
a stronghold or trading station on the Syrian coast
near Laodicea *ad mare*.[67] We must surmise that
they also tried to take booty and to gain a foothold
on the southern coast of Asia Minor. Unhappily
this country is almost unknown archaeologically.
But Dr. Gjerstad who visited Cilicia recently informs
me that there is evidence of Mycenaean colonization
in this district. If Dr. Forrer is right, the Achaean
king had possessed himself of Pamphylia about 1330
B.C. But apart from this it must be presumed that
the Greeks during their voyages along the southern

[66] *Il.* xi. v. 20.

[67] Lively connections with the Mycenaean world are proved by
numerous Mycenaean finds in the recent excavations at Minet el Beida
north of Laodicea *ad mare* on the Syrian coast; see the periodical *Syria*,
X (1929), pp. 285 *et seq.*

coast of Asia Minor had numerous opportunities of coming into conflict with the peoples who lived there, and these were the Lycians and the Cilicians.

The memory of these fights was preserved in the myths and in the epics. Hence the Lycians came to play a prominent part, and the adventures of Bellerophon were localized in Lycia. The woeful signs of the message which he carried from the king of Tiryns to the king of Lycia refer of course to the Minoan script which the Greeks took with them to Cyprus. The battles with the Lycians were celebrated in early epics and were from these introduced into the Trojan epos with that disregard for geography and chronology which is peculiar to epics, when events are incorporated into them. While the Lycians loomed largely in earlier recitals, they became the chief adversaries of the Greeks next to the Trojans themselves in the Trojan cycle.[68]

The same thing happened in the case of the Cilicians. The Greeks had learned to know them also during their voyages toward the east, and for this reason they were mentioned in epics and recitals. The Homeric poet took over the tradition and had heard that they were a mighty people, but not knowing their whereabouts he thought them fit to be the people over whom the father-in-law of the most brilliant hero of the Trojans ruled, just as Hecabe

[68] Wilamowitz, *Die Ilias und Homer* (1916), p. 305, contends that the Ionians introduced the Lycians because their kings claimed descent partly from the Lycian hero Glaucus (Herodotus i. 147); *Inschr. von Magnesia a. M.*, No. 17; O. Kern, *Die Gründungsgeschichte von Magnesia a. M.* (1894). I have above given my opinion of similar instances. The fame of Glaucus is due to the Homeric epics, and that is the reason why the genealogies were attached to him.

came from the mighty Phrygian empire. King
Cinyras of Cyprus who gave Agamemnon an artfully
wrought cuirass may have been introduced into
Homer from the same source.

As far as I can see, this is the most natural explanation of the relevant facts. I have dwelt upon it at
length because it not only corroborates the Mycenaean origin of the Bellerophon myth but also gives
a valuable outlook on the Mycenaean background
of the epics.

I touch only lightly upon another myth connected
with Tiryns, because its association with Mycenaean
times is very uncertain. This is the story of the
daughters of King Proetus, who went mad and,
according to the common version, were healed by
the seer Melampus. The earliest testimony, the
Catalogue of Hesiod, says that Hera punished the
maidens because of their excessive indulgence in
love affairs. In a late epos, the Melampodeia, the
tale is transferred into the usual Dionysiac scheme.
The Proetides are driven mad by Dionysus because
they resisted his cult. Melampus, who is said by
Herodotus to have taught the name and the cult
of Dionysus and the phallic processions, belongs
evidently to the religious movement of the archaic
age in which the cult of Dionysus was received and
regulated. The version according to which Hera
caused the madness is earlier and moreover connected with Tiryns, where Hera was the chief
goddess, but it is impossible to say how old it may be.

It has been remarked pertinently that the myth
of the Proetides has the same basic idea as that of
Io. Although the statement that the Proetides

believed that they had been metamorphosed into
cows occurs only in late writers, the same elements
are conspicuous—the wrath of Hera, the madness,
and the extensive wanderings, but in the case of Io
the love of Zeus is given as the cause, and Argus is
said to have watched Io and to have been killed by
Hermes.   There is no certain clue for unraveling
this myth.   I am content to point to the fact that it
is attached to the Heraeum, which was built upon
a Mycenaean site of importance, and that it especially established the connection of Hera with the
cow.[69]   There is certainly reason to think that the
cult of Hera at the Heraeum is of Mycenaean date,
and this may perhaps be surmised in regard to the
myth, too, although there is no specific proof.   If
some explanation is wanted, it may be guessed that
the ecstatic cult of the nature goddess, with dances,
which is so conspicuous on Mycenaean monuments,
gave rise to this myth, just as the somewhat kindred
ecstatic cult of Dionysus gave rise to many similar
myths in a later age.   But this is of course a mere
guess, and the myth of Io may be dismissed, not
being very essential for our purpose.

At last we come to Argos, the capital of Argolis
in historical times.   In the Mycenaean age it was
but one of the minor sites and its remains from this
age are not important.   Of the myths connected
with the city of Argos, we may pass over that of
the culture hero Phoroneus, who is much less prominent than the hero of Nauplia, Palamedes, and the
eponymous hero Argos; in a later chapter I shall recur to the attempt to make him a rival of Heracles.[70]

[69] See my *Griechische Feste* (1906), pp. 42 *et seq.*   [70] Below p. 212.

The only myth of interest, but, nevertheless, of a
very great interest, is that of the Danaides.

The kernel of this myth was always the murder
on the bridal night of the fifty sons of Aegyptus by
the fifty daughters of Danaüs. The reason why this
mass murder was perpetrated and the relations between the fathers, Danaüs and Aegyptus, differ in
various versions and are of secondary importance.
The events which followed are also related variously,
but it is well to observe that, according to the current
versions, the Danaides were not punished for their
cruel deed.[71]

What does this deed of the Danaides, the murder
of their husbands, signify? The nature symbolism,
according to which this myth like many others
was interpreted formerly, need hardly be discussed
seriously.[72] If we disregard such more or less far-
fetched interpretation, the tale which seems to
present the closest analogy is that of Judith and
Holophernes, the tale of the Jewish woman who
enticed the oppressor of her people into love and
slew him on the bridal night. It may be worth while

[71] Except in a single late version, *Schol. Eurip. Hec.* 886, according
to which Lynceus, the only son of Aegyptus who was saved, put them
to death. P. Friedländer, who treats the myth at length in his dissertation, *Argolica* (Berlin, 1905), pp. 5 *et seq.*, takes this version to be the
oldest, quite arbitrarily. This is one weak point of his reasoning; the
other is that there is no apparent reason why the brother of Danaüs,
ejected from Argos, should retire to Egypt. The well-known myth that
the Danaides were compelled to carry water in perforated vessels is
Hellenistic and was transferred to them from those who were not initiated
into the mysteries. I agree with Robert, *Griech. Heldensage*, p. 277,
that it is an Orphic invention.

[72] The connection of the Danaides with the spring at Lerna,
Apollodorus, ii. 1, 5, 11, and Paus., ii. 24, 2, is superficial. Amymone
was not originally one of the Danaides.

to try to proceed on this analogy. It implies that the motif, which is so conspicuous in the legend of Judith, the heroism of the woman, had been forgotten in the Greek tradition. The Greek shuddered always in telling the story, but if the deed was originally a crime, it is impossible to understand why no punishment followed, or if a punishment was given, why that was forgotten. So much seems to be absolutely certain, that the killing of the husbands, the sons of Aegyptus, was originally no crime. It cannot have been an action neither good nor bad. Was it then a heroic deed?

There is a curious question to which very little attention has been paid. Why are the Danaides so many, not less than fifty? We may understand why, to prove his heroic strength, it is told that Heracles in one night begat fifty sons, but there is no apparent reason why the Danaides should be so many and the killing of their husbands a wholesale massacre. If we take the word Danaides in the original sense of Danaan maidens[73] and not according to the usual interpretation as the daughters of Danaüs, a way to understanding this feature will perhaps be opened; Danaüs is moreover a very shadowy personage.

The current opinion is that the husbands of the Danaides were originally nameless and that they were made sons of Aegyptus only after the Greeks had learned to know Egypt in the seventh century B. C.[74] As they found animals venerated in this

[73] The alternative form Δανααί occurs in a quotation from Hesiod in Strabo, viii, p. 371; frag. 24 Rzach, ed. 3.

[74] E.g. Ed. Meyer, *Forschungen zur alten Geschichte* I (1892), p. 84.

country, they transferred the myth of Io, who
was metamorphosed into a cow, to Egypt, and with
the Io myth that of the Danaides also was transferred
to Egypt; thus their husbands were made sons of
Aegyptus. The elaboration of the cycle is ascribed
to the author of a lost epos, the Danais, of which only
one fragment is preserved, telling that the daughters
of Danaüs armed themselves near the river of the
Nile.[75] This seems prima facie to refer to the killing
of their husbands, and if this is so, the locality
where the drama was enacted was changed. For in
the current version Danaüs and his daughters flee
to Argos, the sons of Aegyptus pursue them and com-
pel them there to the disastrous wedding. To avoid
this contradiction others refer the words to a fight
in which the maidens engaged before leaving Egypt.[76]
This seems to be a very doubtful means of evading
the localization in Egypt, which probably is really
the old version.

The Greeks, however, knew Egypt not only in the
seventh century B. C., but also in the twelfth century
B. C., when Greek tribes and in fact the Danaans
tried to invade Egypt; and we know, moreover,
that these migrating peoples came with wives and
children. There is a circumstance pointing to the
probability that the myth goes back to this time.
For the tribal name of the Danaans is already obsolete in Homer and it is hardly probable that it was
picked up and applied to a myth invented in the
seventh century B. C. If the myth goes back to

[75] *Frag. epic. graec.* ed. Kinkel, p. 78.

[76] For another attempted explanation see Ed. Meyer, *loc. cit.*, p.
82, n. 3.

the time when the Danaans raided Egypt, its origin may be explainable under the conditions of this time. A crowd of Danaan women had been captured and made concubines of Egyptians; they slew their husbands and escaped. The wholesale slaughter of the Greeks on Lemnos by their indigenous wives is a somewhat kindred story, explaining why this island was lost to Greek colonization.[77] This may be the simple underlying fact; certainly it explains why the deed was not considered a crime. It is a simple story from the life of that stormy age, simpler than the dramatic episode of Judith and Holophernes, but the analogy is there.[78]

This explanation of the myth of the Danaïdes as an historical reminiscence from the time when the Danaans attacked Egypt may seem hazardous to many, and I am quite aware of its hypothetical character; but it is perhaps not less probable than other interpretations which have been proposed. If my guess hits the mark, this fable is the only one connected with the city of Argos which goes back into the Mycenaean age. But it is evident that it in fact refers to the whole province of Argos and not to its later capital, with which it was connected only loosely and secondarily. The unimportance of the city of Argos from a mythological standpoint cor-

[77] I agree with Wilamowitz, *Sitzungsberichte der preuss. Akademie der Wissenschaften*, 1906, p. 76, that this is the meaning of the myth, which was very much enlarged and remodeled. The latest treatment, by G. Dumézil, *Le crime des Lemniennes* (1924), takes up other points of view.

[78] In the first edition of his *Geschichte des Altertums*, I (1884), p. 264, Ed. Meyer found a reminiscence of old wanderings of the peoples in the story of the emigration of Danaüs from Egypt; later in his *Forschungen, loc. cit.*, he changed his view.

responds to its obscurity in the Mycenaean age. When Argos became the capital of the province, it tried of course to build up a mythology of its own; we have noticed these efforts, but they cannot deceive anybody.

2. LACONIA

From Argolis, the chief seat of the Mycenaean civilization, we proceed to the southeastern province, Laconia. Several important Mycenaean remains are found here, but they cannot be compared with those of Argolis. The bee-hive tomb at Vaphio near Sparta where the two golden cups, the most beautiful products of Minoan art, were found, with various pieces of jewelry, proves that wealthy princes ruled here in the Mycenaean age. Very remarkable are the finds at Amyclae, showing that the cult of the pre-Greek god Hyacinthus was celebrated in the Mycenaean age. The Menelaeion at Sparta also probably goes back into Mycenaean times; it is in fact the sanctuary of Helen at Therapnae.[1] Elsewhere Mycenaean finds are unimportant.

Before we enter upon the Laconian myths a preliminary question is to be discussed. In historical times Argos claimed the primacy in the Peloponnese; though it was unable to support these claims, it never bowed down completely to Sparta. Its claims found an expression in the myth that Argolis was the inheritance allotted to Temenus, the eldest son of Aristomachus. We shall see how Sparta in this as well as in other cases tried to change and reshape the myths in its own favor. The claims of Argos correspond to the relation between the two provinces

[1] *Annual* of the British School at Athens, XV (1909), pp. 108 *et seq.*

in the Mycenaean age, during which Argos was the most important province and Laconia relatively unimportant, and they go ultimately back into this time, for in later times there is nothing to warrant the predominance of Argos. The reign of King Pheidon about which our information is regretably scarce and uncertain was too ephemeral to have founded such persistently sustained claims.

In Homer the relation between the two provinces is just this. Lacedaemon appears as a vassalage of the king of Mycenae, or rather as a secundogeniture given to his younger brother. That Agamemnon and Menelaus were co-regents, as the Spartan kings were, is one of a series of ill-founded contentions which try to find traces of the conditions of historical Sparta in the Homeric poems. In Homer and in mythology on the whole, Menelaus is clearly subordinate to Agamemnon. There is, however, a well attested version according to which Agamemnon and his son Orestes were at home in Laconia, and this must be taken into consideration, for it would move the seat of the overlord from Argolis to Laconia.

This was a received opinion, at least among some people, at the beginning of the fifth century B. C. Pindarus says in one of his odes that the Atreides, i.e., Agamemnon, died at Amyclae and calls Orestes a Lacedaemonian; in another ode, which praises a victorious athlete from Tenedos, he says that this athlete's ancestors went with Orestes from Amyclae,[2] hinting at the emigration conducted by Penthilus.[3]

[2] Pindarus, *Pyth.*, xi. vv. 24; 47 *et seq.*; and *Nem.*, xi. v. 44 resp.
[3] Above p. 49.

Especially explicit is a passage in Herodotus.[4] The Spartan ambassador replies to King Gelon, who claimed the hegemony in the war against the Persians, that Agamemnon would groan, if he heard that the hegemony was taken from the Spartans by the Syracusan Gelon. Stesichorus, whether he is a citizen of Himera from the seventh century B. C. or a Locrian from about 500 B. C.[5] proffers the same localization.[6] From these passages only one legitimate conclusion may be drawn; viz., that the Spartans tried to appropriate Agamemnon for themselves as the prototype of their hegemony in the Peloponnese, just as the Dorians appropriated Heracles in order to justify their possession of the peninsula. In their war with the Arcadians they transferred the bones of Orestes from Tegea to Sparta.

There seems, however, to be an earlier testimony in a passage in the Odyssey[7] which relates that Agamemnon on his voyage homeward from Troy, coming to Cape Malea was driven by storms out on the sea to the extreme part of the country where Aegisthus resided, but that the gods changed the wind and he alighted with joy in his fatherland. But Aegisthus who had put out watchmen to watch his return, invited him to a meal and killed him and his followers. We may observe that these sentences are not coherent; this is a puzzle to which we return presently. In a preceding passage it is

[4] Herodotus, vii, 159.
[5] Wilamowitz is inclined to think so ("Die griech. Heldensage," I, *Sitzungsberichte der preuss. Akad. der Wissenschaften* 1925, p. 46, n. 1).
[6] In the *Schol. Eurip. Orestes*, v. 46.
[7] *Od.* iv. vv. 514 *et seq.*

related that Aegisthus seduced Clytaemestra and became the ruler of Mycenae, but the murder of Agamemnon is passed over with only two words.[8]

Now for a person voyaging from Troy to Argolis, Cape Malea is evidently out of the way; whilst it would be on the way for one going to Lacedaemon. Observing this fact scholars have analyzed the passages in question with the tools of logic, assuming that the verse about Cape Malea is based upon the localization of Agamemnon as well as of Aegisthus in Lacedaemon.[9] They think that a narrative in which Agamemnon had his residence at Amyclae was worked over in order to make it fit in with the current opinion of his residence at Mycenae. I refrain from criticizing the criticism and remark only that when a poet adapts earlier chants for use in his poems, as certainly has been done here, inconsistencies and errors will be committed very easily and almost unavoidably. Such inconsistencies and errors exist undoubtedly in Homer. In this case they are the words about "the steep mountain of Malea," v. 514, and the two verses 519 and 520. The foregoing verses tell that Agamemnon was driven out on the sea, when he rounded Cape Malea, to the extreme part of the country where Aegisthus resided. The two verses in question add that "when an opportunity for safe return appeared the gods changed the wind again and they came home." The narrative proceeds to tell that they alighted

[8] *Od.* iii. vv. 243 *et seq.*

[9] Ed. Schwartz, "Agamemnon von Sparta und Orestes von Tegea in der Telemachie," *Strassburger Festschrift zur xlvi. Versammlung deutscher Philologen*, 1901, pp. 23 *et seq.* Cp. K. Kunst, "Die Schuld der Klytaimestra," *Wiener Studien*, XLIV (1924–25), pp. 18 *et seq.*

with joy and that Aegisthus laid an ambush for
them and murdered them. The two verses are
incomprehensible in the given situation and there
must be something wrong with them. The reference
to Cape Malea was, as Dr. Kunst observes,[10] taken
over from the description of the calamity befalling
Menelaus at the same place on his return. I agree
with Professor Schwartz that the two verses 519
and 520 were added later in order to smooth over
the discrepancy.[11] A transposition of the two
verses before v. 517, which is adopted by some
editors, does not remove the difficulty.

If the two verses in question are cancelled and if
in v. 514 the southernmost cape of the Argive
peninsula is put instead of Cape Malea, the narrative
proceeds consistently. Agamemnon was driven by
the gale from the landing place in Argolis at which
he aimed, but succeeded in coming ashore at a far-off
place in Argolis where Aegisthus lived; for as a
member of the royal dynasty he must have a castle
and a town. Thus Agamemnon was by fate brought
into the hands of Aegisthus. Why Aegisthus did
not reside at Mycenae after having won Clytaemestra
is an idle question; he did so after having killed
Agamemnon because he therewith took the place
of the Great King. Thus the most probable solution
is that there is behind this passage a minstrel's
error, of which the Spartans have taken advantage
in order to appropriate Agamemnon for themselves.
Furthermore I am inclined to think with Mr.
Harrie[12] that the temple of Alexandra at Sparta

[10] Kunst, *loc. cit.*, p. 23.　　[11] Schwartz, *loc. cit.* p. 25.
[12] I. Harrie, "Zeus Agamemnon," *Archiv für Religionswissenschaft,*
XXIII (1925), pp. 366 *et seq.*

with Agamemnon's memorial has been of importance in establishing the story.

Thus we shall have satisfactorily answered the question as to how Agamemnon and with him Orestes came to be localized at Lacedaemon. In view of the relative importance of the two provinces in the Mycenaean age it is impossible to take the overlord from Mycenae and to transfer him to Lacedaemon.

If we turn to Laconian mythology a curious circumstance is prominent: we have much less to do with personages of heroic mythology than with old gods who were received into it. Helen is an old goddess whose origin belongs to the Mycenaean age and who always was a goddess at Sparta. On reliefs from the second century B. C. we see her image between those of the Dioscuri in the form of a stiff *xoanon* from whose wrists fillets hang down and who wears a kind of calathus on her head.[13] She had two temples at Sparta: one is the so-called Menelaeion, her famous temple at Therapnae which was built upon a Mycenaean site, while another was situated not far from the Platanistas; with the Helen of this temple tree-cult rites were connected.

---

[13] Tod and Wace, *A Catalogue of the Sparta Museum*, pp. 117 and 158. I am now a little more inclined than in my *Minoan-Mycenaean Religion* (p. 458 n. 1) to identify this head-dress of Helen with the basket ἐλένη, in which according to Pollux, x. 191, unspeakable sacred things were carried at the Ἑλενηφόρια. The head-dress looks really more like a basket than like a common *polos* which, according to K. Val. Müller, *Der Polos* (Dissertation, Berlin 1915), was originally a decorative head-dress without any peculiar signification. The Ἑλενηφόρια were formerly said to be an Attic festival, but since Kaibel has established the reading of the manuscripts Δίφιλος δ' ἐν Ἑλαιωνηφοροῦσι in Athenaeus, vi. p. 223 A, this supposition is groundless; our only information is the passage in Pollux.

It is, however, not known to which of these two
temples the festival of Heleneia which was celebrated
in her honor belonged. Her connection with the
tree cult is corroborated by the fact that there was a
plant called *heleneion*, just as the word *hyakinthos*
denotes both a god and a plant. Helen appears
in connection with the tree cult on Rhodes also,
where Helen Dendritis was venerated.[14]

In mythology Helen is, however, localized in
Attica also. Theseus carried her away with the aid
of Peirithous and hid her in the fortress of Aphidna.
The attempts to separate this myth from Aphidna
in Attica have failed.[15] In order to corroborate this
statement it is hardly necessary to refer to the island
called Helene near the coast of Attica and to other
dubious instances.[16] That Helen was rescued by
her brothers the Dioscuri is, however, rightly considered to be a later addition. We state that Helen
was at home in Attica also, and this ought not to be
astonishing, for if she was an old goddess she may
have been venerated in several places. Although
her cult was preserved chiefly at Sparta, she has
left traces in myths elsewhere.

If it is asked why this old pre-Greek goddess
became the pivot of the Trojan war, I can, I believe,

[14] For references for the above statement see my *Minoan-Mycenaean Religion*, pp. 456 *et seq.*

[15] See J. Toepffer, "Theseus and Peisistratos" in his *Beiträge zur
griech. Altertumswissenschaft*, pp. 153 *et seq.*, reprinted from the volume
Aus der Anomia (1890), pp. 36 *et seq.* V. Costanzi, "Il culto di Teseo nell'
Attica," *Religio*, I (1920), pp. 315 *et seq.* Cp. Wilamowitz, "Die griech.
Heldensage II," *Sitzungsberichte der preuss. Akad. der Wissenschaften*,
1925, p. 236.

[16] As Pfuhl does in Pauly-Wissowa's *Realencyklopädie der klass.
Altertumswissenschaft, s. v.* Helena, p. 2829.

see but one explanation. It was peculiar to Helen
to be carried off, by Theseus and by Alexander.
The rape of a goddess is a well-known feature in a
special cult legend; Pluto carries off Kore. Though
at first it may seem astonishing, the rape of Kore and
the rape of Helen are in fact kindred, if we look
away from the Helen of epics and take her as the
old goddess that she was; she is a vegetation goddess,
just as Kore is. In the myth of Theseus, to which I
shall recur later,[17] there is an apparent doublet;
he and his friend Peirithous try to carry off Persephone, who is identified with Kore. That may be
better understood if there was a reminiscence that
Helen was originally akin to Kore-Persephone.

For us the rape of Kore by Pluto looms in the
most sacred light of Greek cult legend and religion;
the rape of Helen presents itself as a frivolous and
scandalous quite profane story; but this difference
may be a result of a development under different
conditions. The myth told that the old pre-Greek
goddess Helen was carried off, but the invading
Greeks did not seize the deep sense of the legend,
only the feature so common in the heroic age, the
feuds of which were caused by the theft either of
cattle or of women, that a woman called Helen was
carried off. When the familiar motif of the rape of
a fair woman was given as the cause of the Trojan
war, the woman was called by the name of the
goddess of whose carrying off the Greeks had heard
but whose cult had fallen into disuse in most places.
Or it is perhaps better to say that Helen was in cult
legend replaced by Kore, who always retained her

[17] Below pp. 170 *et seq.*

dignified position, not being drawn, as was Helen, into the heroic mythology. Helen, consequently, came to be treated as a mortal woman, of course a princess. She was made the queen of the city in which she still was especially venerated, and when introduced into the Trojan cycle she sank still lower, to become the woman who eloped with an Asiatic prince.

I pass over Hyacinthus briefly, only calling attention to the well-known and very interesting fact that his name is evidently pre-Greek and that the site of his temple at Amyclae yielded numerous Mycenaean finds.[18] He is perhaps the most evident instance of the continuity of a Mycenaean cult in the Greek age, but he was superseded by Apollo. Thus the well-known myth arose that he was killed by the god by accident. His death is without doubt a primary fact originating in the Minoan conception of gods who die, viz., vegetation gods. How old the common myth is, it is impossible to decide; in some respects it seems rather late. Of course it must be later than the coming of Apollo.

The brothers of Helen, the Dioscuri, are both as gods and as heroes the most famous in Lacedaemon. They are perhaps the most complex among the Greek gods.[19] Commonly we think of them as youthful horsemen, the models of Spartan youth, and the saviours of men in sudden perils, especially at sea. But they were also house gods and as such widely venerated in Greece. Their symbols

[18] See my *Minoan-Mycenaean Religion*, pp. 403 and 485 *et seq.*

[19] The problem is more complex than appears in Farnell, *Greek Hero Cults*, pp. 175 *et seq.*; e.g. he passes over the very important house cult without a word.

are two amphoras with the *panspermia*, snakes,[20] and the *dokana*, which can only be the beams of a house built of sun-dried bricks. The sacrifices brought to them are meals, *theoxenia*, which occur particularly in the house cult. They are especially connected with the Spartan kings, who took them with them when taking the field.

On the other hand, the Dioscuri are heroes localized at Lacedaemon, sons of Tyndareus and brothers of Helen. In the only passage in which they are mentioned in the Iliad[21] they appear as athletic youths and it is said that the earth already covered them in their fatherland. They are one of the many instances of mythical twins, but they are also venerated as gods. It seems likely that these mythical heroes and these gods were originally separate personages and that they have been united so as to form the Dioscuri as we know them. Homer says that they were dead and buried, i.e., he knows them as heroes only. The discrepancy was later smoothed over by the well-known myths in which one, Pollux, was said to be a god and the other, Castor, a mortal; or that they alternated, living on one day and staying beneath the earth on the next.[22]

The Dioscuri are perhaps related to the Minoan religion. I have discussed this probability in another place,[23] but I am well aware that the matter

[20] In this they resemble Zeus Ktesios, a veritable house god; see my paper, "Zeus Ktesios," *Athen. Mittheilungen*, XXXIII (1908), pp. 279 *et seq.*, and my *Griech. Feste*, pp. 417 *et seq.*

[21] *Il.* iii. vv. 237 *et seq.*

[22] *Od.* xi. vv. 303 *et seq.*

[23] In my *Minoan-Mycenaean Religion*, pp. 469 *et seq.*

is uncertain and I have nothing to add here but a
few words concerning their fight with the Apharetidae, another pair of twins, for other myths about
them are clearly secondary and due chiefly to their
connection with Helen, which can hardly be very
old. The mythographers differ in regard to the cause
of the contest. On one side, it is told that the
Dioscuri and the Apharetidae having together stolen
cattle in Arcadia quarreled about their booty; on
the other, it is said that the Dioscuri carried off the
daughters of Leucippus, who were the brides of the
Apharetidae. Sometimes the two versions are combined. It is generally acknowledged that the former,
being the more primitive, is the older version; the
uniting of both versions into one myth is due to the
epos called Cypria.[24] The Apharetidae appear as
Messenian heroes and their engagement with the
Dioscuri is consequently thought to reflect the
strife between the Messenians and the Spartans, but
the place of the fight was near Sparta, according
to Lycophron, who follows the Cypria.[25] Thus it is
possible that the myth was originally enacted at
Lacedaemon and that it is earlier than the hostility
between the Messenians and the Spartans, but it is
not possible to surmise how old it is, and above all,
there is no evidence whereby to connect it with the
Mycenaean age.

[24] These results attained by G. Wentzel in his excellent dissertation
Ἐπικλήσεις θεῶν (Göttingen 1890), V., pp. 18 *et seq.*, are generally
recognized.

[25] Lycophron, *Alexandra*, v. 559. Paus. iii. 11. 11, mentions the
memorial of Aphareus on the market place of Sparta, and (iii. 13, 1)
near the Skias of the same city the tombs of Idas and Lynceus, but himself finds it probable that they were buried in Messenia.

Concluding these considerations we may state that
Laconia on the one hand has Mycenaean remains but
fewer and less important remains than those of
Argolis, and that on the other hand it has some myths
but fewer and less important myths and especially
fewer heroic myths, than Argolis.

3. THE DOMINION OF PYLOS

West of Laconia and separated from it by the
high and steep Mount Taygetus is Messenia, but
the boundaries of this province toward the north
are not so neatly fixed as those of Laconia. In historical times they varied not a little.[1] Triphylia,
the coastal district north of Messenia between Neda
and Alpheus, was long a province in its own right,
and thus can hardly be reckoned as part of one of
the great provinces until the Eleans subjugated it
together with the district of Olympia, Pisatis, in
the middle of the fifth century B. C. Later the
Arcadians laid claim on Triphylia. We have to
turn to archaeology and mythology in order to see
what parts of the southwestern Peloponnese are
to be reckoned with in the early age.

That we are able to discern the traces of Mycenaean settlements in Messenia better than we
previously could is to a great extent due to the
strenuous work which Dr. Valmin through several
years has devoted to this province, together with
the earlier explorations of other scholars. Contrary
to its expansion in Argolis, Boeotia, and Attica,
Mycenaean civilization in the western Peloponnese

[1] For the latest discussion see N. Valmin, *Études topographiques
sur la Messénie ancienne* (Dissertation, Lund 1930), pp. 5 *et seq.*

clings to the coast, with one exception, which will be discussed below. This is unparalleled elsewhere in Mycenaean Greece except in southern Thessaly. A nice tholos tomb was found at Kampos on the eastern side of the Messenian gulf. The seven cities which Agamemnon promised to Achilles are not identified, with two exceptions, but relying upon these identified places scholars believe them all to have been situated around the gulf. Some Mycenaean sherds, but as yet very few, have been found in sites near this coast, at Samarina, Pidima, and Karteroli. The upper plain is as yet devoid of Mycenaean remains.[2] On the western coast a few Mycenaean finds were made at Mothone and at Cyparissia. A really important Mycenaean site was that Pylus near which the island of Sphacteria is situated. A little toward the north at Tragana are a prehistoric acropolis and two tholos tombs, of which one has been excavated and has yielded beautiful late Mycenaean vases. Near by at Osman Aga are other tholos tombs.[3]

The place in the western Peloponnese where the most important discoveries from the Mycenaean age have been made is the village of Kakovatos on the coast about six miles north of the mouth of the Neda and the boundary of Messenia. Here are an acropolis with remains of walls, a palace, Mycenaean sherds, and three tholos tombs of fair size; though they

[2] Another very remarkable fact is that no Geometric ceramics are found in Messenia.

[3] Excavated by Professor Kourouniotes, see *Ephemeris archaiologike*, 1914, p. 99 *et seq.*; cp. *Bulletin de correspondence hellénique*, L (1926), pp. 552 *et seq.* The tombs must be dated to LH III, not with Kourouniotes to LH II.

have been robbed, enough remains to show that they once were very rich. Especially notable are the beautiful ceramics belonging to the second Mycenaean period. To the same period belong also the ceramics found in the tholus tomb of the Messenian Pylos, and others from Kleidi, which is on the coast somewhat north of Kakovatos, near Samikon, and which Professor Dörpfeld identifies with the Homeric Arene.[4] Following certain ancient authors who sought the Homeric Pylos in this neighborhood, he put forward the opinion that the Mycenaean site at Kakovatos is to be identified with the Homeric Pylos, the city of Nestor. This view has attracted attention to this place and is widely accepted, but is also contested.

To the west of the Upper Messenian plain is the plain of Sulima through which the railway to Cyparissia now passes. Here Dr. Valmin made interesting discoveries.[5] The two plains are separated by a ridge now called Malthi. On this ridge was a Mycenaean settlement built upon an earlier Helladic one, with an apsidal house. A Mycenaean house of fairly large proportions has been excavated. In the plain below this ridge are two tholos tombs of which one has been excavated, and a little farther toward the west near Kopanaki four others have been discovered, of which one has been cleared. The tombs excavated had been thoroughly plundered so that the finds were poor; they belong to

---

[4] *Athen. Mittheilungen*, XXXIII (1908), p. 321.

[5] See his dissertation quoted n. 1, pp. 103 and 112 *et seq.* and his papers, "Two Tholos Tombs at Bodia in Eastern Triphylia," *Bulletin of the R. Society of Letters of Lund*, 1926–27, pp. 53 *et seq.*; also his "Continued Explorations in Eastern Triphylia," *ibid.*, 1927–28, pp. 171 *et seq.*

the Late Mycenaean period, thus proving that the Mycenaean settlement in the Sulima plain is decidedly later than that on the western coast. The great number of tholos tombs shows that this district in the interior but not far from the western coast had a certain importance in the Late Mycenaean age.

This tract, viz., westernmost Messenia and Triphylia, was thus much more covered with Mycenaean settlements than any other in the western Peloponnese, while finds from the Mycenaean age are elsewhere very scarce. It appears that the Mycenaean settlers came over the sea, first taking possession of some suitable points on the coast and only at a late period proceeding along the river of Cyparissia upward to the Sulima plain. The settlers in this plain cannot have come from the south or east, for the Upper Messenian plain shows no traces of Mycenaean habitation.

This fairly dense Mycenaean population on the western coast of the Peloponnese cannot but be brought into relation with the Homeric tradition of the dominion of Nestor, king of Pylos. Dr. Leaf passed over this dominion in his suggestive book on *Homer and History*, but it is worth an inquiry since archaeological discoveries have lent color to the old tradition and to the fragments of a Pylian epos incorporated into Homer. But here the perplexing question arises: Which site was Nestor's Pylos? Professor Dörpfeld holds it to be identical with Kakovatos, but many scholars adhere to the old opinion that it was the Messenian Pylos. The settlements of the Sulima plain are separated by a considerable distance from those on the coast and hardly contribute to the solution of this problem; access to them may be a little more difficult from the Messenian Pylos than from Kakovatos-Pylos.

It is of course a good argument in support of Professor Dörpfeld's opinion that the site of Kakovatos was evidently the most important in this region, to judge from the number, size, and richness of its tholos tombs; it is moreover, according to the finds, earlier than the Messenian Pylos. The journey of Telemachus in a carriage from Pylos to Sparta, described in the Odyssey, has been vigorously discussed in this connection;[6] I pass over it because the question cannot be solved with certainty; I think that too much importance has been attached to it. Dörpfeld's other arguments, drawn from the Pylian epos incorporated into Homer, a source which ought to possess far better local information than the late poem of the Telemachia, seem to be irrefutable. The war with the Epeans or Eleans on the borders of the river of Alpheus, the situation of the town besieged by the Elean foes of the Pylians—Thryoessa, far-off at Alpheus in the extreme part of the sandy Pylos[7] —prove that the Pylian dominion extended to this river and included Triphylia and Pisatis. There was also friendly intercourse with the Eleans; Nestor was victorious in the funeral games of Amarynceus, an Epean prince.[8] That the Pylians had intercourse principally with the Eleans or Epeans makes it more probable that Kakovatos rather than the distant Messenian Pylos was Nestor's Pylos. Even the war with the Arcadians[9] is better suited for the Triphy-

[6] *Od.* iii. vv. 447 *et seq.*; the journey back, xv. vv. 182 *et seq.*
[7] *Il.* xi. vv. 670 *et seq.*   [8] *Il.* xxiii. v. 630.   [9] *Il.* vii. v. 133.

lian Pylos than for the Messenian. The latter town
may have belonged to the dominion but the capital
was Kakovatos-Pylos.

Thus the extent of the dominion of Pylos is
determined except for the problem involved in the
much discussed verses of the Iliad in which Agamemnon promises to give to Achilles, if he lets himself be
appeased, along with the hand of his daughter,
seven towns all near the sea at the extreme of the
sandy Pylos.[10] Most of these towns were unknown
in historical times and their situation is uncertain,
but Cardamyle is situated on the eastern side of the
Messenian gulf and Pherae is identified with Pharai
near the innermost recess of the gulf. Consequently
the inference is that the other towns also were
situated around the gulf,[11] and from this the further
conclusion is deduced that the dominion of Pylos
included the whole of the historical province of
Messenia. It seems, however, not certain that the
word "extreme," νέαται Πύλου, necessarily is to be
understood "in the extreme part of the dominion of
Pylos," as it certainly must be in the case of
Thryoessa. The translation "at the confines of the
dominion of Pylos" is also possible, and if this is
adopted nothing is said of the political situation of
the seven towns. This may certainly have varied.
For if Agamemnon promises to give away the seven
towns they must needs be in his hands; he cannot
give away what is in the possession of a vassal, the
prince of Pylos. This passage implies that the
seven towns on the Messenian gulf did not belong

[10] *Il.* xi. vv. 291 *et seq.*

[11] The last discussion in Valmin's dissertation, pp. 206 *et seq.*

to the dominion of Pylos but bordered on it. Only
the latter interpretation can be admitted here, if it
is not to be surmised that the poet has taken over
the phrase carelessly from the Pylian epos.

In view of this discussion it is comprehensible that
scholars have thought according to the usual geographical units and have identified the dominion of
Pylos with the historical province of Messenia in
general, perhaps with the addition of Triphylia.
But this has, in my opinion, vitiated the problem.
The boundaries were not the same in the Mycenaean
age as in the historical age. The fact that the Mycenaean civilization at the beginning of its second
period gained a foothold on the coast and only much
later spread inward to the plain of Sulima proves
that the Mycenaeans came oversea. Both the
Messenian and the Triphylian Pylos are typical
Viking towns founded at suitable places near the
coast far from the base of emigration.[12] Thence the
Mycenaeans spread inward at a later time only.
The fact that a denser Mycenaean habitation is
found only in the Sulima plain, the Upper Messenian
plain showing no traces of Mycenaean settlements,
proves that the Mycenaean center was on the western
coast. In the beginning the Mycenaean Vikings
may have passed the Messenian gulf without stop-
ping, if they did not perhaps come from the Corinth-

[12] N. Gardiner, *Olympia*, p. 35, believes that the invaders came overland from Argolis, because Kakovatos is harborless; but he remarks,
p. 38, that nowhere else has such a quantity of amber been found as
was found here, and sees herein an unmistakable evidence of a trade
route from the head of the Adriatic. The two statements seem to contra-
dict each other somewhat, but I should be more inclined to agree with
the latter. The best harbor in an early age is a fine sand shore on which
the ships can be drawn up, such as exists at the "sandy" Pylos.

ian gulf. Later on they tried to gain a foothold
even on the coasts of the Messenian gulf, and this is
reflected in the Homeric passage concerning the
seven Messenian towns.

The fact that the Mycenaean civilization came to
the western Peloponnese oversea is retained by the
mythical tradition according to which the Minyans
immigrated to these parts. Much has been written
about the Minyans of Orchomenus and we must
recur to them and their relations with Pylos at length
in a later chapter. Here I only state that the tradition cannot be disregarded and that its reliability is
proved by the mention in the Iliad of a river,
Minyeios, in the district of Pylos.[13] Discussing its
identity, Strabo proposes that it got its name either
from the Minyans who came with Neleus' wife,
Chloris, from Orchomenus in Boeotia, or from the
Minyans who were descendants of the Argonauts and
from Lemnos were expelled to Laconia and from there
to Triphylia.[14] His theories are in themselves of
no value, being only attempts to explain the per-
sistent tradition of Minyans in Triphylia. This
tradition is corroborated by genealogies which seem
not to be idle inventions, nor does it seem to be an
idle tradition that the descendants of Neleus and
the Pylians emigrated to Ionia. Since it is possible
to treat this tradition fully only in connection with
the problem of the Minyans, we shall recur to it
in another chapter.[15] Here I add only the observation
that it appears in the Pylian epos, of which fragments
were incorporated into Homer, that the situation
of the Pylians was precarious.

[13] *Il.* xi. v. 722.   [14] Strabo, viii. p. 347.   [15] Below pp. 143 *et seq.*

We have to consider what is left of this Pylian epos.[16] Its contents are extremely little concerned with mythology, for its character is more historical, as is frequently the case with epics. Professor Robert thinks that even if the episodes in Homer are derived from an Ionian epos, the myths originally belonged to the Pylians whose natural foes were the Arcadians.[17] Professor Wilamowitz gives voice to another opinion.[18] He calls attention to the Pylian origin of the Colophonians and thinks that the Pylian epos originated in the town of Colophon in Asia Minor. In order to disprove its Pylian origin he proceeds to point to some geographical impossibilities and errors in the description of the war and the march of the troops, drawing the inference that the situation of Pylos was undetermined. The name Pylos, he thinks, designated, originally, the entrance of the Nether World, then the western part of the Peloponnese, and finally a certain locality but never a town.

Certainly the Gate of the Underworld and Nestor's Pylos were mixed together in a myth to which we shall recur presently, but that does not prove that Nestor's Pylos was originally that Gate. That would be the same mythological point of view which once made Troy the castle East of the Sun and West of the Moon. Pylos appears in the epos as a

[16] A. Lörcher, *Wie, wo, wann ist die Ilias entstanden?* (1920), attributes great importance to the many passages concerning Nestor and gives the title "Die Nestoris" to one of his chapters. But the inference that this preference given to Nestor and the Pylians came about because the Iliad was conceived at Olympia at the games is very unlikely.

[17] C. Robert, *Die griech. Heldensage*, p. 191.

[18] Wilamowitz, *Die Ilias und Homer* (1916), pp. 207 *et seq.*

real town, and the geographical inconsistencies are not good arguments, for as Professor Wilamowitz himself remarks, epics are always careless in regard to geography and distances; but it ought to be added that this carelessness does not disprove the real existence of the places and the original connections of the myths with them. It is unlikely that such inconsistencies prove that the epos originated among people who were ignorant of the actual geography of the places mentioned; blunders were sure to creep in during the repeated rehandling of the epics.

I cannot but think that the Pylian epos originated, as epics usually do, among people who were concerned with the events described, viz., among the Pylians themselves; that with them it came to Ionia, where parts were incorporated into the Iliad; and that its contents are historical traditions subjected to epical and mythical remodeling. At all events they are not mere fiction.[19]

The story is remarkable that Heracles, evidently at the head of the Epeans or in their company, had dealt severe blows to the Pylians and killed eleven sons of Neleus, only the youngest one, Nestor, being left.[20] That is no glorious tradition and consequently we may believe that it has some real foundation; viz., that the Pylians had been very severely dealt with by their foes in Elis. The story must, however, be compared with another often

---

[19] It is not to be wondered at that the Pylians are called Achaeans, for they were pre-Dorians, or that their foes are called both Epeans and Eleans; Epeans is the name of a tribe, Elis of a province (Ἦλις Lat. *vallis*, ϝαλις, ϝαλειοι are the native forms); i.e., a local name from which that of the inhabitants was derived.

[20] *Il.* xi. vv. 689 *et seq.*

quoted episode; viz., that Heracles wounded Hades, fighting with him at Pylos among the Dead.[21] It is justly recognized, and we shall have more to say of it when we come to Heracles,[22] that this Pylos is the Gate of the Underworld and that the myth is an old form of Heracles' victory over Death. Because of the resemblance of the names it was applied to the city of Pylos and thus Heracles became the foe of the Pylians. It is the oldest of his Deeds and the starting point for these, and has perhaps given rise to the idea that Heracles was a leader and a hero of the Dorians.

The Pylian epos which, in fact, glorified the last struggles of the old Viking empire against the invaders was certainly not conceived in a foreign country by people to whom the Pylians were mythical figures only. To quote Professor Robert, its mythical contents are extraordinarily small. But even if Professor Wilamowitz' view is accepted, the fact remains that epical traditions of a certain richness cling to the western coast of the Peloponnese and that the same tract is the only one on this side of the peninsula which is comparatively rich in Mycenaean remains. The traditions may be more historical than mythical; if so, their value is the same or still greater for our purpose. For the traditions here treated are such as are handled by epics. Epical traditions and Mycenaean remains cover the same district.

[21] *Il.* v. vv. 395 *et seq.*

[22] Below pp. 203 *et seq.* For the evidence see E. Drerup, *Das fünfte Buch der Ilias* (1913), p. 180 *et seq.*

4. THE REST OF THE PELOPONNESE

If we now turn to the remaining parts of the Peloponnesian peninsula, to Arcadia, the central mountain land, to Elis, the northwestern district, and to Achaea, the coastal province on the south side of the Corinthian gulf, Mycenaean remains are remarkably scarce.   Finds from Achaea were first reported quite recently: late Mycenaean tombs at Goumenitza near Kalavryta,[1] chamber tombs near Prostovitza on the west slopes of Mount Erymanthus, chamber tombs and three tholos tombs near Chalandritza, twelve miles south of Patras.[2] Only the last mentioned find seems to be of any importance; and the report, barely mentions that and gives no details.   In Arcadia Mycenaean remains seem to be still less important; most remarkable are the tholos tombs at Sarandapotamos near Tegea, of which one has been explored.[3] Elis has yielded still less, Olympia a single Mycenaean sherd, and the hill where ancient Pisa was situated a few sherds.[4]

To this scarcity of Mycenaean finds the paucity of myths closely corresponds.   Arcadia has a number of curious old-fashioned cults and even myths, but

[1] *Deltion archaiologikon*, IX (1924–25), App. pp. 14 *et seq.*

[2] *Journal of Hellenic Studies*, XLIX (1929), p. 235.   Recent finds *ibid.*, L (1930), p. 241 and *Bulletin de correspondence Hellénique*, LIII (1929), p. 501 *et seq.*

[3] Not published but mentioned by Dr. Fimmen, *loc. cit.*, p. 10.

[4] Dörpfeld, *Athen. Mittheilungen*, XXXIII (1908), p. 319, does not mention anything Mycenaean; in the *Archäologischer Anzeiger*, 1909, p. 121, it is expressly stated "nothing Mycenaean," but as the very conscientious Dr. Fimmen, who knew the materials personally, mentions Mycenaean ceramics, some, though not considerable, Mycenaean finds must have been made in the meantime.

the most interesting of these are divine, not heroic myths, e.g., those of Calliste and of Auge. The few heroic myths are of a late make. Atalanta is sometimes said to be an Arcadian, sometimes a Boeotian; she is perhaps one of those folk-tale personages who were not localized originally and of whom stories were told in different places.

In Elis likewise the number of myths is very few. Salmoneus, the eponymous hero of the town of Salmone at Alpheus, has been much discussed lately and has been thought to be a reflection of an old kingly magician.[5] This is probably true and shows that his importance for heroic mythology is small. His myth was a local sacral myth which was attached to the Pylian-Thessalian genealogy.[6] It is a curious and, from the point of view of the history of Greek religion, interesting fact that the most famous seers and soothsayers are connected with Elis. The Iamidae and the Clytiadae did service at Olympia,[7] and the celebrated mythical seers Melampus and Bias are said to be sons of the Elean hero Amythaon, who was connected genealogically with Neleus. For our purpose these myths have hardly any interest; their elaboration is probably due to the religious ideas of the early archaic age.

It would have been a sheer miracle if the foundation of the Olympian games had not been projected into the heroic age and surrounded with myths. Our concern is not to enucleate the origin of these

[5] J. G. Frazer, *The Golden Bough* (ed. 3), I, p. 310, and II, p. 181. S. Reinach, *Cultes, Myths et Religions*, II (1906), pp. 159 *et seq.*

[6] Cp. below p. 141.

[7] L. Weniger, "Die Seher von Olympia," *Archiv für Religionswissenschaft*, XVIII (1915), pp. 53 *et seq.*

famous games and their mythical history, which has been discussed very vividly,[8] but to try to see how it agrees with our general principles. Except for a single sherd, Mycenaean remains are absolutely lacking at Olympia, which has been searched thoroughly, and they are few and insignificant at the neighboring town of Pisa, which in an earlier age controlled the games. The myths attached to Olympia ought consequently to be later creations, even if earlier elements were used in arranging them. Their relatively late date is indicated by the fact that quite a number of aetiologic myths concerning the foundation of the games exist but that none was generally accepted so as to oust the others.

Pausanias has two quaint myths,[9] one is that Heracles—who here is said to be one of the Idaean Dactyls to whose care the child Zeus was entrusted—with his four brothers founded the games;[10] the other is that Zeus himself founded them after his victory over Cronus. Both are apparently late inventions and need not detain us.

More widespread is another myth according to which Heracles instituted the games, having killed the Molione.[11] These strong twins have apparently been borrowed from the Pylian myth. Nestor men-

[8] Summary in N. Gardiner, *Olympia* (1925), p. 58, *et seq.* A sound criticism of the speculative hypotheses in H. J. Rose, *The Greek Agones* in *Aberystwyth Studies*, III (1922), p. 1 *et seq.* Last treatment by R. Vallois, "L'origine des jeux olympiques," *Revue des études anciennes*, XXVIII (1926), pp. 305 *et seq.*, and XXXI (1929), pp. 113 *et seq.*

[9] Paus. v. 7, 8 *et seq.*

[10] Cp. Vallois *loc. cit.* (1926). This myth seems to be connected with certain facts in the actual cult. It is judged very contemptuously by Farnell, *Greek Hero Cults*, pp. 125 *et seq.*

[11] Pindarus, *Ol.* x. v. 26 *et seq.*; Apollodorus, ii. 7, 2, 5, etc.

tions them twice; he says that they took part in the war on the side of the Epeans and that he nearly killed them,[12] and in another passage he says that they were victorious in the chariot race at the funeral games of Amarynceus at Bouprasion.[13] Heracles killed them in the course of a war which he waged against King Augeias of Elis because Augeias had withheld the fee which he had promised him for the cleaning of his stables. Augeias appears in the Pylian epos as king of Elis.[14] In this epos Heracles was the foe of the Pylians; in the myth here treated he is the foe of the Eleans.

This change may perhaps be connected with a change in the dominating population. The Eleans of the historical age spoke a northwestern dialect; they were a northwestern tribe, kindred of the Aetolians, who had traversed the Strait of Naupactus. If the Dorians who invaded the Peloponnese took the same way, they came earlier and were ousted by the Eleans. This view implies of course that the Epeans who warred with the Pylians belonged to the earlier Dorian invasion. In the Homeric age the last invasion had already taken place, and Homer confused of course Epeans and Eleans, but, as we remarked, the latter name is a local and not a tribal one. However this hypothesis may be judged, the myth of Heracles' war with Augeias and his killing of the Molione is apparently a late creation, composed of elements of which certain parts were taken from the Pylian cycle.[15]

[12] *Il.* xi. vv. 709 *et seq.*   [13] *Il.* xxiii. v. 638.   [14] *Il.* xi. vv. 701 and 739.

[15] N. Gardiner, *Olympia*, p. 60, calls it justly a part and parcel of the myth of the return of the Heraclidae.

Much more celebrated is the myth of Pelops and
Oenomaus which was chosen as the subject of the
sculptures in the east pediment of the temple of
Zeus at Olympia. We have seen above[16] that
Pelops was the eponymous hero of the tribe of the
Pelopes, which gave its name to the Peloponnesian
peninsula, and that he was made an ancestor of the
Atreidae. Oenomaus appears curiously isolated; he
is not attached to the genealogy of the Elean kings.
The goal of the race is by some authors said to have
been on the Corinthian isthmus; personages and
events of the myth were localized partly in the northeastern Peloponnese, partly even on Lesbos. Thus
the inference is near at hand that the myth was
transferred to Olympia from Lesbos[17] or from the
northeastern Peloponnese.[18] It must, however, be
conceded that there is nothing which proves with
certainty that these localizations are earlier than its
localization at Olympia.[19]

More important is the fact to which several
scholars have pointed that the running of the course
originally implied not a race but the carrying off of
the bride according to the primitive custom known
also to the Greeks. This is a rather common
mythical motif.[20] It appears that the myth of the
race of Pelops and Oenomaus was remodeled pro-

[16] Above p. 44.
[17] Robert, *Die griech. Heldensage*, pp. 209 *et seq.*; with some modifications J. Kakridis in his book 'Αραί (Athens 1929), and in the periodical
Hermes, lxvi (1928), pp. 119 *et seq.*
[18] Weiszäcker in Roscher's *Lexikon der Mythologie*, III, pp. 767 *et seq.*
[19] Vallois, *loc. cit.* (1929), p. 122.
[20] The race for the bride is a fairly common motif used in tales of
the suitors of the Danaides, of Penelope, of Pallene, and of Thebe,
the eponymous heroine of Thebes beneath Mt. Plakos.

foundly in order to be applied to Olympia. It is
uncertain where it was originally at home.

For our point of view the important fact is that
neither in this nor in other myths concerning the
institution of the Olympian games is there anything
which can be referred to the Mycenaean age. Just
as Mycenaean remains are lacking at Olympia, so
the myths attached to Olympia do not cling to that
place from Mycenaean times. They are recent
inventions transferred from other places or remodeled
with some use of earlier elements. We must be
content with this general statement; here, as often,
it is impossible to discern how the myths were
developed in the archaic age.

5. THE IONIAN ISLANDS

Odysseus has his home on Ithaca, and the scene
of the greater part of the Odyssey is laid on that
island. Since the search for Mycenaean remains
according to the guidance of the Homeric myths
had been rewarded so brilliantly at Mycenae and
at Troy, it is intelligible that Mr. Schliemann
planned and Professor Dörpfeld attempted to carry
out the plan to discover Odysseus' palace on Ithaca.
Of course Professor Dörpfeld holds the opinion that
old Ithaca was in reality Leucas. We need not
discuss that vexed question here. On both islands
the search for Mycenaean remains failed, generally
speaking; all that was found were some few sherds
such as appear even in countries distant from Greece.[1]

[1] W. Dörpfeld, *Alt-Ithaka* (1927), p. 150 (Ithaca), pp. 283 and 337
(different sites on Leucas). It is impossible to know what value is to
be attributed to a recent newspaper statement that there were found on

Why the search for Mycenaean remains failed is
clear. One of the premisses was erroneous. For
the myth of Odysseus is not a heroic myth but a
romance.[2] A romance may choose and localize its
heroes in an arbitrary manner; thus the localization
of the plot is unreliable. It may be transferred from
one place to another in a loose manner which some
scholars think fit for heroic mythology also. The
failure of the search for the palace of Odysseus
proves from the negative side the view maintained
in these lectures.

On the other hand, apart from the story of his
return, Odysseus is one of the most prominent
Homeric heroes and plays a most important part in
the Iliad. That seems to prove that he, as well as
other heroes, belonged to the old stock. His very
name shows signs of great antiquity. The ending
is the one common in the earlier stratum of heroic
names, -eus, and the varying forms, Odysseus,
Olytteus, etc.,[3] present a perplexing philological
problem and prove the ancient origin of the name;
for later names are regularly so formed that their
origin is clear.

Odysseus lived at Ithaca, be it the historical
Ithaca, or Leucas. Although he himself plays a very

Ithaca "des restes très importants d'agglomérations mycéniennes et
promycéniennes." See *Journal of Hellenic Studies*, XLIX (1929), p. 235.
If that is literally true, it would reverse my arguments, but I think it
safest to wait and see. I have not seen the correspondence which has
been going on this autumn (1930) in the *Times* concerning Ithaca. Cp.
Bulletin de correspondence hellenique, LIII (1929), p. 505.

    [2] Here I am in agreement with Wilamowitz, *Die Ilias und Homer*,
pp. 281 *et seq.*

    [3] Collected e.g. by J. Schmidt in Roscher's *Lexikon der Mythologie*,
iii. pp. 645 *et seq.*

prominent part in the Iliad, his country and his
people are mentioned only twice. In the rather
late scene where Helen from the walls of Troy points
out the Greek heroes to the Trojans, she says that
he was bred in the rocky country of Ithaca;[4] and in
another place the herald Eurybates is said to be an
Ithacan.[5] On the other hand, when Odysseus'
people are mentioned in the mustering of the troops
by Agamemnon, they are said to be Cephallenians.[6]
In the Odyssey Odysseus lives on Ithaca and is
twice called an Ithacan, but he is called not king
of Ithaca but king of the Cephallenians. This occurs
in the late narrative of his meeting with his old
father Laërtes.[7] He fears that the Ithacans may
send messages to the towns of the Cephallenians.
Remembering the prowess of his youth, Laërtes
calls himself king of the Cephallenians, and some
verses later[8] Antinous' father complains that Odysseus killed the bravest of the Cephallenians. The
name of the island of Cephallenia is, however,
absent from Homer, the four islands of which the
dominion of Odysseus is composed being called
Ithaca, Dulichion, Same, and Zacynthus.

These passages are all late and it may be inferred
that a late name intruded itself, just as in the Pylian
epos the Epeans were called Eleans. But the relation between the names of the country and of the
people is here reversed. The Eleans have their
name from the country of Elis, the people of the
Kephallenes, as the Greek form is, have given their
name to the island of Cephallenia, which in the

---

[4] *Il.* iii. v. 201. [6] *Il.* iv. v. 330. [8] *Od.* xxiv. v. 429.
[5] *Il.* ii. v. 184. [7] *Od.* xxiv. vv. 350 *et seq.*

Homeric age was called by another name, be it
Dulichion, as Professor Dörpfeld and his followers
think, be it Same as the old opinion is.[9]

To this view the finds from the Mycenaean age
correspond in a certain manner. While very few
Mycenaean remains, not more than in foreign places,
have been found on Ithaca and on Leucas, such finds
are more considerable on Cephallenia, including
four tholos tombs and a series of chamber tombs
and other tombs near Diaka, with sub-Mycenaean
pottery.[10] To these finds, registered by Dr. Fimmen,
are to be added not inconsiderable finds of pottery,
bronze utensils, etc., from a habitation at Orkopeda
on the peninsula of Pale.[11] Thus archaeological
facts seem to prove that the epical tradition of the
dominion of the Cephallenians is old; it belonged,
however, to a very late period of the Mycenaean
age and was of no great importance.

There are, however, certain objections to be considered. Attention has been called to the fact that
the name of the Kephallenes, in the Dorian dialect
Kephallanes, has the same ending as several tribal
names of northwestern Greece, e.g., Ainianes, Atin-
tanes, Athamanes, etc., and from this fact the conclusion is drawn that the Kephallenes were a northwestern tribe. If this is so, they must have invaded
the islands at the beginning of the historical age;
that is, at a very late period of epic poetry, and have
given their name to the island after the Homeric
age. The name of the island of Cephallenia appears
for the first time in Herodotus. It cannot be denied

[9] Cp. Wilamowitz, *Homerische Untersuchungen* (1884), p. 73.

[10] *Deltion archaiologikon*, V (1919), pp. 92 *et seq.*

[11] *Ibid.*, VI. (1920–21), pp. 175 *et seq.*

that this is possible; and if it is really what happened, the above inference must be withdrawn.[12]

It appears that this is a very uncertain matter, but its importance for our chief purpose is slight. Moreover, I am obliged to confess that I am unable to guess why Odysseus was localized precisely on Ithaca. It may be explained, if with Professor Wilamowitz we take Ithakoi to be a tribal name which was applied to the island later,[13] just as the tribal name of the Cephallenians was applied to the island of Cephallenia, but this also is not more than a guess. It ought, however, to be well observed that no old cycle of myths is attached to Odysseus. The story of his return to his faithfully abiding wife is a romance; his adventures on the sea are sailors' stories, such as are told by a sea-faring people; and were *en vogue* during the epoch of the Greek colonization. Originally they were not bound up with a certain person but were attached to one person or to another who seemed suitable, and Odysseus was suitable as king of an empire of far-off islands. Other myths of Odysseus are still later. The fame of Odysseus is due to these late myths and to the genius of a poet who depicted his character as that of the wise and cunning man and thus made him an important personage in the Iliad. He has no mythological cycle of his own but was put into the foreground during the development of Homeric

[12] The contention that tribal names ending in *-ānes* and *-ēnes* are exclusively northwestern is not absolutely certain. If Athamas is the eponymous hero of the Athamanes, which, however, is very uncertain (cp. below pp. 133 *et seq.*), this would prove that tribal names with this ending had already appeared in the Mycenaean age.

[13] Wilamowitz, *Die Heimkehr des Odysseus* (1927), p. 187.

epics. And this corresponds closely to the state of things in this outlying part of Greece, as archaeology shows them to have been in the Mycenaean age.

6. SOUTHERN BOEOTIA

Boeotia comes next to Argolis and takes the second place in the richness both of its myths and of its Mycenaean remains. There we find two important Mycenaean cities; though the perversity of Fate has left less than elsewhere of past splendor, there is enough to prove that they once were mighty and populous. We find the large and strong fortress of Gla and the extensive works for the improvement of cultivation by the draining of the lake of Copais, which better than anything prove the high standard of Mycenaean civilization in peaceful work; they are far superior to the roads radiating from Mycenae, and I shall recur to them in a later place.

But if we take a survey of the province as a whole in regard to Mycenaean remains, they do not appear to be so numerous as might be expected from these outstanding examples,[1] in fact, elsewhere in Boeotia both Mycenaean habitations and isolated finds seem to be scarce.[2] Not to speak of Argolis, Attica is

[1] See D. Fimmen, "Die Besiedelung Böotiens bis in frühgriechische Zeit," *Neue Jahrbücher für klass. Altertumswissenschaft*, XXIX (1912), pp. 524 *et seq.*, supplemented by his *Kretisch-mykenische Kultur*, pp. 5 *et seq.*

[2] The Mycenaean remains unearthed at Eutresis between Thebes and Creusis on the Corinthian gulf are not numerous, but in Mycenaean times the place was fortified with a heavy Cyclopean wall. See Hetty Goldman, *Excavations at Eutresis* (Fogg Art Museum, Harvard University, 1927), p. 82 *et seq.* The like at Haliartus, *Annual* of the British School at Athens, XXVIII (1926–27), p. 129; the walls *ibid.* XXVII (1925–26), p. 82.

much more thickly strewn with Mycenaean sites,
tombs, and finds. This state of things is only partly
due to the lack of exploration and knowledge of
Mycenaean remains in Boeotia. This province has
not been so thoroughly searched as have Argolis
and Attica, but much attention has been paid to
Boeotia also, and it is hardly likely that such an
explanation would cover the whole truth. It seems
as if Boeotia had been a kind of new land of the
Mycenaean civilization which, coming of course
from the south, occupied two great centers and
penetrated less into the country. The draining
of the lake of Copais, which provided a vast area
of arable land for the profit of the town doing the
work corroborates this view.

This is of course only a suggestion and it may be
judged on its own merits. For our purpose the important fact is the existence of Mycenaean centers.
I begin with Thebes, postponing the mention of
the others until I treat their myths. Extensive
remains of a Mycenaean palace have been found at
Thebes; unhappily it was possible to excavate them
only partly, because they are situated in the midst of
the modern town.[3] This was the emplacement of
ancient Thebes also, and this continuous habitation
of the site was of course catastrophic to the Mycenaean remains. In spite of this, enough is left to
show the outstanding importance of Mycenaean
Thebes. Especially remarkable are fragments of
wall paintings belonging to an earlier period than

[3] They were explored by Professor Keramopoullos; see *Ephemeris
archaiologike*, 1909, p. 57 *et seq.*; *Praktika*, 1911, p. 143 *et seq.*; 1912,
p. 85 *et seq.* For a summary see the *American Journal of Archaeology*,
XXXIV (1930), p. 219 *et seq.*

those of Orchomenus,[4] a potter's kiln, and a number
of big stirrup jars or fragments of such jars with
painted short inscriptions.[5] Further, a great number
of tombs with rich contents has been found,[6] proving
that Thebes had a prosperous and numerous population in the Mycenaean age.

Thus, though the later ages have been fatal to
the Mycenaean remains of Thebes, enough is left
to show that the city was a most important center
of Mycenaean civilization; and the myths attached
to Thebes are of a corresponding richness and importance. It would perhaps be sufficient to point to
the well-known Theban cycles of myths, but they
show some peculiar features which make it a duty
to enter upon them more closely, in spite of the uncertainty which is inevitably bound up with research
of this kind.

The Theban cycles were treated in post-Homeric
epics of which we have some slight knowledge and
were especially taken up and favored by the great
tragic poets. The chief figure is Oedipus. Professor
Robert has treated his myths exhaustively and has
given a model piece of mythographical research in
his great work *Oidipus;* here we must try to get

[4] See *Tiryns*, II, p. 199. Cp. G. Rodenwaldt, *Der Fries des Megaron
von Mykenai* (1921), p. 69, n. 152; and in regard of the dating of the
earlier period, W. Lamb, in the *Annual* of the British School at Athens,
XXV (1921–23), p. 254 *et seq.*

[5] For a brief mention see my *Minoan-Mycenaean Religion*, p. 20,
n. 8. J. Sundwall discussed the script in the periodical *Klio*, XXII
(1928–29), p. 228 *et seq.* A. W. Persson in his interesting attempt to
decipher the Minoan-Mycenaean script reads on three of the Theban
jars *ku-te-me-se va-na tei-vo-e*, which very much resembles Κάδμος ϝάναξ
Θηβῶν (*Schrift und Sprache in Alt-Kreta*, Program of the Promotion of
Doctors of Letters, Uppsala, 1930, p. 28 *et seq.*).

[6] A. Keramopoullos, *Deltion archaiologikon*, III (1917), p. 25 *et seq.*

behind the traditional myths and see what their origin and their connections with the Mycenaean age may be. I cannot share Professor Robert's opinion that Oedipus is an old depossessed god.[7] From the fact that three of the tombs and cult places ascribed to Oedipus are certainly late, Professor Robert draws the conclusion that the fourth, the tomb at Eteonus in Boeotia, was the original and old one. Oedipus is, however, no old vegetation god but simply a *Märchen*-hero, a folk-tale personage who, by vanquishing the sphinx won the hand of the queen and the kingdom, although this simple and common motif was complicated by the addition of a great many others. That his name is a descriptive one, corroborates this view. Such a mythical personage has of course no tomb; even that at Eteonus is a late creation.[8] Nor can I side with Professor Rose who takes Oedipus to be a historical personage, a prince who had been exposed as a child and who at the head of a Corinthian army conquered Thebes, slew King Laius, and wedded Queen Epikaste, his mother.[9] He fully recognizes the folk-tale elements but thinks that Oedipus is a nickname. In view of the fact that it is one of the few characteristic *Märchen* names in Greek mythology, I am persuaded that the origin of Oedipus is to be found not in history but in folk-tales.

[7] C. Robert, *Oidipus*, I (1915), p. 44 *et seq.* For a criticism see L. R. Farnell, *Greek Hero Cults* (1921), p. 332 *et seq.*

[8] Cp. my review of Robert's book in *Göttingischer gelehrter Anzeiger* (1922), pp. 36 *et seq.*

[9] H. J. Rose, *Modern Methods in Classical Mythology* (St. Andrews, 1930), p. 24 *et seq.* An analysis from the point of view of folk-tale motifs is made by S. Luria in *Raccolta di scritti in onore di F. Ramorino* (1930), p. 289 *et seq.* I prefer to leave the treasure of Thisbe out of account.

The myth was localized at Thebes; consequently Oedipus became king of Thebes and was inserted in the genealogy of the kingly Theban house. A detailed analysis of the Oedipus cycle is out of place here, but I am bound to point to certain circumstances of importance for our subject. To begin with I remark that the reception of folk-tale motifs in this cycle, just as, e.g., in the Perseus cycle, shows its popularity and age.

Concerning the ancestors of Oedipus a few words will suffice. His grandfather Labdacus is an empty name, and if the guess deriving his name from the name of the letter, *labda*, Λ, hits the mark, he is of very late origin. On the other hand, the myth in its developed form implies an important rôle for Oedipus' father.

If the myth of Oedipus told only that he guessed the riddle of the sphinx, or simply that he slew her and in reward won the hand of the queen and with her the kingdom, it would have been a very simple folk-tale of a well-known kind. But other motifs were added, drawn from the conflicts in family and ethical life of an early people: the queen was his mother and the man he slew his father. The addition of these motifs created the real Oedipus myth and its essential greatness. In a later chapter[10] we shall treat the naming of the mythical personages and we shall see that the name Oedipus belongs to a class of names, rare in Greek mythology but of frequent occurence in folk-tales, in which the hero's name is descriptive of certain peculiar characteristics which he possesses. Oedipus signifies "the man with

[10] See below pp. 189 *et seq.*

the swollen feet." The formation of the name is of great antiquity, showing a kind of derivation which was obsolete in the Greek language of the historic age.[11] The feature that his feet were pierced, though irrational as has been said, is bound up with the story that as a newborn child he was exposed to die, but was saved, and when grown up was recognized by his parents. This motif is on the other hand essential only in connection with the myth telling that Oedipus married his mother. That is to say, in this case, because of the formation of the name, we are able to state that the tale of the exposure of Oedipus and of his marrying his mother was joined in an age which long preceded the historical age with the folk-tale of the young man who by guessing the riddle of the sphinx won the queen and the kingdom. I confidently ascribe the origin of this myth complex to the Mycenaean age.

Folk-tales have a logic of their own which sometimes is rather penetrating, though it may seem

[11] H. Petersson in my above-quoted (p. 103 n. 8) review, p. 45. I repeat Petersson's convincing argument: It is evident that the first compound part of Οἰδίπους is connected with the stem in οἰδάω, οἰδέω, but the difficulty consisting in the difference of vowels (ι instead of α, ε) has not been overcome. There exists, however, a type of corresponding words and compounds such as κυδρός and Κυδιάνειρα, and this type is found in Sanskrit and Old Persian also. (See J. Wackernagel, "Vermischte Beiträge zur griech. Sprachkunde," *Programm* zur Rektoratsfeier der Universität Basel (1897), p. 8 *et seq.*) If we suppose that a Greek adjective *οἰδρός once existed, the formation of the name Οἰδίπους falls in with this type, and the existence of this adjective may be assumed with much probability, formations corresponding to it being found in other languages; e.g., Old German *eitar*, "poison," from Old Teutonic *aitra*, "venomous tumor;" Indo-eur. *oid-ro*, Lettish *idra*, "rotten marrow of a tree." Cp. P. Kretschmer, in *Glotta* XII (1923), p. 59, but I cannot approve of his chthonic interpretation of Oedipus.

puzzling to us. When it was asked how the queen
became a widow, the myth answered by applying
another motif of the same kind: Oedipus had without
knowing it killed his father. Thus the terrific logic
of events was still more emphasized. The slaying
of his father is not so essential for the myth and
may have been added later; but this motif also is
certainly very old,[12] and with it the cycle is established in all its essential parts. Other features are
more loosely bound up with it and must be passed
over here.[13] The history of Greek literature proves
that this myth was perhaps the most dramatic of
all Greek myths. I venture to think that in its
essential parts it was already created in the Mycenaean age and attached to Thebes. The reasons for
its localization at Thebes we are of course unable
to discover or to guess—they may have been quite
fortuitous, as often happens in localizing current
tales—but a necessary condition for the recognition
of this localization was that Thebes in this age was a
famous town.

The second part of the Theban cycle is from our
point of view perhaps of still greater interest. This
cycle resembles the cycle of Mycenae in that the
kernels of the first part of each—the Oedipus and the
Perseus myth respectively are closely linked up
with folk-tales; whereas the second parts—the myths
of the Atreidae and of the Seven against Thebes
respectively—belong to those myths which have a
historical aspect and kernel. With certain scholars
I have assumed this historical kernel in the case of

[12] The earliest mention is found in the Nekyia, *Od.*, xi. v. 273.
[13] Cp. my above-quoted (p. 103, n. 8) review.

the Atreidae, and in making the same assumption in regard to the War of the Seven against Thebes I only follow the footsteps of Wilamowitz, Ed. Meyer, and Robert, who take this myth to be a historical reminiscence of a war waged against Thebes by a confederation of Argive princes.[14]

But the matter is not so simple as it may appear. Difficulties arose when the myth of the war was joined with the myth of Oedipus, and we must try to grasp these. The common form of the myth is well known. The two sons of Oedipus, Eteocles and Polyneices, quarreled about the throne; Polyneices was driven out by his brother, and collected with the help of the Argive prince Adrastus the great army of the Seven, but failed to conquer Thebes; he and his brother slew each other in the battle, the army was routed, and the other leaders were killed, except Amphiaraus, who was swallowed alive by the earth. The sons of the Seven marched a second time against Thebes with an army, conquered, and destroyed the town. This complex form of the myth was known to Homer, for in the fifth book of the Iliad[15] it is related that Tydeus, one of the Seven, went to Thebes as a messenger, and that he challenged and vanquished all the Cadmeans in athletic contests. In a later passage in the preceding book,[16] the same adventure is told more fully; it is added that Tydeus came to Mycenae accompanied by Polyneices in

[14] Wilamowitz, *Hermes*, XXVI (1891), p. 240, and "Die griech. Heldensage, I," *Sitzungsberichte der preuss. Akad. der Wissenschaften,* 1925, p. 58; Robert, *Oidipus,* I, p. 120; Ed. Meyer, *Geschichte des Altertums,* II, p. 189 *et seq.*

[15] *Il.* v. v. 800 *et seq.*

[16] *Il.* iv. v. 370 *et seq.*

order to collect soldiers, and in his reply to Agamemnon, Sthenelus, the comrade of Tydeus' son Diomedes, says that he and his fellows conquered Thebes of the Seven Gates.

On the other hand, it is told in another passage of the Iliad that Mecisteus, who according to later sources was a brother of Adrastus, went to Thebes after the fall of Oedipus, to his funeral games, and vanquished all the Cadmeans.[17] Moreover, a passage in the Nekyia[18] says that Oedipus ruled at Thebes, enduring many evils, even after the discovery of his crimes. Professor Robert is quite right in rejecting the attempts to harmonize this version with the usual ones.[19] We have to admit frankly that the last-quoted Homeric version tells that Oedipus, even after having recognized the frightful deeds of which he was guilty, ruled as king at Thebes and eventually met his death in a war. This version recurs in Hesiod,[20] where it is said that Zeus destroyed the generation of the heroes in two great wars, some of them beneath Thebes of the Seven Gates, warring because of Oedipus' sheep, and others whom he conducted in the ships oversea to Troy because of the fair-haired Helen.

Professor Robert argues conclusively that in this version Oedipus lives, is king and leader in a great war; and this must be admitted; but when he tries to point out the war in question I cannot follow him. He reminds us of the many wars which the

[17] *Il.* xxiii. v. 678 *et seq.*
[18] *Od.* xi. v. 273 *et seq.*
[19] Robert, *Oidipus*, I, p. 115.
[20] Hesiod, *Works and Days*, vv. 161 *et seq.*

Thebans waged, according to the myths, with their traditional foes the Minyans, the Teleboans, and others, and concludes that the war in which Oedipus fell, according to the Iliad, cannot be the War of the Seven against Thebes.[21] This last-mentioned was only one of the many wars which the Thebans fought with their neighbors in the mythical age. He thinks that the epos called the Thebais fused all these wars into one Great War.

This solution of the difficulty is only seemingly easy. For the passages quoted from Homer and Hesiod, which differ from the usual version, refer evidently, as Professor Robert admits, to the same war, and if the war because of Oedipus' sheep was one of the many casual wars which myths attribute to Thebes, how was it possible that Hesiod puts it on the same footing as the most famous war of mythology, that against Troy, and counts it as the second in which the generation of the heroes perished? This being so, it is established beyond possible doubt that the war in which Oedipus fell was the one Great War of Thebes, just as there was one Great War of Troy, although mythology knew other wars of the Trojans too. That is to say, Professor Robert's theory is no real solution of the dilemma and another way must be found.

From the standpoint of principles Professor Robert's view of the Theban war is the same as that advanced by Professor Bethe in regard to the Trojan war.[22] He thinks that of old only scattered elements of myths existed, although he admits that the War

[21] Robert, *Oidipus*, I. p. 121.
[22] Cp. above p. 6 *et seq.*

of the Seven has a historical kernel going back into
the Mycenaean age. But it was only one of many
wars, he says. He tries to demonstrate this opinion
by proving that the two foremost of the Seven,
Tydeus and Amphiaraus, were not Peloponnesians
by origin but were brought into connection with
Adrastus, being made his sons-in-law. He thinks
that emigrants to Ionia from Euboea, Boeotia, and
Argos brought their myths with them and that these
separate myths originating in different provinces of
the mainland coalesced in Ionia into the cycle of the
War of the Seven, and that the myth of the hostile
brothers was invented in order to give a cause for
this war.[23] In a following chapter he attempts to
reconstruct the epos which created this cycle, the
Thebais. I pass over his reconstruction and his
criticism of the earlier reconstruction of this epos by
Professor Bethe.[24]

Here also I am unable to embrace the opinion that
the great mythical ideas were conceived in a later
age, say in the seventh century B.C. Of course
Thebes may have waged many wars in the prehistoric
age, but popular recollection was unable to keep
them apart in the lapse of the centuries, and one
war became at an early date more prominent than
others. Consequently I consider it as granted that
old mythology knew one great war against Thebes,
as it knew one great war against Troy, and these
two wars were the most famous wars of the mythical age. This is the kernel of the question. The
simple mythical fact stated above was of course

[23] Robert, *Oidipus*, I, p. 143 *et seq.*
[24] E. Bethe in his brilliant book *Thebanische Heldenlieder* (1891).

not sufficient, the myth had to tell details too, and we may surmise that these were likely to be varied and enlarged. It is only natural that the most famous king of Thebes was made the leader in this war. The cause of the war does not take hold on popular fancy. Cattle-lifting is a very common pastime among early peoples, who breed cattle and value them highly, as the Greeks did, and it is accordingly very frequently given as the cause of wars in the myths just as is the abduction of a woman.

On the other hand, the Theban cycle was distinguished by the reception of motifs, already mentioned above,[25] which were derived from the ethical conflicts and family life of an early people. Still another familiar motif of this kind is that of the hostile brothers. Mythology knows plenty of such pairs, e.g., Proetus and Acrisius, Romulus and Remus, and many others. The hostility of the brothers gave a very good reason for the war: one brother had been expelled by the other and tried to regain his throne. It may moreover be surmised that an accident of this kind happened more than once in the heroic age. When such a quarrel was given as the cause of the war, Oedipus was out of place: not he but another, Eteocles, must be made king and leader of the Thebans in the Great War.

It seems to me to be difficult to decide what was the original form of the myth in this respect, whether Oedipus himself or one of the hostile brothers was the Theban leader in the Great War. Oedipus is manifestly an intrusive personage in the myth of the War, for he belongs originally to a different

[25] Above p. 104.

cycle; but because of his mythological fame he was
connected with the Great War also. For the same
reason he was introduced into the story of the hostile
brothers, and made their father. This led to quite a
series of difficulties which mythical fiction did not
succeed in solving in a probable manner. These
difficulties appear in the two questions: who was
the mother of the brothers, and what happened in
the time between the discovery of the crime of
Oedipus and the Great War? I do not enter upon
these questions, which are of no importance for this
discussion.[26]

We turn to the other side, to the foes of the
Thebans, who also are essential to the myth. We
are wont to regard the Theban war from the standpoint of the besieged, whilst we regard the Trojan
war from the standpoint of the besiegers. There is
a certain reason for these different standpoints,
because, unlike the Trojan war, the Theban war
ended in the failure of the besiegers; but this point
of view ought not to be so overemphasized as to
make the foes of Thebes of only incidental importance. On the contrary, the myth, as we know it,
takes a far greater interest in the leaders of the
hostile party than in the Theban leaders; the latter
are, except for Eteocles, rather insignificant mythical
personages. There is not the least reason for supposing that the rôles have been reversed in importance.

The foes too belong to the original myth, but in
such a series of heroes, names are apt to be changed,
left out, or added. How old the canonical number of
seven may be, is of course uncertain, although it is

[26] I touched upon them in my review quoted p. 103, n. 8, pp. 43 *et seq.*

intimately bound up with the myth as we know it. But this number may have determined the number of the gates of Thebes, for, as it has been observed, the historical city of Thebes never had seven gates. There is, however, one personage who is essential and hardly can have been subject to a change; namely, the leader of the hostile army, Adrastus; and this is in fact acknowledged by the scholars who think that the historical kernel of the myth is an expedition of Argive princes against Thebes. The myth of the War of the Seven was not created at Thebes but like other myths was a product of the general creative genius of the Greeks and was told everywhere. This inference follows from the localization of Adrastus.

Adrastus belongs to the northeastern Peloponnese, but as to the town where he ruled mythological sources differ. He is commonly said to be king of Sicyon, and the special reason for this is Herodotus' account of how Cleisthenes, the tyrant of Sicyon, managed to get rid of his cult by introducing the cult of his death-foe Melanippus.[27] Herodotus says that Adrastus had a heroön on the market place of Sicyon, but a learned Hellenistic author contends that this heroön was a cenotaph and that his real tomb was at Megara.[28] Such localizations must always be regarded with a certain diffidence, because well-known hero names were applied to nameless tombs and cults, or ousted less known names. Thus it may be understood that a hero might have two or more tombs, no one of which was necessarily the

[27] Herodotus, v. 67.
[28] Dieuchidas in the *Scholion* to Pindarus, *Nem.*, ix. v. 30.

real one.[29] The story of how Adrastus became king
of Sicyon gives grounds for suspicion. He is said to
be the son of Talaus, the king of Argos, and of the
daughter of Polybus, the king of Sicyon. Expelled
from Argos because of a quarrel, he went to Sicyon
and inherited the kingdom from his mother's father.
Talaus is said to be the son of Bias, a brother of
Melampus, the seer who, during the reign of King
Anaxagoras, cured the women stricken with frenzy
by Dionysus. This is a later version of the myth of
the daughters of Proetus, which belongs to Tiryns,
and may be dismissed. Adrastus was not king of
the city of Argos, though he is genealogically annexed
to the kingly house of Argos. We may safely say
that he ruled as king somewhere in the province of
Argos, but we cannot tell for certain which Argive
city was his.

That Adrastus was king in some other Argive town
and leader of the expedition against Thebes is not
incompatible with the overlordship of the king of
Mycenae as it is described in Homer. Myths and
monuments prove that Mycenae was the richest and
mightiest city, but they prove also that there were
several other rich and mighty cities in Argolis. We
have taken their rulers to be vassals of the king of
Mycenae, but we have also emphasized the facts
that the power of the suzerain depended on his
personal energy and that the vassals strove to assert
their independence, a goal which was attained at
last at the breakdown of Mycenaean power and
civilization. There is place for many changes and

[29] I think it hardly necessary to discuss the hypothesis that Adrastus
originally was a name of the Lord of the Underworld. I cannot see
why it should not be a purely human name.

vicissitudes in the half-millenium, more or less,
during which the Mycenaean age lasted. We know
now, e.g., that the great constructions at Tiryns
belong to a very late period of the Mycenaean age,
about 1200 B. C. This flourishing of Tiryns seems
to imply a decline of the power of Mycenae. When
the suzerain's power was decaying, an energetic
and successful prince of some other city may have
tried to play politics in his own interests. He may
have collected soldiers and appeared as leader of an
expedition for the purpose of establishing a dominion
of his own in a neighboring province, just as William
the Conqueror did. Adrastus seems to have been
such a personage, using certain circumstances in
order to make himself ruler of Thebes.

The series of the Seven heroes was, as we have
observed, subject to changes, but some of the heroes,
especially Amphiaraus and Tydeus, appear in all
versions as more important than the others. Amphiaraus is already in the Odyssey inserted into the
genealogy of the seer Melampus and of the kingly
house of Argos, and is said to be a son-in-law of
Adrastus, but we have seen that this genealogy is
not trustworthy.[30] The fact that Amphiaraus is at
home in Boeotia is established by cults so important
that they cannot be suspected to be later creations.
He had a sanctuary at Oropus on the confines of
Attica where, giving oracles during sleep, he cured
the sick. Another oracle of his, already famous in
the times of Croesus, seems, according to Herodotus,[31]
to have been near Thebes. We are unable to say
whether it was identical with his temple at Harma

[30] *Od.* xv. v. 225 *et seq.*; see above p. 114.   [31] Herodotus, viii. 134.

in Boeotia mentioned by Strabo, or with his temple at Potniae between Plataeae and Thebes, mentioned by Pausanias.[32] The myth telling that he was swallowed alive by the earth is consistent and without any doubt part of the old tradition. It is of course an aetiologic myth meant to explain why Amphiaraus was thought of as living beneath the earth and why his cult place was under the ground, like that of Trophonius at Lebadeia.[33] We have to admit that a Boeotian cult hero was received into the myth of the Seven against Thebes.

The fact that Tydeus always is said to be a son of the Aetolian king of Calydon, though versions differ in regard to his mother, seems to prove that this genealogy is old and trustworthy and that Tydeus is at home in Aetolia. He also is made a son-in-law of Adrastus. Tydeus' name is one of the old type and moreover his character shows traces of a high and crude antiquity which was detested by the Homeric age. He belongs to that older generation of heroes who possessed an admirable strength and did valiant deeds but met an evil fate.[34] His violent temper and his hasty deeds are prominent characteristics. Like so many other heroes he was exiled because he had slain a relative; that is a consistent feature of the tradition, although there are variations as to the names and the number of the slain. Further, he is always represented as the special protégé of the goddess Athena. He appears as a

[32] Paus. ix. 8, 3. Strabo, ix, p. 404.

[33] This is a valid objection to Farnell's euhemeristic view, *Greek Hero Cults*, p. 58 *et seq.*

[34] E.g., Meleager. This feeling seems to me to underlie the passage *Il.* i. v. 266 *et seq.* also.

knight-errant, capable of valorous but also of cruel
deeds, a character consistent with the stormy
Mycenaean age but antiquated in the more humanized Homeric society, which set up higher moral
standards than did the Mycenaean Vikings. This
character is certainly a heritage from Mycenaean
times.

Of the others, Capaneus is the most interesting.
His genealogy and localization are unknown. The
fact that his son Sthenelus always appears in Homer
as the faithful comrade of Diomedes, Tydeus' son,
gives perhaps a hint at an old connection even
between the fathers. His character is depicted as
exactly like that of Tydeus. Striving to conquer
Thebes, he defied even Zeus. The myth, first found
in Euripides, that at his funeral his wife Euadne
threw herself upon the flaming pyre of her husband,
is very remarkable. For it is absolutely inconceivable that such a myth was invented under the conditions which we know to have existed in Greece
from Homer onward; but the custom is well attested
for certain Aryan peoples. Among the Thracians,
the Indians, and the Scandinavians of the Viking age
the wife accompanied her husband in death in this
terrible manner. From the funeral of Patroclus as
described in Homer we know that captives were
killed in order to accompany the deceased into the
Other World, and this description is recognized as a
most valuable testimony of old, crude funeral customs.[35] In several cases it has been assumed that the
same custom has left traces in Mycenaean burials,
and though this supposition is certainly wrong in

[35] By E. Rodhe, *Psyche* (ed. 10, 1925), I. p. 14 *et seq.*

certain cases, e.g., in regard to the shaft-graves at
Mycenae, and in others is doubtful, the discovery of
the untouched burials in the bee-hive tomb at Dendra
proves that a similar custom actually existed. One
of the sacrificial pits in the tomb contained half-
burned animal and human bones which must have
survived from a sacrifice at the funeral, and the
king and the queen were buried at the same time.
Professor Persson thinks it likely that in fact we here
have an instance of the self-sacrifice of the queen at
her husband's funeral.[36]   At all events we have an
example of human sacrifice at the funeral. The
myth of Euadne's voluntary death on her husband's
pyre is pre-Greek and, I venture to think, a precious
testimony as to Mycenaean funeral customs.

We have, consequently, good reason to think that
the three foremost of the Seven have come down from
Mycenaean times; but at least two of these three
were not Argives or Peloponnesians, one being a
Boeotian and the other an Aetolian. Professor
Robert has duly emphasized this fact,[37] and according
to his point of view he draws the inference that both
had waged a war of their own against Thebes, that
the emigrants from Boeotia and Aetolia respectively
had brought the myths of these wars with them to
Ionia, and that there the wars had been fused with
other wars by the Ionian epic poetry, so that the
cycle of the Great War of the Seven against Thebes
was formed.

[36] A. W. Persson, *Kungagraven i Dendra* (1928), p. 130 *et seq.*

[37] It matters little that he thinks that both Amphiaraus and Tydeus
(in regard to Tydeus I cannot see why) belong to the tribe of the
Graikoi, which was settled on both sides of the Euripus: Robert, *Oidipus*,
I., p. 121.

I cannot see any reasonable ground for this supposition except the preconceived opinion that the
great mythical cycles were first formed by the
Ionian minstrels by the fusion of several minor
myths into one cycle. We have found reasons to
suppose that the idea of one Great War against
Thebes was an old heritage from the Mycenaean
age, and we have seen that the leader and the three
most prominent heroes go back into the same times.
Hence it is a fair inference that the cycle in its
outlines also goes back into the Mycenaean age.
For a great war and a few prominent personages,
among them the leader, are intimately bound up
with each other. Certainly one of the Seven is a
Boeotian hero and another an Aetolian knight-errant,
but why should not the Argive aggressor have
secured the help of a valorous knight-errant and a
Boeotian adversary of Thebes, or, at least, why
should not the myth have presented him as doing
so? In historical times it is almost a rule that
discord between neighbors provides the lever for
aggression by foreigners. These are of course
nothing but possibilities, but they are mentioned in
order to show that there is no interior improbability
in drawing the inference which the myth makes
likely; namely, that not only the idea of the Great
War against Thebes but also its chief heroes have
come down from Mycenaean times.

Concerning other parts of the cycle I am unable
to proffer any well founded opinion. Eriphyle, the
sister of Adrastus and the wife of Amphiaraus, and
her treacherous conduct toward her husband, have
a prominent place, but I see no means for reaching

any opinion as to the time when this motif was joined with the cycle, or as to the time when Amphiaraus and Tydeus were made sons-in-law of Adrastus.

The feeling that a great undertaking ought not to end with a great disaster has created the myth of the Epigonoi, the sons of the Seven, who conquered and sacked Thebes. This myth is obviously late, some scholars think very late. It may be post-Mycenaean, but cautiousness bids me to leave the question undecided.[38] One of the Epigonoi, Diomedes, derives certainly from Mycenaean times.

There is another well-known Theban myth which cannot be passed over in silence, although it is very difficult to judge and will not be of much importance for our purpose—the myth of Cadmus, the founder of Thebes. The opinion now current[39] reverses the traditional view. Cadmus is assumed to be at home at Miletus, where a noble family counted him as its ancestor. Not far from Miletus there were a mountain and a river both called Cadmus and the inhabitants of Priene were called Cadmeans.[40] At Miletus the tradition arose which ascribed the introduction of the Phoenician alphabet to Cadmus. Even the genealogy which makes Cadmus a brother of Phoenix, Cilix, and Thasos is said to point to Asia Minor. The deduction will of course be that Cadmus was at a rather late age transferred from Ionia to Thebes.

[38] Robert, *Griech. Heldensage*, p. 949 *et seq.*; and Wilamowitz, *Hermes*, XXVI (1891), p. 239, hold that it is very late.

[39] Summarized by K. Latte in his article in Pauly-Wissowa's *Realenzyklopädie der klass. Altertumswissenschaft.*

[40] The sources are quoted by O. Crusius in his able article in Roscher's *Lexikon der Mythologie*, II, p. 872 *et seq.*

In Homer Cadmus is mentioned only once, as Ino's father;[41] in Hesiod's Theogony he occurs as husband of Harmonia and father of Semele, Ino, and others.[42] Here at last the myth seems to be fully developed. The salient point is, however, another; viz., that Homer always calls the Thebans Cadmeans;[43] the town is on the contrary called Thebe or Thebae. The names of the people, Cadmeans, and of the acropolis, Cadmea, cannot of course be separated from the hero Cadmus, and this proves the lack of foundation of the current opinion. For it is not to be believed that epic poetry would have given the inhabitants of the old town of Thebes a name derived from a hero who at the time was quite recently invented and transferred from Asia Minor to Boeotia. The names of tribes and peoples belong generally to the old epic stock, and epic poetry is quite unwilling to receive recent names, especially for old famous peoples. That the inhabitants of Thebes were called Cadmeans is one of the not uncommon cases in which a town and its inhabitants had different names; e.g., Ilios and the Trojans, Orchomenus and the Minyans, etc. It is further to be observed that Boeotia is richer than other Greek provinces in old tribal names. One of these was the name of the Cadmeans and with that Cadmus is linked inseparably. Professor Crusius came nearer to the truth than later writers, though he neglected the last mentioned argument

[41] *Od.* v. v. 333 *et seq.*

[42] Hesiod, *Theogony*, v. 937 and v. 975.

[43] Καδμείωνες or Καδμεῖοι, occurs eight times; Θηβαῖος occurs in the Odyssey, as an epithet of the seer Teiresias only.

and argued only from the oldest, rather scanty sources.[44]

If Cadmus is the old eponymous hero of the Cadmeans, the people who inhabited Thebes, we are bound to find an explanation for the mythical fact that he was made a Phoenician immigrant and that wide wanderings were ascribed to him which have found an expression in his genealogy also. It will, however, be necessary to take up another important detail of his myth before proceeding to this question.

The myth of Cadmus is the foundation myth of Thebes in the strict sense of the term. The oracle commanded Cadmus to follow a cow and to found a town on the spot where she lay down. When she did so, he intended to sacrifice her, but in fetching water for the sacrifice he encountered the dragon of Ares and slew him. He sowed the dragon's teeth, and from them men grew up, the Spartoi, who killed one another until only five were left. For expiation he had to do service to Ares for a long year; at the end of this time he received the god's daughter, Harmonia, for his bride, and the wedding was celebrated with great pomp.

It is a curious fact that this is a true foundation myth; the site of the town is determined by divine intervention, the origin of the people and of the noble families is explained. Such myths are numerous but they are almost always told of colonies or of towns, such as Rome and Carthage, put on an equality with them. It will be hard to find another true foundation myth referring to a town in Greece,

[44] I am glad to note that Dr. Fimmen embraces the same opinion (*Neue Jahrbücher für das klass. Altertum*, XXIX (1912), p. 534 *et seq.*).

except perhaps in the case of Alos in Thessaly.[45] I
do not of course take the many etymological myths
into account; their late make is so transparent that
it is needless to dwell upon them.[46] There are not a
few myths telling how the walls of a city were built.
E.g., Apollo and Poseidon built the walls of Troy
for King Laomedon, the Cyclopes the walls of
Tiryns for King Proetus, and Athena helped in erect-
ing the walls of the Acropolis of Athens. But these
legends are not foundation myths in the true sense
of the word; the existence of the city is presupposed
and they relate only how it was fortified. They are
evidently late aetiologic myths.

Except for these rather doubtful or worthless
instances, only one other example may be cited, and

[45] The town of Alos in Thessaly has a foundation myth. Its founder
is said to be either Aloeus (*Schol. Apoll. Rhod.* i. v. 482 = Hesiod, *frag.*
9 Rzach, ed. 3; the town is here said to be Aetolian) or Athamas (*Schol.
Apoll. Rhod.* ii. v. 514). The myth runs: An oracle commanded Athamas
to settle on the spot where he would be entertained by wild beasts. He
encountered wolves devouring their prey, and as they fled he settled in
that country and called it Athamania; or he founded a town on the spot
and called it Alos from his wanderings (ἄλη) or from his servant maid
Alos (*Et. magnum*, p. 70, 8; Steph. Byz. *s. v.* 'Αθαμανία). Though the
myth differs in regard to the locality, and the usual etymological interpretation is prominent, it undeniably has features which appear to be
old. It is impossible to say how old it may be, but it ought not to be
forgotten that the foundation legend was implied by the mythical fact
that Athamas went from Boeotia to Thessaly. Another myth tells that
Ilus, the eponymous hero of the city of Ilion, went out from Phrygia
with fifty youths and fifty maidens, following a cow, and founded the
city of Ilion where she lay down. This myth appears only in Apollodor,
ii. 12, 3, and is a late invention.

[46] E.g. the myth that Perseus founded the city of Mycenae where he
lost the chape (μύκη) of his sword, Paus., ii. 16, 3; or the myth that
Coroebus founded Tripodiskos in Megara where the tripod which he
carried from Delphi fell from his shoulders, Paus., i. 43, 8.

that also concerns Thebes. It is told that this city
was founded by Amphion and Zethus. The best
known feature is that these twin brothers built the
walls of Thebes; hence one may reasonably be inclined to consider this myth as one of the common
type describing the erection of the city walls; but
as early as in the Nekyia it is expressly stated that
the brothers founded the city of Thebes of the Seven
Gates and built the walls.[47] The well-known version
of the myth occurs, however, first in the Antiope of
Euripides, the earlier tradition being very meager.
It has a feature which is found in true foundation
myths. The twins were exposed to die but were
saved by shepherds, just as were Romulus and
Remus or Cyrus. But as told by Euripides the myth
is not a foundation myth. The brothers recognized
their mother and punished their stepmother Dirce.
It is supposed that the city of Thebes existed already,
for their stepfather Lycus is king of Thebes. We
have no way of knowing what may have been the
earlier form of the myth which Euripides used and
transformed. We cannot say whether or not it was
a true foundation myth. The constantly recurring
fact is that Amphion and Zethus built the walls of
Thebes and from this detail alone we can surmise
that it is old. The statement in the Nekyia that the
brothers founded the city may be deduced simply
from their building its walls.

Thus Thebes has one foundation myth, or perhaps
two. At all events Amphion and Zethus appear to
be intrusive in the Theban cycle. They fit very
badly into it. That is the reason why Professor

[47] *Od.* xi. v. 262 *et seq.*

Robert, relying upon a passage in Apollodorus, ascribes them to another Boeotian town, Hyria.[48] But even so we do not get rid of the most embarrassing fact, that they built the walls of Thebes, for it is related only that they lived at Hyria and were exiled because of a murder; i.e., there is nothing to prove that the supposed foundation myth belongs to the town of Hyria. We should not demand consistency and sequence of myths; both these myths were attributed to one town without consideration of how they fitted together. The inconsistencies appeared when the myths were brought into a kind of pseudo-historical system by means of genealogies.

The remarkable fact is that Thebes in contrast to other Greek towns has a true foundation myth. It is very easy to understand why the colonies have foundation myths and the cities in Greece have not. The founding of a colony was a fact which was present to all; the towns in Greece, on the contrary, had very often been inhabited since immemorial times; many of them show traces of human habitation not only from Mycenaean but from pre-Mycenaean times also. Therefore foundation myths were precluded; they were out of place. Thus I am inclined to believe that the Theban foundation myth is really a reminiscence of a historical fact and that a Mycenaean tribe really founded a new town here. If this is so, it falls in with the opinion which I gave above that Boeotia was an outpost of Mycenaean civilization. The site of Thebes was of course inhabited in pre-Mycenaean times, but what has

[48] Robert, *Oidipus*, I, p. 398, referring to Apollodor, iii. 10, 1. 1, from Hellanicus.

been found from this age is not so much as to be a serious objection to this view.[49]

If I am right, an old myth, of course handed down from Mycenaean times, told that Thebes was founded by the eponymous hero of the tribe which inhabited the town, the Cadmeans. The founder, Cadmus, came consequently from abroad. The old myth did not tell or had forgotten whence he came, and the field was left open for guesses. At the beginning of the historical age the foreigners who constantly visited Greece were the Phoenicians.[50] If we take these conditions into consideration, we may perhaps be able to understand why the myth hit upon the idea of making Cadmus a Phoenician. At that time other foreigners were hardly known in Greece, and as Cadmus was acknowledged to be a foreigner, he became a Phoenician. The myth of

[49] Keramopoullos in *Deltion archaiologikon*, III (1917), p. 2 *et seq.* A nest of pre-Mycenaean vases mentioned in the *Journal of Hellenic Studies*, XLIX (1929), p. 233. In 1929 sherds of Minyan ware and some sherds of good L. H. II. pottery were found beneath a wall of the palace of the period before the reconstruction; see *American Journal of Archaeology*, XXXIV (1930), p. 220.

[50] The name of the Phoenicians (Φοίνικες) signifies etymologically "the Red Men." According to a sagacious hypothesis put forth by H. R. Hall, *Proceedings* of the Society of Biblical Archaeology, XXXI (1909), p. 282, "the Red Men" were originally Minoan colonists from Crete and the name was later transferred to the Phoenicians of the Syrian coast. Such a hypothesis would of course very well explain the special features of the myth which are treated above. But I cannot accept this explanation because there is overwhelming evidence that the Mycenaean civilization was introduced into Greece by Greek Vikings and not by Minoan colonists. A. Fick, *Vorgriechische Ortsnamen* (1905), p. 123 *et seq.* and R. Burrows, *The Discoveries in Crete* (1907), p. 141 advanced the opinion that this name was first applied to all the brown-complexioned people whom the Greeks met and only later restricted to the Semites of Canaan.

his wanderings, which are somewhat similar to the voyages of the Phoenicians in the Aegean, and his genealogy were but consequences of his alleged Phoenician origin. The fact that his name recurs in Ionia is more probably to be explained by the theory that emigrants from Boeotia brought him with them, counted him as their ancestor, and applied his name to certain localities than by the opposite hypothesis that he came from Ionia to Boeotia, which involves unsurmountable difficulties. We know, moreover, that the immigrants in Ionia were a very mixed lot.

7. NORTHERN BOEOTIA AND THESSALY

Just as Thebes is the center of Southern Boeotia, Orchomenus is the center of the northern part of the province, together with the great and fertile plain at the lake of Copais. Orchomenus has always been famous for its bee-hive tomb, the so-called treasury of Minyas, which now is ruined but rivals the best examples of these stately domes at Mycenae. Mr. Schliemann made excavations at Orchomenus also. A Bavarian expedition took up the work at the beginning of this century and discovered important remains from the Mycenaean and the pre-Mycenaean ages.[1] Most remarkable and important are the numerous fragments of painted stucco. They once covered the walls of a palace of which no stone is left. Nor has any trace of other buildings

[1] H. Bulle, "Orchomenos," I, "Die älteren Ansiedelungsschichten," *Abhandlungen der bayerischen Akademie der Wissenschaften*, I. Kl., XXIV: 2 (1907); II, E. Kunze, *Die neolithische Keramik, ibid.* N. F. III (1931).

from the Mycenaean age been discovered, but the wall paintings suffice to prove that a palace was once standing at Orchomenus like those in Argolis and at Thebes, decorated by the hands of Mycenaean craftsmen. The paintings of Orchomenus are later in date than those of Thebes. A single specimen of a jar inscribed with Minoan characters was also found.

The most conspicuous architectural monument which the Mycenaean age left in Boeotia is, however, the large palace which was erected on the small island of Gla in the lake of Copais.[2] The area enclosed by the ring-wall is more than ten times as large as the area enclosed at Tiryns, but it shows only very slight traces of habitation. Even ceramics and other small finds are scarce. The very name of this mighty castle was forgotten. It is sometimes supposed to be old Arne, but this identification has been contested and is hardly probable. Other identifications are not more likely.[3] This is a kind of riddle, but one may suppose that something happened here like that which seems to have happened at Midea, the Mycenaean fortress in Argolis which has the largest area of any but plays very little part in myths;[4] viz., that the palace was inhabited

[2] *Bulletin de correspondence hellénique*, XVIII (1894), p. 271 *et seq.*; Tsoundas-Manatt, *The Mycenaean Age* (1897), p. 375 *et seq.* Cp. F. Noack, *Homerische Paläste* (1903), p. 19.

[3] Phlegya: A. W. Gomme, "The ancient name of Gla," in *Essays and Studies to W. Ridgeway* (1913), p. 116 *et seq.* Glechon: T. W. Allen, *Classical Review*, XVII (1903), p. 239 *et seq.* This equation is contested by A. W. Persson, *Schrift und Sprache in Alt-Kreta* (Uppsala, 1930), p. 29, n. 2, who points to the fact that the name of Gla is of Turkish origin.

[4] See above p. 182.

for a short time only and abandoned so early that its memory was obliterated. This supposition is consistent with the lack of ceramics and other small finds.

Further, one of the most extensive undertakings which ever was carried out in prehistoric Greece is not to be forgotten, the draining of the lake of Copais. Modern observations prove that the system of ditches with stone embankments which was built on the bottom of the lake in order to conduct its water to the *katavothra*, is ancient and in all probability belongs to Mycenaean times, as ancient tradition implies.[5] The immense attempt was also made to excavate tunnels through the mountains which separate the lake from the Euripus, but this work is of a later date.

If we, according to our principles, ask for the cycle of myths corresponding to the Mycenaean center of Orchomenus, the answer will be the myth of the Minyans. Since K. O. Müller more than a hundred years ago published his famous book on Orchomenus and the Minyans this tribe has loomed very large in the modern conception of Greek mythology. Criticism has, however, been directed against the mythical importance attributed to the Minyans,[6] and it is fair to acknowledge that old mythology has not very much to tell about the Minyans. The

[5] *Bulletin de correspondance hellénique*, XVI (1892), p. 121 *et seq.*; Frazer in his commentary on Pausanias, vol. V, p. 110 *et seq.*; survey by Geiger in Pauly-Wissowa's *Realenzyklopädie der klass. Altertumswissenschaft*, s. v. Kopais, XI, p. 1351 *et seq.*

[6] By Fimmen, "Die Besiedelung Böotiens bis in frühgriechische Zeit," *Neue Jahrbücher für das klass. Altertum*, XXIX (1912), p. 536 *et seq.*, and by Robert, *Die griechische Heldensage*, p. 56.

great fame of the Minyans came in later days when
the Argonauts were said to be Minyans. Hence it
is inferred that the Argonauts are pseudo-Minyans,
so called because many of them and especially Iason,
were descended from Minyas' daughters.

It is frankly to be admitted that here seems to be
an exception to the rule laid down that the mythical
importance of a town corresponds to its importance
in the Mycenaean age and civilization. Although
our knowledge of the Boeotian cities in this age is
only too fragmentary, so that it is difficult to discern
their relative importance, according to the remains
Orchomenus seems to rival Thebes, as myths say
it did; but there is no cycle of myths connected
with Orchomenus which in popularity and fame can
be at all compared with the Theban cycle.

The mythical history of Orchomenus related by
Pausanias[7] is a mosaic pieced together of incoherent
and disparate elements. Of the first two kings,
Andreus and Eteocles, the former is a mere name,
the latter seems to be an old figure but has in fact
no myth of his own; he belongs to aetiologic hieratic
mythology as the founder of the cult of the Charites
at Orchomenus. If Dr. Forrer, who believed that
he discovered the names of these two kings in
Hittite documents, is right, their historical existence
would be proved; but although I am inclined to
think that Dr. Forrer is right in the chief point, the
existence of an Achaean empire extending to the
southern coast of Asia Minor in the fourteenth and
thirteenth centuries B.C., these identifications of

[7] Paus. ix. 34, 6–37.

names are extremely questionable and are better left out of account.[8]

This is, however, not the whole truth. Homer has two significant references to Orchomenus. In the Nekyia it is said that Neleus, the king of Pylos, married Chloris, the youngest daughter of the Iaside Amphion, the king of Orchomenus;[9] and in another passage[10] Orchomenus and Thebes in Egypt are mentioned side by side as the richest towns of the world. The eleventh book of the Iliad, the embassy to Achilles, in which this passage is found, is of course a relatively late poem and many scholars take the mention of the Egyptian capital to be a sign of its late date, but quite recently the opposite opinion was advanced by Miss Lorimer.[11] She remarks that Echenaton transferred his capital elsewhere in the first half of the fourteenth century B. C. and that Rameses II finally abandoned Thebes as the royal residence. She thinks that the raiding

---

[8] E. Forrer, *Mitteilungen der deutschen Orientgesellschaft*, No. 63 (1924); recent survey in the *Reallexikon der Assyriologie* s. v. Ahhijava, and in his article, "La découverte de la Grèce mycénienne dans les textes cunéiformes de l' empire Hittite," *Revue des études grecques*, XLIII (1930), p. 279 *et seq.* His assertions gave rise to lively polemics. They were contested by J. Friedrich, "Werden in den hettitischen Keilinschriften Griechen erwähnt?" *Kleinasiatische Forschungen*, I (1927), p. 87 *et seq.*; Forrer's reply: "Für die Griechen in den Boghaz-köi Inschriften," *ibid.*, p. 273 *et seq.* P. Kretschmer, "Zur Frage der griechischen Namen in den hethitischen Texten," *Glotta*, XVIII (1930), p. 161 *et seq.*, is inclined to support Forrer.

[9] *Od.* xi. v. 281 *et seq.*; v. 459 is of no importance.

[10] *Il.* ix. v. 379 *et seq.*

[11] In the *Journal of Hellenic Studies*, XLIX (1929), p. 153 *et seq.* A late date is advanced by Wilamowitz, *Die Heimkehr des Odysseus* (1927), p. 173.

northerners after about 1200 B. C. would not have
been able to penetrate as far as Thebes and that
consequently it looks as if the references to Thebes
were derived from the fifteenth century B. C. There
is an undeniable probability in this view, and it
ought to be added that during the reign of the
Theban priest-kings the Greeks did not come to
Egypt—it was the dark intermediate age—and that
Thebes was sacked thoroughly by the Assyrians in
663 B. C.[12] The Greek mercenaries who went to
Egypt during the reign of the Sait kings in the
beginning of the Orientalizing period[13] saw a ruined
city. The glory of Thebes was irrevocably past.

A clue to the answer to this delicate question is
given by the Egyptian objects found in Greece.[14]
The great mass belong either to the XVIIIth or to
the XXVIth dynasty; a few are more indistinctly
labeled as belonging to the XXIId–XXVIth dynasties. Objects from the intermediate period are scarce
and insignificant, the most notable exception being
those found in the so-called tomb of Isis at Eleusis,
which belong to the XXth–XXIId dynasties. That
is to say, there is evidence of brisk connections with
Egypt in the fifteenth to the thirteenth centuries
B.C. and then again in the Orientalizing period from
its beginning in the middle of the seventh century

[12] For the thoroughness of the sack see *Cambridge Ancient History*
III, p. 285.

[13] The date of the mercenaries' inscriptions from Abu Simbel is
now fixed with certainty in the reign of Psammetich II. (593–588 B. C.):
G. Lefebure, "Ποτασιμπτώ," *Bulletin de la société archéologique d'Alex-
andrie*, No. 21 (1925), p. 48 *et seq.*

[14] They are now very easy to survey in the useful compilation of
J. D. S. Pendlebury, *Aegyptiaca, A Catalogue of Egyptian objects in the
Aegean area* (1930).

B.C., viz., in the period after the sack of Thebes. This certainly gives considerable support to Miss Lorimer's opinion.

From the Homeric verses mentioned above it appears that the fame of Orchomenus was as great in the age of Homer as in that of K. O. Müller. This fame derives probably from the Mycenaean age, for in the later Geometric and in the Orientalizing periods its great glory was gone.

If we turn to the myths, we do not find any proper Orchomenian cycle of myths; but Orchomenus and the Minyans appear very often in a great many mythical connections, and we must try to find out what their rôle was in the early age of Greece. The clues which we are compelled to use are the localizations of the myths and the genealogies, but the latter must always be regarded with a certain diffidence and the localizations cannot be accepted without additional proofs. We must try to find out the results of such an analysis.

Minyas himself is nothing but the eponymous hero of the tribe and has no myths of his own. The myth of his daughters who resisted the cult of Dionysus and went mad is well known, but belongs to the late type of Dionysiac myths, which are of no importance for our subject.

The myth of Athamas is on the contrary very important. Athamas is believed to be the eponymous hero of the tribe of the Athamanes.[15] This tribe had never any importance in Greek history; it lived on Mount Pindus and sometime belonged

---

[15] This suggestion seems doubtful; there is a difference in the forms, 'Αθαμᾶνες but gen. 'Αθάμαντος.

in historical times to the Molossian kingdom. If
this view concerning Athamas is right, the Athamanes must have been a relict, driven up into the
mountains, of a tribe which once dominated a much
larger district toward the southeast, but this seems
at least doubtful. For our inquiry this idea may be
put aside.

I need not relate the well-known myth of Athamas,
his children by Nephele, Phrixus and Helle, their
stepmother Ino, and their escape from the sacrifice,
riding on the ram. Happily the elements from which
this myth was derived are discernible, and what I
observed many years ago[16] still holds good. The
kernel of the myth is the sacrifice of a member of
the house of Athamas; such a rite was practiced
at Halus in Thessaly even in historical times. This
kernel was enlarged and developed in various
manners. According to another and simpler version,[17] Athamas himself, not Phrixus was the
sacrifice. Drought, failing of the crops, and hunger
are always given as the causes of this sacrifice, and
this is consistent with old cult customs which
required human sacrifices to avert such calamities.

From this point of view it is possible to explain
the outstanding rôle of the fleece in the myth.
On the top of Mount Pelion there was a sanctuary
of Zeus Acraeus to which a procession went in the
severest heat of the summer, about the time of the
rising of Sirius; the men were girt with sheep fleeces.
This Zeus is the cloud-gatherer and rain-giver, and
the procession is in accord with quite a number of

[16] In my *Griechische Feste* (1906), p. 10 *et seq.*
[17] Herodotus, vii. 197.

similar customs the aim of which was rain-magic.
That the fleece served as a means for weather-magic
is proved by various known facts.[18]   Hence we are
able to understand the curious fact that the Cloud,
Nephele, is said to be the wife of Athamas.   She
is the longed for rain-cloud which in another instance
of weather-magic, people saw rising from the well
of Hagno on Mount Lykaion.[19]

The historical sacrifice of the Athamantidae took
place at Halus in southern Thessaly in the cult of
Zeus Laphystius; consequently Athamas is said to
be at home in Thessaly.   Around Halus was the
field of Athamas,[20] but there is no Mount Laphystion.
The mountain with this name is situated in Boeotia,
between Coronea and Orchomenus.   We do not know
the source of Pausanias' statement[21] that the sacrifice of Phrixus took place on this mountain—it may
be an inference, but such an inference is right, for
since there is no other mountain with this name, it
is evident that this Boeotian mountain was the origi-

[18] See my *Griechische Feste*, p. 8.

[19] Paus. viii. 38, 3.   It is interesting that the Cloud appears in another
Thessalian myth also, that of Ixion.   (Concerning the Phlegyans see
below pp. 150 *et seq.*)   A cloud instead of Hera was given him for a wife.
He was punished by being attached to a fiery wheel whirling around in
the air; this can hardly be anything but the lightning.   We find in this
myth the same elements.   Cp. also the myth of Salmoneus who nowadays
is considered to be a kingly sorcerer and rain-magician and who is
attached to the same genealogy.   The story that Ixion cunningly precipitated his father-in-law into a pit of burning charcoal refers perhaps
to the custom of fire-festivals in Central Greece; cp. my article "Fire-
festivals in Ancient Greece," *Journal of Hellenic Studies*, XLIII (1923),
p. 144 *et seq.*

[20] According to Apollonius Rhodius, ii. v. 154.

[21] Paus. ix. 34, 5.

nal home of the cult of Zeus Laphystius.[22]   It follows
of course that Athamas himself and the cult originally
belonged to the Boeotian Mount Laphystius and,
like many other cults, was transferred to another
place.

This localization, depending on the cult, is corroborated by the numerous traces of Athamas,
preserved in myths around the lake of Copais.
Athamas is said to have founded the town of Acrae-
phia at the east side of the lake,[23] and here, says
Pausanias, there was also a field of Athamas as
one proceeded on the direct road to the lake.[24]
Quite a number of his sons are mentioned as eponymous heroes and founders of various Boeotian towns
and localities, Ptous as early as the time of the
epic poet Asius.[25]

Consequently the statements that Athamas was
a son of Minyas,[26] that he was king of Orchomenus,
and lived there,[27] are not unfounded.   He is of old
connected with the plain around the lake of Copais
and with Mount Laphystion; that is, with the
district of Orchomenus.

With the myth of Athamas is connected that of
the Argonauts.   The Argonauts set out to fetch the
golden fleece from Colchis.   The harbor from which
they sailed was Iolcus near ancient Pagasae and

[22] The scene of the madness of the Minyades was laid on the same
mountain, *Schol. Lycophr. Alex.* v. 1237, and it is given as an *aition*
of the festival of Agrionia in Orchomenus; see my *Griechische Feste*, p.
273 *et seq.*

[23] Steph. Byz. *s. v.*

[24] Paus. ix. 24, 1.

[25] See Robert, *Griechische Heldensage*, p. 44.

[26] *Schol. Apoll. Rhod.*, i. v. 230.

[27] Hellanicus, *ibid.*, III. v. 265, cp. i. v. 763.

modern Volo in Thessaly, and here the famous cycle
of myths corresponds to the Mycenaean remains,
for Iolcus was the northernmost Mycenaean town.
Mycenaean sherds and minor finds are reported
from all Thessaly, just as they are from other
provinces of Greece,[28] but only scattered minor and
unimportant finds have come from parts of the
province other than from the neighborhood of
Iolcus.[29] There the remains are so numerous and
important as to prove that Iolcus was an important
center in the Mycenaean age. It is now generally
acknowledged that Professor Tsoundas discovered
the site of old Iolcus on a hill in the plain of Volo,
called Old Volo or the Kastro of Volo.[30] This hill
consists of remains of old habitations. Many late
Mycenaean sherds and some vases were discovered.[31]
Recently it has been reported that trial excavations
were undertaken on this hill, and that remains of a
Mycenaean palace built upon neolithic layers were
unearthed. It appears to have been extensive and
well built; the floor was covered with cement and
the walls with painted stucco.[32] It is to be regretted
that no more detailed report is forthcoming of this
apparently interesting discovery. The really convincing facts are the rich finds from the Mycenaean
age in the neighborhood of Iolcus. At Kapakli

[28] See the lists in Fimmen, Die kretisch-mykenische Kultur, p. 2 et
seq., and in Wace and Thompson, Prehistoric Thessaly (1912), p. 8 et seq.
and p. 206 et seq.

[29] Cp. the article "Iolkos" by Stählin in Pauly-Wissowa's Realenzyklopädie der klass. Altertumswissenschaft.

[30] Chr. Tsoundas, Αἱ προϊστορικαὶ ἀκροπόλεις Διμηνίου καὶ Σέσκλου,
(1908), p. 16.

[31] Wace and Thompson, loc. cit., p. 207; cp. p. 2.

[32] Bulletin de corespondence hellénique, xlv (1921), p. 530.

quite near Iolcus Dr. Kuruniotes excavated a tholos tomb which was almost untouched and yielded rich finds, especially gold objects; this has been one of the richest and most important discoveries of remains from the Mycenaean age. The vases are referred to the second Mycenaean period.[33] To the same period are ascribed vases found in tombs on a small peninsula just south of Volo within the area of what formerly was called old Pagasae but more justly is called Demetrias.[34]

Less than an hour to the west Professor Tsoundas excavated the mound of Dimini, where two tholos tombs were discovered, and another neighboring mound, Sesklo,[35] with a small tholos tomb which yielded late Mycenaean vases. Proceeding toward the west we come to the Phthiotic Thebes, with a ring-wall of uncertain date. Mycenaean terracottas, sherds, and painted stucco were found here. Halus, farther toward the south, near the sea, is not yet explored, but the old town is surrounded by Cyclopean walls which may be Mycenaean. In the village of Goura in the interior on the northern slope of Mount Othrys another tholos tomb was discovered by peasants, but the contents were dispersed so that nothing can be said of it with certainty.

It appears that the Mycenaean civilization had an important center in Iolcus and, as we observed above, this corresponds to the localization of the famous cycle of the Argonauts in that place. After this

[33] Wace and Thompson, *loc. cit.*, p. 206.

[34] Beloch in *Klio*, xi (1911), p. 442 *et seq.*; cp. his *Griechische Geschichte*, iv:1 (ed. 2), p. 224, n. 1.

[35] Sesklo is identified with the ancient town of Aison or Aisonia by Robert, *Griechische Heldensage*, p. 34 and n. 4.

survey of the Mycenaean remains in Thessaly we
come back to the fact that the Argonauts are said
to be Minyans. We find this statement in Pindarus;[36]
Herodotus has much to tell about the Minyans;[37]
and Apollonius Rhodius still more. Modern scholars
generally embrace the view that they are pseudo-
Minyans, accepting the opinion professed by Apollonius Rhodius and his scholiast that they were so
called because they and especially Iason were
descended from the daughters of Minyas. But
Buttmann, whose paper on the Minyans[38] is forgotten but is more solid than Müller's book, remarked
justly that the myth gives us no reason whatever
why the inhabitants of Iolcus were called Minyans;[39]
the name is one of these ever recurring old stock
expressions which the poets use by tradition without
knowing their sense. The statement of Apollonius
Rhodius and his scholiast[40] is no real explanation
but merely an attempt to explain the old stock
expression: in order to give a reason why the Argonauts were called Minyans they made them sons of
Minyas' daughters, for they could not be made
sons of Minyas himself. Buttmann's conclusion
that the real reason was that the Minyans inhabited
not only northern Boeotia but also southern Thessaly seems to be well founded. The Argonauts were
not called Minyans because they were descended

---

[36] Pindarus, *Pyth.*, iv. v. 69.

[37] Herodotus, iv. 145–150.

[38] Ph. Buttmann, *Mythologus* (1829), ii. p. 203.

[39] This is first mentioned by Simonides ἐν τοῖς Συμμίκτοις according to *Schol. Apollon. Rhod.*, i. v. 763. Whether this Simonides is from
Ceos or the younger Simonides from Amorgus is doubtful.

[40] Apollon. Rhod. i. v. 230 and the scholion ad 1.

from Minyas' daughters: these genealogies were invented in order to give a reason for the traditional phrase describing the Argonauts as Minyans.

The myth itself corroborates this connection, for the goal of the expedition is the fetching of the golden fleece, the fleece is inseparable from the cult of Zeus Laphystius, and the original home of this cult is Mount Laphystion, south of Orchomenus. It follows that the cycle, that of the Athamantidae and the Argonauts, is connected with both northern Boeotia and southern Thessaly, and this is comprehensible if we accept Buttmann's conclusion that the Minyans inhabited not only northern Boeotia but also the seaboard toward the north, including southern Thessaly.[41]

This conclusion is corroborated by cults and place names common to Boeotia and southern Thessaly. In addition to the cult of Zeus Laphystius, which was our starting point, that of Athena Itonia may be especially mentioned. Among place names the Phthiotic Thebes was mentioned above. There is a Coronea not only in Boeotia but in Thessaly also, situated on the northern slopes of Mount Othrys. Another Orchomenus in Thessaly is mentioned by several authors,[42] and lastly, a Thessalian town Minya is known by an inscription.[43] This is too much to be accidental and testifies to ethnical interrelations between the districts.

In this light the varying genealogies must be considered. Athamas is by Hellanicus said to be

---

[41] Buttmann, *loc. cit.*, II, p. 207.

[42] See Robert, *Griechische Heldensage*, p. 57.

[43] *Inscr. graecae*, IX:2, No. 521 from Larissa; Steph. Byz. *s. v.*

the son of Minyas; in the common genealogy he is the son of Aeolus. Aeolus is clearly a late creation, the eponymous hero of the Aeolian tribe. In this genealogy Athamas is the brother of Cretheus, Salmoneus, Sisyphus, and Perieres, king of Messenia. The two latter are undoubtedly late creations. Even Cretheus is not much more than a genealogical connecting link, the father of Aison, Pheres, and Amythaon, who in turn are nothing but eponymous heroes, Aison and Pheres of two Thessalian towns, but curiously enough Amythaon of the district of Amythaonia near the Triphylian Pylos.[44] The source of this genealogy is, however, late and here we merely state the fact of its existence.

With Tyro, the daughter of Salmoneus and wife of Cretheus, we strike old ground. She is mentioned in the Odyssey, together with Alcmene and Mycene, as one of the most famous heroines.[45] Her story is fully told in the Nekyia[46] but without certain features which are conspicuous later. But here a bewildering state of things appears. Where is Tyro at home and where is the scene of her love affair with Poseidon from which sprang the twins Pelias and Neleus? She is said to be the daughter of Salmoneus, and Salmoneus is the eponymous hero of the town of Salmone in the Alpheus Valley. Her wedding takes place in the river of Enipeus. There is a large river with this name in Thessaly but also another of the same name, a small tributary to Alpheus in Pisatis. She is the wife of the Thes-

---

[44] According to Rhianos in Steph. Byz. *s. v.*

[45] *Od.* ii. v. 120.

[46] *Od.* xi. v. 235 *et seq.*

salian hero Cretheus and by him mother of the Thessalian heroes Aison and Pheres, but she is also mother of the Triphylian hero Amythaon. Of the twins whom she bore to Poseidon one, Pelias, is closely related to Thessaly; the other, Neleus, as closely to Pylos.

Attempts have been made to find out whether Tyro is at home in Thessaly or in Pisatis.[47] I think this is lost labor. We are unable to come to any decision and have plainly and solely to admit that Tyro from of old was connected both with Thessaly and with Pisatis-Pylos. Two heroes may be made brothers without being originally related, e.g., Cretheus and Sisyphus; but if they are said to be twins, obviously their relation cannot be fortuitous. The mythical connections between Thessaly and Pylos, including the neighboring Pisatis, which belonged to the dominion of Pylos, are recognized facts. The genealogy is closely interwoven with these interrelations, which must be founded on some reality.

In this connection the passage in the Nekyia quoted above[48] deserves attention. Here it is said that Neleus married Chloris, the youngest daughter of the Iaside Amphion, who was king of Orchomenus. This links the genealogy of the house ruling at Pylos with Minyan Orchomenus. The passage involves a heresy and even modern mythographers are not fond of heresies. But it is highly improbable that such a passing mention of a famous hero contains a chance invention: the passage is certainly derived

[47] Robert, "Tyro," *Hermes*, li (1916), p. 290 *et seq.*
[48] Above p. 86.

from old tradition which was abandoned later
because it could not be fitted into the prevailing
quasi-historical scheme.   Amphion is said to be
king of Orchomenus and an Iasides.   Greek mythographers have deduced from this passage a King
Iasius or Iasus, the husband of Persephone, a
daughter of Minyas,[49] of course an invention without
any value.   We have only to admit that the story
that a Pylian queen was a daughter of the king of
Orchomenus reflects the connections of the Minyans
with the dominion of Pylos; moreover these connections are corroborated in other ways, especially by
the mention in Homer of a river Minyeios near
Pylos,[50] evidence the value of which is generally
recognized even by scholars who are skeptical in
regard to the myths of the Minyans.

There is nothing new in what has been set forth
here.   It is recognized that the interrelations between
the Thessalian and the Pylian heroes are too close
and manifold not to be of ancient and genuine
origin; furthermore, the connections between the
Minyans and the Pylians are acknowledged even
by those whose opinions are opposed to the wide
distribution attributed to the Minyans.   The in-
evitable conclusion from these two facts should
receive only its due emphasis, viz., that as Pylos was
closely connected on one hand with Thessaly and
on the other with the Minyans, the connections of

[49] Paus. ix. 36, 8, and Pherecydes frag. 117 Jacoby. It is, of course,
amazing to find Persephone as his wife. I think that the explanation
may be found in the Homeric passage *Od.* v. v. 125 *et seq.* concerning
Demeter's wedding with Iasion; the daughter was substituted for her
mother.

[50] *Il.* xi. v. 722.

the Minyans with Thessaly cannot have been late inventions.

The interrelations between northern Boeotia and southern Thessaly on one hand and the west coast of the Peloponnese on the other cannot be arbitrary inventions. There is some reason for even such mythological connections, but we ought to realize that they are a most embarrassing fact. As far as we know Greek history there is no trace of relations between these two very distant districts. These relations are, however, proved to have existed and to have been very lively. It follows that they existed in prehistoric times. For nobody will be inclined to ascribe their origin and development to the dark intermediate age between the downfall of the Mycenaean civilization and the rise of culture in the Geometric period. They belong consequently to the Mycenaean age. This view is supported and stressed by the fact that both districts were centers of Mycenaean civilization.

In order to understand this embarrassing fact, it is useful to consider another case, the amphictyony of Calaureia,[51] which comprised the towns of Prasiai, Nauplia, Hermione, Epidaurus, Aegina, Athens, and the Minyan Orchomenus;[52] i.e., seaside towns on the Argive peninsula and in Attica, and the inland town of Orchomenus in Boeotia. Two German scholars observed that Mycenaean sherds are found

[51] Wilamowitz, "Die Amphiktyonie von Kalaurea," *Nachrichten der Gesellschaft der Wissenschaften zu Göttingen, phil.-hist. Kl.*, 1896, p. 158 *et seq.*, esp. p. 169 *et seq.* contested K. O. Müller's hypothesis of the prehistoric origin of the league of Calaureia. I hope that it will seem more probable in the light of the new evidence adduced.

[52] According to Strabon, viii. p. 374.

in all these towns and therefore they ascribed this amphictyony to the Mycenaean age.[53] That opinion was contested[54] and is of course not established beyond doubt, but the really important question is why the Minyan Orchomenus which was situated in the interior of Boeotia was a member of this league of seaboard towns.[55] The league must needs belong to an age in which Orchomenus had interests on the sea, and this was not the historical age so far as we know it. But this position of Orchomenus agrees with the wealth ascribed to it in the Iliad.

Furthermore, another observation drawn from mythology may be added. The fleet gathered in a Boeotian harbor, Aulis, and set out thence for Troy. This rallying place has aroused wonder for, it has been said, the king of Mycenae being the commander-in-chief, one would expect the fleet to gather in some harbor of Argolis. Dr. Leaf has tried to show that Aulis was most unsuitable as the rallying place of a fleet. He demonstrates, however, a little too much; for it would follow from his arguments that Chalkis never can have been a trading place from which colonists and merchants sailed. We have to admit that Aulis was the harbor of Boeotia on its western coast, no other being

[53] A. Frickenhaus and W. Müller in the *Athenische Mitteilungen,* XXXVI (1911), p. 37.

[54] By Fimmen in the *Neue Jahrbücher für das klass. Altertum,* XXIX (1912), p. 537.

[55] E. Curtius in *Hermes,* X (1876), p. 388, solved this difficulty violently by cancelling the words "the Minyan." Arbitrarily he supposed Orchomenus to be the Arcadian town with this name and consequently wondered why Argos was omitted. The underlying presumption is that the league was one of Argive inland states, contrary to the evident fact that the league centers around the Saronian gulf.

available.[56] A myth is not consistent; it connects
facts from different ages in an arbitrary manner:
though the two facts mentioned are not consistent we
have to admit both, only realizing that they originally
belonged to different contexts. The other great
sea expedition of the Greek myths, that of the Argonauts, started from a harbor also said to have been
Minyan, Iolcus. Both Aulis and Iolcus are situated
on the seaboard, covered by the Minyan name.[57]

If we put these traces of a sea power concentrated
in the tracts inhabited by the Minyans together
with the great wealth ascribed in Homer to Orchomenus, the solution is at hand. The Minyans were
a trading people. That trade was considerable in
the late Mycenaean age is certain; vases of this
period are found in many foreign countries, especially
in Sicily and southern Italy. The harbors of the
Minyans, of which Iolcus was one, were on the
coast; but their chief city was inland Orchomenus,
the wealth of which depended also on the fertile

[56] W. Leaf, *Homer and History* (1916), p. 99 *et seq.*, relies upon
geography and the "Mediterranean Pilot" according to which Aulis is
said to be a most impossible harbor for the gathering of a fleet. He
concludes that the assembly at Aulis did not belong to the old myth but
was added by a Boeotian poet. I do not, of course, take the gathering
of the fleet at Aulis to be a historical fact, but I want only to point out
that the story is not so silly as it appears in Leaf. Boeotia had no other
harbor on its eastern coast, it must for good or for bad rely on Aulis
for its trade. This fact would be sufficient reason to a poet for representing Aulis as the rallying place of the fleet. In the archaic age Chalcis
certainly took over part of the Boeotian trade.

[57] Near Aulis is Hyria, where Amphion and Zethus are said to have
lived (cp. above p. 125), and where the Rhampsinites legend was localized
and applied to King Hyrieus. One is inclined to suppose that there was
a bee-hive tomb at Hyria which gave cause for the localizing of the story
there.

plains recovered by the draining of the lake of Copais. There is nothing improbable in the fact that the chief town of this trading people was an inland town. Perhaps its inhabitants tilled the ground in autumn and spring and went to sea during the summer, as Hesiod describes the Boeotian peasants of his time as doing and as did the peasants of Gotland, the great trading center of the Baltic sea in the Middle Ages.

This trade and sea power lead to an understanding of the connections of the Minyans with the western coast of the Peloponnese. We have seen above[58] that the dominion of Pylos is a typical seaside state founded by people who came oversea. I should not venture to say that it was founded by the Minyans, for the finds in both the towns which are said to be the Homeric Pylos are earlier than anything found in the Minyan area, even if some of the finds in Thessaly are ascribed to the second Mycenaean period,[59] but I think it to be a fair inference that Pylos served as an intermediate station for the Minyan trade. This will give a satisfactory explanation of the connections discussed above.

I cannot end this reasoning without giving a hint as to the possible trade routes, in spite of the great uncertainty of the matter. The Minyans may have sailed round the Peloponnese in order to reach Pylos, but it is also possible that they took a shorter route. Orchomenus is not much more distant from the Corinthian gulf than from the Euripus.

[58] Cp. above p. 85.

[59] Above p. 138. Wace and Thompson, *Prehistoric Thessaly*, p. 8 *et seq.*, and p. 206.

The Minyans may have taken the road past Delphi and Crisa to the harbor of Cirrha.[60]   Not only the oracle of Delphi but also the wealth of the temple are mentioned in Homer,[61] and Delphi was already a cult place in the Mycenaean age.   Remains of this cult have been found on the very spot where the temple and the great altar were built and in another place, in the suburb called Marmaria.   West of the temple precinct is a Mycenaean cemetery with a small tholos tomb.[62]   It may be guessed that Delphi in this age was not only a cult place but also a trading station.   Thus its rise to wealth and importance may be better understood.

Finally, it may be asked what bearing this view has on our scanty and hypothetical knowledge of the history of the Mycenaean age.   The greatest center of Mycenaean power is found in Argolis, where the remains are both the richest and the earliest.   History and mythology point to connections toward the south and the southeast, with Crete and the Orient, especially with Egypt.   The power of Mycenae and Argolis must be related in our minds with the destruction of Cnossus, the downfall of Minoan civilization, and the raids which reached the Delta of the Nile.   The inhabitants of Argolis were Vikings in the usual sense of the word.   But the Vikings known to history were not only pirates but tradesmen also, and the same may be

[60] An unimportant Mycenaean tomb was found accidentally near Itea, the modern harbor town of Delphi, *Deltion archaiologikon*, VI (1920–21), p. 147.

[61] *Il.* ix. v. 405; the oracle *Od.* viii. v. 80 and xi. v. 581.

[62] See my *Minoan-Mycenaean Religion*, p. 400 *et seq.*; cp. Evans, *The Palace of Minos*, II, p. 832 *et seq.*

supposed in regard to the Mycenaeans, even in regard to the inhabitants of Argolis.

It has been supposed that Mycenae owed its wealth to its control of trade. Its situation is favorable for trading not only to the southward on the Argive gulf but also to the northward on the Corinthian gulf. To corroborate this opinion the roads radiating from Mycenae toward the south and the north are referred to.[63] There may be a certain truth in this view but I cannot help thinking that the rulers of Mycenae were more warring than trading kings.

It has been remarked that the overwhelming power of Mycenae covers only a part of the Mycenaean age and that we have to suppose several changes and vicissitudes in the political status and power of the various towns during this age. The northerly connections of Mycenae and Argolis explain, as was observed above, the unlucky attempt to conquer Thebes, an episode the memory of which was preserved in myths.

It is comprehensible that when the great expedition toward the east came to an end, the people turned more and more to trading, not, however, without incidental piracy. The Phoenicians acted similarly, for trade and piracy were closely bound up even in the Homeric age. It seems as if this late period of the Mycenaean age was represented

[63] This view was put forth by V. Bérard, *Les Phéniciens et l'Odyssée*, I (1902–03), p. 11 and p. 78, according to whom Mycenae was a fortress built at a junction of the mountain passes for the purpose of levying taxes on all traffic going through. It was modified by G. Murray, *The Rise of the Greek Epic* (ed. 3; 1923), p. 57, who thought that Mycenae kept open a safe trade route between the northern and the southern sea. For a sound criticism see W. Leaf, *Homer and History*, p. 220 *et seq.* For the roads see R. Steffen, *Karten von Mykenai* (1884), Text, p. 8 *et seq.*

especially by the Minyans. Their sea power seems to
be a fact as well as their connection with the distant
dominion of Pylos. They were more a trading than
a warring people. Epical poetry prefers to chant
great and valorous deeds in war and has a certain
disesteem for trade. Thus it has little to say about
the Minyan Orchomenus, but the recollection of
the wealth of the city and the importance of its
people loomed in the background of tradition.

There were great sea expeditions starting from
Minyan harbors, which were the most lively in
Greece in the late Mycenaean age. For this reason
the myth told that the expedition which set out
for Troy gathered in the harbor of Aulis, but according to a still older tradition the king of Mycenae was
made its commander-in-chief. Another expedition,
bound up with Minyan myths, acquired a fame of
its own, the expedition which fetched the golden
fleece from Colchis. It started from Iolcus, the
Minyan center on the Gulf of Volo.

I cannot leave this subject without adding another
observation. When treating the other provinces of
Greece we have generally had to speak of cities,
not of tribes; in this chapter almost the reverse takes
place. We have spoken of a tribe which had two
great centers, many minor ones, and several harbors.
This falls in with the conditions of old Boeotia as
described by tradition;[64] various tribes never play
so great a part in old tradition in any province as
in that of Boeotia. In addition to the Minyans,
we have first the Phlegyans who are mentioned
as early as in the Homeric poems and by later authors

[64] See Fimmen's article mentioned p. 129, n. 6.

are described as a reckless and impious people. It is notable that they, like the Minyans, belong both to Thessaly and to Boeotia. Probably they were a tribe to the rear of the Minyans who tried to push forward and invade the neighboring civilized country. Other tribes are the Temmikes, the Aones, the Graikoi, the Gephyraioi, and the Hyantes, but we know too little of them to say what their importance was and to which ages they belonged.

Perhaps we have here a picture of the continual attempted invasions by Greek tribes coming down from the north and striving to invade Greece. One of these tribes, the Minyans, took over the Mycenaean civilization during its late period when the warring enterprises toward the east already belonged to the past. They were cut off from the routes toward the south and the southeast by the inhabitants of Argolis. Consequently they turned toward the northeast, or, perhaps going overland and across the Corinthian gulf, they went toward the west. According to the conditions of the time they turned to trading or to cultivation of their land, but these peaceful occupations diminished their importance in mythology.

The Minyan power declined; things were changing rapidly in this age. The Minyans were exposed to the pressure of the tribes in their rear coming down from the mountains in the north and northwest, but they seem to have had foes in the south too. For the myths telling of their war with Thebes probably have a historical background. Our sources are late. Euripides is the first who mentions Heracles as the vanquisher of the Minyans and the liberator of

Thebes.[65] Diodorus has an extensive and picturesque
tale of how Heracles overcame the Minyans and their
king Erginus, who had conquered Thebes and made
it tributary to Orchomenus.[66] Another version is
that Heracles blocked the *katavothra* through which
the lake of Copais was drained, so that the district
of Orchomenus was inundated.[67] It is the same fact,
the catastrophe which overtook the power of Orchomenus, in various mythological settings. In the
latter version it is combined with the fact that the
plain made dry by the draining of the lake of Copais
was again flooded, but the blocking of the *katavothra*
may have come about through negligence. That
the Minyans of Orchomenus lost their power through
a disastrous war with Thebes is a generally received
opinion.

It is hardly possible to proffer any well founded
opinion as to the time at which this war took place.
Dr. Fimmen's opinion[68] that the inhabitants of
Thebes were the Boeotians who immigrated into
the province to which they gave their name seems
unlikely to be correct. Our information concerning
their immigration is given by Thucydides,[69] who says
that they came from Thessaly; and it seems a priori
probable that they came from the north or northwest,
not from the south or southeast. The war with
Thebes is probably earlier. What was left of the
Minyan power was destroyed when the Dorians
invaded both Boeotia and Thessaly and overturned

---

[65] Euripides, *Heracles*, v. 48 and v. 220.
[66] Diodorus, iv. 10; cp. Apollodorus, ii. 4, 11.
[67] Diodorus, iv. 18; Paus. ix. 38, 7.
[68] Fimmen, *loc. cit.*, p. 538.
[69] Thucydides, i. 12.

the old conditions. One of the components of the historical Boeotian dialect is Doric or more justly West Greek. Some of the Minyans seem to have emigrated. There are traces showing that they took part in the colonization of the western coast of Asia Minor at the very end of the Mycenaean age. Herodotus enumerates many peoples of whom the Asiatic Ionians were composed and among these are the Minyans of Orchomenus.[70] Further, Pherecydes says that the Minyan king Athamas founded Teos,[71] and Anacreon therefore calls this town, in which he was born, an Athamantian town.[72]

In Ionia we encounter the Pylians again. According to Strabo, the colonization of Ionia was begun by Androclus, a son of Codrus, the last king of Athens.[73] According to Pausanias, Codrus' father, Melanthus, was a descendant of Neleus who, together with many Pylians, had been expelled by the Heracleidae.[74] Neleus, a son of Codrus, founded Miletus and other sons founded other towns. Priene was founded by Neleus' son Aepytus, who has the same name as an Arcadian hero, and Colophon was, according to Mimnermus, founded by the Pylian Andraimon. Teos, which first was founded by Athamas, is said to have been founded for a second time by Nauclus, Codrus' son.

These foundation legends are reshaped by the logographers, and the tendency to make Athens the mother city of the Ionian towns in Asia Minor

[70] Herodotus, i. 146.
[71] In *Schol. Plat. Hipparch.*, p. 229 D; Frag. 102 Jacoby.
[72] In Strabo, xii. p. 633.
[73] Strabo, xiv. p. 632.
[74] Paus. ii. 18, 8.

appears clearly. Pausanias says that the Pylians expelled by the Heracleidae emigrated to Athens, where Melanthus, a descendant of Neleus, became king instead of Thymoites, a descendant of Theseus. Hellanicus says that Erythrae was one of the Ionian towns founded by Codrus' son Neleus.[75]

There cannot be any doubt that the participation of the Pylians in founding the Ionian towns on the western coast of Asia Minor is the fundamental fact, and this fact the logographers tried to harmonize with the claims of Athens to be their mother city. Therefore a double of Neleus was invented and made a son of Codrus; therefore, also, the expelled Pylians are said to have emigrated first to Attica and from Attica to Ionia; and therefore the last kings of Athens are said to be descendants of Neleus. For it was natural to connect the colonization of Ionia, if it was due to the Athenians, with the end of the kingdom at Athens and the emigration of the kingly family. Attica may have contributed to the colonization of Ionia, but the fact ought not to be overlooked that in the old form of the legends the Pylians play the foremost part.

This is probably a historical fact. For the Mycenaean dominion of Pylos was conquered by the immigrating Dorians, and it is only natural that the old ruling classes and part of the people should have emigrated. That they took the way eastward to Ionia is to be explained by their connections with the Minyans, of whom a part took the same way when they were ousted by other tribes. There is every chance that old, good tradition is preserved in

[75] Hellanicus in his *Atthis* quoted by Harpocration *s. v.* 'Ερυθραῖοι.

these foundation legends, which go back into the sixth century B. C.; they give us a valuable outlook on the migrations of the peoples in the stormy age which put a definite end to the Mycenaean civilization and led to the colonization of the western coast of Asia Minor, a movement which archaeological evidence proves to belong to this time. This gives the finishing touch to the picture of the sea-faring Minyan people, whose connections were so wide and who evidently played a very important part in the late Mycenaean age.

The question may be put to which of the great Greek tribes the Minyans belonged. That they are connected genealogically with the Aeolians, Aeolus being put at the head of their genealogy, does not prove anything, for this genealogy was invented at a time when Boeotia and Orchomenus were considered to be Aeolian. Nor is it good evidence that the Orchomenians of the historical age spoke the common Boeotian dialect. For the areas of the various dialects have changed thoroughly because of the migrations. There seems to me to be a certain probability that the Minyans were Ionians—in the first place because they contributed so largely to the colonization of Ionia. The Greek colonists of Ionia were very mixed, but its language proves of course the predominance of the Ionian element. Secondly, Euboea was Ionian and it is only natural to suppose that the Minyans inhabited this island also and when expelled from the mainland retired to it. The existence of not a few Mycenaean remains in Euboea, among which are small bee-hive tombs, proves that the island shared in the Mycenaean

civilization; moreover, there is a town called Eretria
in Euboea as well as in Thessaly, just as Boeotian
place names recur in Thessaly.

These considerations are of a certain importance
in connection with the few words which I have to
add concerning other Thessalian myths, primarily
the myth of Achilles. Like Boeotia, Thessaly is a
country of many tribes, Achaeans, Myrmidons,
Hellens, Magnetes, Dolopes, Perrhaiboi, etc., thus
reproducing the conditions that we find in historical
times in the mountain countries to the west, where
a great number of small tribes were living. It will
be well to keep in mind the steady push of tribes
referred to above.

Achilles[76] owes his fame and his glory to the great
poet who made him the chief personage of the Iliad.
His mythical importance ought not to be measured
accordingly, but he belongs certainly to old mythology. For we have seen that folk-tale motifs were
attached especially to old mythical heroes, and such
motifs are conspicuous in the myth of Achilles. He
was born of Thetis, a sea nymph, to a mortal, Peleus,
who wrestled with her and won her in spite of her
metamorphoses. Here we have a widely spread
motif of fairy tales, which shows that Thetis originally was no goddess but a nymph.

The myth of Achilles is, however, to be tested in
order to see if it, like others, has any historical
background. The Iliad includes, in the dominion of
Peleus, Phthia and Hellas, both populated by the
tribe of the Myrmidons. The name of Phthia is
preserved in historical times in Achaia Phthiotis in

[76] Cp. Wilamowitz, "Die griechische Heldensage," II, *Sitzungsberichte der preuss. Akademie der Wissenschaften* (1925), p. 239 *et seq.*

which the Phthiotic Thebes was situated; it is the
tract north of Mount Othrys and west of the Paga-
saean gulf. It is to be supposed that in an earlier
time it included the northern coast of the gulf and
Mount Pelion also, because of the relation of the
name of Peleus and his myth to Mount Pelion
whose eponymous hero he is.

In regard to Hellas, I think that Dr. Leaf is
eminently right in taking it to be the Spercheus
Valley,[77] for as Spercheus is the river near which
Achilles is brought up, every other view will involve
unsolvable difficulties. The myth which makes the
man of Mount Pelion the father of the votary of
Spercheus supposes that these two districts were
united, viz., that they were inhabited by the same
tribe, the Myrmidons. This is the northern part of
the region covered by the Minyans.

There is no direct proof showing that the myth of
Achilles goes back into the Mycenaean age, in fact
he has no cycle; nor is there any proof to the contrary.
But supposing that it does so by reason of its apparent antiquity and connections with the folk-tale,
we must tentatively try to see how the above statements fall in with what has been set forth concerning
the Minyans.

We have supposed that there was a steady push of
tribes coming down from the north and northwest
and that the Minyans were expelled, first of course
from Thessaly, and retired in the other direction,
to Boeotia, to Euboea, and finally to Asia Minor.
If they were Ionians, as we surmised, the newcomers
were Achaeans, after whom the country was called

[77] W. Leaf, *Homer and History*, p. 110 *et seq.*

Achaea with the distinguishing epithet the Phthiotic.
The dialect of this region is Doric but with Aeolic
traces.[78] That is to say, the Achaeans possessed
themselves of Thessaly, and after them the Dorians,
but the Dorian element was much stronger in the
southern part of the province. Thus it seems that
the Achaean tribe of the Myrmidons represents an
intermediate stage between the domination of the
Minyans and the final Dorian invasion.

The rest of Thessaly, where Mycenaean remains
are unimportant, has no important myths. Most
known because of many works of art, is the battle of
the Centaurs and the Lapiths. This battle appears
in art, however, much later than their battle with an
archer, who perhaps may be called Heracles. Centaurs without any adversary appear in the earliest
art of the archaic period and as early as the Late
Mycenaean age.[79] It is to be observed that they are

[78] O. Kern, *Neue Jahrbücher für das klass. Altertum*, XIII (1904)
p. 16 *et seq.* The inscriptions show, however, the northwest κοινή.
Chadwick's identification of the Achaeans and Achilles with the northwestern Greek tribes in his *Heroic Age* (1912) p. 280, *et seq.*, is unfor-
tunate. These arrived in Greece latest, even after the Dorians whom
Homer neglects.

[79] See above p. 34 and n. 31. The representation on the M. M. gem
in Baur's list (= Evans, *Scripta Minoa*, I, p. 11, fig. 5b) does not show
a centaur. Terracottas and bronzes representing centaurs appear as
early as the Geometric period; e.g., at Olympia, where some of them are
from the deepest layers, a winged centaur is represented on a Dipylon
cup. The representations of the centaurs' combat with an archer goes
back perhaps into the eighth century B. C.; whilst those of their combat
with the Lapiths begin with the sixth century. This combat is, however,
mentioned *Od.* xxi. v. 295 *et seq.*, and *Il.* i. v. 263 *et seq.* P. V. C. Baur,
The Centaurs in Ancient Art (1912). The subject was treated recently
by P. Demargne, *Bulletin de correspondance hellénique*, LIII (1929),
p. 117 *et seq.*; but his assumption that the centaur was borrowed from
Oriental art seems questionable in view of the fact that there are no good
Oriental prototypes.

met with in other provinces too, in Aetolia in the
story of Nessus and in Arcadia in the story of
Pholus. They appear consequently to be a mythical
conception common to the Greeks,[80] but according
to the prevailing Greek ideas their myths were
localized in definite but various places, of which
Thessaly was only one. The real riddle is the
connections of their foes, the Lapiths. I return to
this question in the chapter on the Attic myths.

8. ATTICA

Attica is strewn with Mycenaean remains. Best
known are those from the Acropolis of Athens. The
hill is surrounded by an old Cyclopean wall which
follows the natural sinuosities of the rock and is
probably of Mycenaean date. On the Acropolis
are the remains of Mycenaean buildings, and beneath
the so-called old temple of Athena are walls of a
Mycenaean palace with column bases. Not a few
Mycenaean sherds were found here during the excavations, but they are all of a late period. Notable
but little known is a hoard of bronze utensils found
near the Cyclopean wall.[1] Tombs with sub-Mycenaean pottery were found on the southern slope of
the Acropolis.

A fairly large bee-hive tomb was explored at
Menidi, old Acharnae, and yielded interesting finds.
A most remarkable fact is that the cult at this tomb

---

[80] I am, however, unable to believe in the recent attempt by G.
Dumézil, *Le problème des Centaures* (1929), to make them an old Aryan
heritage.

[1] Now at last easily accessible in O. Montelius, *La Grèce préclassique*,
I, p. 153.

was continued down to the time of the Peloponnesian war.[2] At Aphidna in northern Attica Professors Wide and Kjellberg excavated long ago a big tumulus. This excavation is remarkable because here for the first time Middle Helladic vases were found in a regular excavation and taken up in scientific discussion. The place was inhabited in the Mycenaean age also. The acropolis was not explored, but walls of an uncertain date are recorded and on the terraces toward the east Mycenaean sherds were found. We shall presently see that the mythological importance of this site is such that it ought to be searched more thoroughly. In the interior of the province two or three necropolises were discovered near the modern village of Markopoulo in the Mesogaia. At Spata on the road from Athens to Marathon Mycenaean chamber tombs were found which contained not a few remains of funeral furniture.[3] In a cave called Lychnospelaion on Mount Parnes Mycenaean sherds of a late style were discovered.[4]

On the eastern coast there are several Mycenaean sites. At Brauron, an unexplored acropolis with traces of walls, both pre-Mycenaean and Mycenaean sherds have been found. In a neighboring hill are Mycenaean chamber tombs and others have been found not far to the south, at Porto Raphti, north of the small bay; south of it is the site of old Prasiai.

[2] See my *Minoan-Mycenaean Religion*, p. 524 *et seq.*

[3] A survey in H. Gropengiesser, *Die Gräber von Attika* (Dissertation, Heidelberg, 1907). Recent discoveries of Mycenaean tombs at Porto-Raphti, Pikermi, Velanideza, and Vourvatsi, *Deltion archaiologikon*, XI (1927–28), App. p. 59 *et seq.*

[4] See my *Minoan-Mycenaean Religion*, p. 61 *et seq.*

At Thorikus near Cape Sunium houses with sherds, belonging partly to pre-Mycenaean, partly to Mycenaean times, have been discovered. There is also a small tholos tomb there, and another in the neighborhood. On the western coast several Mycenaean chamber tombs have been found near Haliki (Halai Aixonides), south of Athens. Mycenaean sherds are mentioned as having been found at Phaleron.

Eleusis is a Mycenaean site. Mycenaean and pre-Mycenaean sherds were collected on the surface of the acropolis and in other places also. There is a small tholos tomb, and other traces of Mycenaean occupation have been found.[5] The opinion that the oldest walls of the sacred precinct and of the hall of mysteries go back to the Mycenaean age[6] is, however, contested.[7]

Thus Mycenaean remains are scattered over all Attica and prove that this province was deeply penetrated by Mycenaean civilization; but on the other hand they are not very significant and cannot be compared with those of Boeotia, not to speak of those of Argolis. To this state of things the mythical importance of Attica corresponds closely. In the great days of Athens the Athenians and their great poets strove to surround the city with a mythical glory corresponding to its renown in their own age; but it is recognized that the prominence of Attic mythology is late; we ought not to let ourselves be deceived by it. In reality heroic mythology in

[5] F. Noack, *Eleusis* (1927), p. 15.
[6] A. W. Persson, *Archiv für Religionswissenschaft*, XXI (1922), p. 292 *et seq.*
[7] Noack, *loc. cit.*, p. 14.

Attica is on the whole poor, with one great exception, the Theseus cycle—but this is a special case to which we must recur at length below. It is a well-known and curious fact that the Athenians play a most unimportant part in Homer.

The list of the Athenian kings is a rather late compilation, pieced together from different elements and various heroes, who often were doubled in order to make up a sufficiently long list and to smooth over discrepancies. It need not detain us for long. Certain of the kings belong, moreover, to hieratic mythology.

The name of the aboriginal king, Cecrops, shows an ending well known from tribal names, *-ops*, plur. *-opes*, and from this it has been inferred that he was the eponymous hero of a vanished tribe formerly inhabiting Athens. Such an explanation is possible but cannot be demonstrated. The name of the second king appears in two forms, Erichthonius and the abbreviated form Erechtheus, but there cannot be any doubt concerning their fundamental identity, although Erichthonius and Erechtheus have been split up into two persons. The name is etymologically clear. Erichthonius is derived from χθών, "earth," with the prefix ἐρι-, "much." For certain reasons which cannot be repeated here I have inferred that Erichthonius is originally the Divine Child, the newborn spirit of vegetation, of whom there are many traces in connection with the Minoan-Mycenaean religion.[8] King Pandion is also doubled; he has hardly any importance for our subject. The connection of his myths with Megara is notable.

---

[8] In my *Minoan-Mycenaean Religion*, p. 490 *et seq.*

They can have been created only in the early historical period in which Athens strove to extend its
power to the Megaris and succeeded in possessing
itself of the island of Salamis, which belonged to
Megara, and of its hero Aias. By reason of this
tendency Megarian myths were joined with Attic
ones.

Other Attic myths, among which the best known
are those of Ion, of Cephalus and Procris, and of
Procne and Philomele, may be passed over as being
of slight importance for our subject; in other respects
they are interesting, but they cannot be proved to
have any connection with the Mycenaean age.

The most famous of all Athenian myths remains
the great Theseus cycle.[9] It is generally and justly
recognized that the mythical fame and glory of
Theseus grew and developed together with the power
and glory of the state of Athens and the self-con-
sciousness of its people. Theseus was made the
national hero of Athens, the aspirations of which
were, as usually happened, projected back into the
mythical age. In the Athenian monuments of the
earlier archaic period Heracles is prominent and
Theseus almost absent. From the days of the Peisis-
tratidae Theseus gains ever more ground until, during its heyday in the fifth century B. C., he is made

[9] In addition to Robert's exhaustive treatment of the cycle in his
Griechische Heldensage, p. 676 *et seq.*, in which earlier papers are quoted
fully, the short but searching analysis by Wilamowitz, "Die griechische
Heldensage," II, *Sitzungsberichte der preuss. Akademie der Wissenschaften*,
1925, p. 234 *et seq.* is especially to be consulted. Cp. also the paper of
V. Costanzi already quoted, p. 74 n. 15 and E. Kjellberg, "Zur Entwick-
lung der attischen Theseussage" in *Strena philologica Upsaliensis* (1922),
p. 270 *et seq.* A. v. Salis, *Theseus und Ariadne* (1930) appeared only after
this section was written.

the hero of the Athenian democracy, the founder
of the Athenian state through the synoecism and
of the democratic institutions of Athens.

In the development of the Theseus cycle the tendency appears clearly to make it rival the Heracles
cycle, i.e., to create a series of adventures and great
deeds attributed to Theseus resembling those performed by Heracles, who, according to the monuments, was very popular in Athens in the early
archaic age. There must, however, have been an
old kernel around which these accretions were able
to crystallize.

The later group of the cycle comprises the adventures of Theseus on his way from Troezen to Athens;
they appear first on late black-figured vases.[10]
According to Pausanias,[11] Sinis is localized on the
Isthmus, near Cenchreai, a harbor of Corinth on
the Saronian gulf. Crommyon, where Theseus slew
the wild sow, was a village on the boundary between
Megara and Corinth, to which it belonged in historical times. Sciron dwelt on the steep rocks on the
shores of Geraneia, nowadays called *Kakais Skalais*,
south of Megara. Cercyon lived near Eleusis, and
Procrustes farther westward on the river called
Cephissus, which flowed through the Thriasian plain;
or on the mountain of Corydallus, which must be
identified with Mount Aegaleos, the mountain which
separates the Thriasian and the Athenian plains.

These localizations show very definitely the tendency which appears in the myths of Pandion and

[10] E. Buschor in Furtwängler and Reichhold, *Griech. Vasenmalerei*,
Text, III, p. 119 *et seq.*, gives a survey of vase paintings representing
Theseus and his adventures.
[11] Paus. ii. 1, 4.

Nisus[12] to carry the mythological claims of Athens
to the Isthmus and to Megara, and here they extend
to Eleusis also, which Athens succeeded in conquering
in the seventh century B. C. As to the importance of
such claims there is an illuminating story told by
Plutarch[13] that when the Spartans were called upon
as arbitrators in the contention of Athens and
Megara concerning the island of Salamis, they
adjudicated the island to Athens because it is said
in Homer that Aias of Salamis placed his ships on
the same place as the Athenians. If the hero of
Athens, Theseus, had liberated these tracts from
wild beasts and highwaymen his city had a mythical
title to lay claim to them. Athens annexed Eleusis
in the seventh century B. C. and succeeded in wrest-
ing the island of Salamis from the Megarians in the
first half of the sixth century B. C. Mythology
proves that its aspirations went farther.

Consequently these myths cannot be older, at
least as applied to Theseus, than the early historical
age. There may have been earlier myths made over
and reshaped in order that they might be attached
to Theseus, but we do not know what these myths
may have been, nor are they of any importance for
our purpose.

Next to these exploits of Theseus on his way from
Troezen to Athens we have to consider the myth of
his birth and his youth before these deeds. He is a
son of the Athenian king Aegeus, who in obedience
to an oracle went to Troezen and there wedded
Aithra, the daughter of King Pittheus of Troezen.
This town is situated on the northern shore of the

---

[12] Cp. below p. 178.   [13] Plutarch, *Solon*, chap. 10.

Argive peninsula, not far from its easternmost end.
Theseus' son Hippolytus had a sanctuary at Troezen.
Aithra, Pittheus' daughter, is first mentioned in
the Iliad as a servant of Helen.[14]

Here opinions differ. Professor Wilamowitz admits no doubt that Theseus was originally at home
at Troezen.[15] Professor Robert gives voice to the
opinion that the myth of the birth of Theseus was
created in the sixth century B. C.[16] It may be
adduced as an argument for the former view that
the northern shore of the Argive peninsula is said
to have been inhabited by Ionians in early times,[17]
but on the other hand it is a serious objection to
the antiquity of the myth that nothing Mycenaean,
not even a single sherd, has been found at Troezen,
though remains have been sought for.[18] The town
seems to be a post-Mycenaean foundation.

It cannot possibly be doubted that Theseus is
at home in Attica, for the really and undoubtedly
old myths about him, namely, the myths of the
Marathonian bull, of the rape of Ariadne, and of
the rape of Helen, are localized here, and these
myths unquestionably go back into the Mycenaean
age. Then it would seem amazing if he were born
and bred in Troezen and not in Attica, and we had
another case similar to that of Heracles.[19] But

[14] *Il.* iii v. 144.

[15] Wilamowitz, *loc. cit.*, p. 235.

[16] Robert, *loc. cit.*, p. 708.

[17] The passages concern Epidaurus; quotations in Busolt, *Griech.
Geschichte* (ed. 2), I, p. 216, n. 7.

[18] *Athenische Mitteilungen*, XXXVI (1911), p. 33.

[19] The exploits of Heracles belong to Tiryns and his birth story
to Thebes; see below p. 200 *et seq.*

this can hardly be so. Theseus is no hero common to the Greek people or even to the Ionians, but is of local Attic origin. The father of his mother, Pittheus, is the eponymous hero of the demos of Pithus, a member of which is called a Pittheus. Its exact situation is not known, but as it belonged to the seventh tribe, Cecropis, together with Athmonon, Phlya, and Sypalettus, it is reasonably inferred that it may be sought for to the southwest of Mount Pentelicon. Thus Pittheus belongs certainly to Attica and his genealogical connection with Pelops was invented later, after his being transferred to the Peloponnese.

Professor Wilamowitz thinks that Theseus' mother Aithra must be at home at Troezen, because there is no trace of her in Attica. That is true, but on the other hand the trace of her in Troezenian cult legend is not of much value. For that she founded the temple of Athena Apaturia on the island of Sphairia[20] is a hieratic legend of indeterminate and probably rather late date. If Pittheus' daughter Aithra really is a Troezenian, it is very curious that in the Iliad she appears as one of the servants of Helen. For this presupposes the further development of the myth of Helen's rape by Theseus; viz., that Helen was rescued by her brothers, the Dioscuri, who abducted Theseus' mother as a captive. The book of the Iliad in which the passage is found belongs of course to its later parts, but in spite of this its date is so early that it seems difficult to suppose that a Troezenian legend transferred to Attica should be current at that time. For the

[20] Paus. II, 33, 1.

myth must have been a current one, from the casual manner in which it is mentioned. The passage is not of such a nature as the Athenians would have introduced in order to enhance the mythical fame of Athens, which is almost passed over in Homer. Therefore it seems probable that Aithra, like her father, was originally at home in Attica, although it ought to be stated that there is no trace of her there. The myths of Hippolytus and Phaidra are more loosely connected with Theseus and are of hardly any importance for our subject.

We have seen that there are certain reasons for assuming that the grandfather of Theseus and probably even his mother were originally at home in Attica, but it is not to be concealed that this view implies difficulties, for we cannot see any definite reason why they were localized at Troezen. Although the political aspirations of Athens were directed to the Megaris and the Isthmus, it would be hazardous to guess that they laid claim to Troezen; i.e., to the southern coast of the Saronian gulf, also. The birth of Theseus at Troezen is connected with his wandering through the Isthmus but is not a necessary premiss for it. There may have existed some myths or cults at Troezen by which the myth of Theseus was attracted, since it had transgressed the boundaries of Attica, but I am unable to point to such cults or myths;[21] I can only point to the

[21] There is no cult or myth at Troezen which can be proved to be of great antiquity; cp. S. Wide, *De sacris Troezeniorum, etc.* (Dissertation, Uppsala, 1888). In the temple of Artemis Soteira were altars of the gods ruling underground and Dionysus was said to have here brought up his mother Semele from the Underworld, but this myth is localized elsewhere also and affords no sufficient clue.

fact that the same tribe that inhabited Attica once lived in the Argive peninsula also. Happily this intricate question is of no importance for our main purpose, for even if Theseus' ancestors should be Troezenian, it can not be proved that they belong to a Mycenaean myth. At all events the birth story is a later addition.

Three deeds of Theseus remain which are of earlier origin. The capture of the bull of Marathon by Theseus is a close parallel to the capture of the Cretan bull by Heracles; the bulls were identified by the ancient mythographers. In this case it is supposed that, in contrast to what usually happened, a deed of Theseus was transferred to Heracles.[22] I cannot see any necessary reason for assuming such a transference; nor can I see why Professor Bethe identifies the Marathonian bull with the Minotaur.[23] Bulls were among the beasts of chase, and hunting such big game was a valued pastime in the Mycenaean age. Such a simple adventure was told of more than one hero.[24] Professor Bethe is right in stating that this deed belongs originally to Theseus as well as to Heracles.[25] There may be so much truth in his identification of the Minotaur with the Marathonian bull that the myth of the latter was the starting point for developing the Minotaur myth.

This deed of Theseus is represented in vase pictures at an earlier date than his other deeds,[26] and this

---

[22] Wilamowitz, *Herakles*, I. p. 302; in opposition to this the myth is localized in Argolis by P. Friedländer, *Herakles* (1907), p. 37.

[23] E. Bethe, "Minos," *Rheinisches Museum*, LXV (1910), p. 223.

[24] E.g. of Argos; see below p. 212.

[25] Bethe, *loc. cit.*, p. 218 *et seq.*

[26] References in Robert, *Griech. Heldensage*, p. 678, n. 1.

fact is of a certain value, although the earliest
representations belong to the sixth century B. C.
More important is the localization of the myth at
Marathon in northeastern Attica in that part of
the province to which the old Theseus myths belong.
It is very probable that this myth belongs to the
old stock, although this cannot be demonstrated
with arguments of absolute certainty.

The two remaining myths, the rape of Ariadne
and the rape of Helen—their parallelism ought to
be noticed from the outset—can with certainty be
proved to go back to the Mycenaean age. In.
discussing the Laconian myths[27] I spoke of the
abduction of Helen by Theseus and stated that all
attempts have failed to separate this myth from
Aphidna in northern Attica, a site with an unexplored
acropolis which was inhabited in Mycenaean times,
not very far to the northwest from the plain of
Marathon. Helen belongs to Attica also. In the
epos called Cypria she was said to be a daughter
of Nemesis, who had a temple at Rhamnus on the
coast north of Marathon.[28] But in this connection
of Helen with Nemesis, the goddess of retaliation,
there appears a certain speculative strain which
makes its date doubtful, and probably late; and I
have to acknowledge that the goddess Nemesis as
a cult goddess still seems to me to be an unsolved
riddle. I should not venture to emphasize this
connection. We saw further that Helen is a pre-
Greek goddess of vegetation whose peculiarity it is
to be carried off, just as Kore was carried off by

[27] Above p. 74 et seq.

[28] Cp. Wide in the Athenische Mitteilungen, XXI (1896), p. 387.

Pluto. Thus we have a pre-Greek hieratic myth, the rape of the goddess of vegetation by a god, which was made a heroic myth in various ways. This myth was secularized by the Greek invaders and transferred to an Asiatic prince by epic poetry. It may be asked if the case of Theseus is similar. I am distinctly disinclined to believe so, for in two other myths, those of Ariadne and of Persephone, Theseus appears as the abductor of a goddess of vegetation. He may have been originally the chief male personage of the old hieratic myth.[29]

The myth telling how Theseus, with the help of Ariadne, entered the Labyrinth, slew the Minotaur, rescued the Athenian children, and sailed away, taking Ariadne with him, is well known. Of all the myths from the Greek mainland, it has the most numerous and evident relations with Crete and the Minoan world, so that there cannot be any reasonable doubt that it goes back into the Mycenaean age and moreover to that early part of this age in which Crete and Cnossus still flourished and were powerful. It is generally recognized to contain reminiscences from the Minoan age.

[29] The real significance of the myth of the abduction of Kore by Pluto was well explained by F. M. Cornford in *Studies and Essays presented to Sir W. Ridgeway* (1913), p. 153 *et seq*. Kore is the Corn-maiden, the grains which after the harvest are laid down in the subterranean silos or jars to be preserved until the sowing; she is here in the power of Pluto, the God of Wealth, i.e., precisely, of the store of corn by which men live. These subterranean stores being called θησαυροί, I considered whether the name Θησεύς which seems to be derived from the same stem is to be explained according to this view as the "One who puts the corn down" (cp. Latin *Conditor*), but this guess seems to me to be too uncertain to be mentioned except in a note, although it fits in admirably with the opinion advanced in the text.

I have collected and discussed in earlier works[30] the evidence concerning Ariadne and need not repeat the discussion here. The conclusion is that Ariadne seems to be a goddess of vegetation derived from Minoan times. She was venerated especially on the islands of the Aegean but is said to have had a festival in the Opuntian Locris too. The salient feature of her myths is her death, which was told in various versions, but there was also a joyous festival in her honor. Once she is said to have hanged herself like Helen Dendritis. The most perplexing myth is, however, the Homeric one, according to which she was killed by Artemis on the island of Dia, because of information given by Dionysus.[31] In the common myth Ariadne is the wife of Dionysus. I have explained these contradicting myths by the assumption that the Minoan vegetation goddess Ariadne entered into competition with the kindred cult of Dionysus, and on one hand was vanquished and ousted by him, or on the other hand became associated with his cult.[32]

Both Ariadne and Helen are pre-Greek vegetation goddesses, and there are some similarities in detail between them also, to which I have pointed in another place.[33] The most salient similarity is, however, that both were carried off by Theseus. I cannot but find the same pre-Greek myth here, the carrying off of the vegetation goddess, in two different versions. Consequently I take this to be

[30] In my *Griechische Feste*, p. 382 *et seq.*, and in my *Minoan-Mycenaean Religion*, p. 451 *et seq.*
[31] *Od.* xi. v. 323.
[32] In my *Griechische Feste*, loc. cit.
[33] In my *Minoan-Mycenaean Religion*, p. 453.

the kernel of the Theseus myth and I have expressed
my belief that Theseus is originally the chief male
personage in the myth of the rape and that he was
transferred to heroic mythology because the immigrated Greeks did not grasp the sacred nature of the
myth. Another form of the same myth, with other
names, was preserved in the tradition of the mysteries, which seem to be a survival of Minoan
religious ideas. This myth is akin to another sacred
vegetation myth the Minoan origin of which I
have tried to show, the myth of the Divine Child.

This view of the rape of Ariadne and of the rape
of Helen is supported by the third myth in which
Theseus appears carrying off a woman or, to speak
more exactly, the myth in which he attempts to
carry off the queen of the Nether World, Persephone.[34] It is highly improbable that this attempt
was originally considered a crime; success would have
been the crowning end of the hero's career, just as
the victory over Hades or the fetching of Cerberus
crowned the career of Heracles. But the attempt of
Theseus failed; he and his friend Peirithous, whom
he accompanied and on whose behalf he undertook
the adventure, according to the current myth were
magically held fast on their seats in the Underworld.
The myth must be understood in a different way.

Persephone was identified with Kore, the vegetation goddess carried off by Pluto, who was identified
with the Ruler of the Dead. Consequently Theseus
appears here also in his old rôle as carrying off the
vegetation goddess; but, as this goddess was identified with the Queen of the Dead, his deed appeared of

[34] First mentioned in the very last part of the Nekyia, *Od.*, ix., v. 631.

course to be an attempt to vanquish the Empire of
Death. This attempt was bound to fail according
to current Greek ideas concerning the all-conquering
and irresistible power of Death. The earlier and
contrary conception of the victory over Death and
the Empire of the Dead was preserved in the Heracles
myth in traces only, and these were but half understood. Here the current conception won; the
Vegetation Goddess was thought to be identical
with the Queen of the Nether World, and thus
Theseus was doomed to remain in the Underworld.

The real difficulty of this myth lies in another
point. It is told that Peirithous helped Theseus to
carry off Helen. But Helen was given over to
Theseus, who was therefore obliged to help his
friend to carry off another woman, and Peirithous
conceived a desire for the Queen of the Nether
World. So much is clear, that the friendship of
Theseus and Peirithous serves as a means to harmonize two parallel myths which else would seem to
be incompatible. The difficulty hinted at lies not
in the friendship of the two heroes, for such a close
friendship is a frequent feature of myth and folk-
tale; it consists in the localization of Peirithous, for
he is always said to be a Thessalian and king of the
Lapiths. It is very difficult to find a sufficient
reason why a Thessalian hero was brought to
Attica;[35] the connection between the two heroes

[35] According to the principles I follow, I am unable to approve of
the treatment by J. Toepffer in his *Beiträge zur griech. Altertumswissenschaft*, 1897, p. 148 *et seq.*, reprinted from the volume *Aus der Anomia*
(1890), p. 30 *et seq.* He takes up K. O. Müller's lines relying on the verse,
Il. i. 265, which introduces Theseus among the Lapiths, but this verse
is absent from good manuscripts and was taken from the *Scutum Herculis*
of Hesiod, as Wilamowitz emphasizes again, *loc. cit.*, p. 237.

is, moreover, close and consistent. However, there is a family of Peirithoidai in Attica after whom a demos belonging to the phyle of Oineis and situated a little to the west of Athens was named. Peirithous was of course the eponymous hero of this family, and thus it is possible to imagine why he and Theseus were connected.[36] Both were localized in Attica, not very far from each other. But why is this hero said to be a Thessalian and king of the Lapiths? I see no other way than to surmise that the Attic Peirithous was identified with a better known Thessalian hero of the same name, king of the Lapiths. Such homonymies occur in Greek mythology.

The myth of the rape of Ariadne was enlarged and complicated, the adventures of Theseus at Cnossus being added. Ariadne saved him from the Labyrinth, giving him the thread as a guide—clearly a folk-tale motif—or a crown by the splendor of which the Labyrinth was illuminated. The latter is of course a late and rather silly explanatory myth, for the crown was originally a wreath, which is appropriate to the vegetation goddess.[37] It is depicted earlier than any other detail of the Theseus myth. A late Geometric vase picture[38] shows a man embarking on a ship and leading a woman who carries a crown or a wreath in the other hand. Though myths elsewhere are almost absent from Geometric vases, there is no sufficient reason for denying that

[36] Cp. Wilamowitz, *loc. cit.*, p. 238.

[37] It is so represented, e. g., on the famous cup of Euphronius, Furtwängler and Reichhold, *Griech. Vasenmalerei*, pl. v.

[38] *Journal of Hellenic Studies*, XIX (1899), pl. 8; C. Robert, *Archäologische Hermeneutik* (1919), p. 38, fig. 24.

the myth of Theseus and Ariadne is represented in this late and characteristic picture.

That the myth of the Labyrinth is a reminiscence of the vast complexity of the palace at Cnossus is generally admitted, and I need not dwell upon this point nor speak of the etymology and explanation of the name.[39] I wish only to emphasize that this myth must needs go back to the time during which the palace at Cnossus was still standing in its old splendor; i.e., to the time before the final sack of Cnossus about 1400 B. C.

It is generally acknowledged that the myth of the Minotaur also is a reminiscence from the Minoan age, but as to its explanation opinions differ. The current opinion is that the bull-cult and the bull-god played a prominent part in the Minoan religion, but in fact there is no good evidence for this opinion. In the Minoan monuments, which often depict scenes from the bull-ring and from bull-hunting, there is nothing to prove that this was anything other than a popular, profane pastime.[40] Both youths and girls entered the bull-ring and took part in its performances, of which the public was exceedingly fond. They were of course trained for this perilous kind of sport; possibly the Minoans compelled captives to take up these fights, just as the Romans sometimes compelled captives to fight in the arena as gladiators. This pastime accounts for the origin of the myth of the Minotaur, especially if we take the detail into consideration that both girls and youths were sacrificed to the monster. A

[39] From λάβρυς, double axe; I have discussed it in my *Minoan-Mycenaean Religion*, p. 189 *et seq.*

[40] See my *Minoan-Mycenaean Religion*, p. 322.

vague reminiscence of the vast palace at Cnossus,
which seemed to a simple man to be a true labyrinth
in which everybody was unavoidably lost, and a
mythologically transformed reminiscence of the perilous bull-fights in which captive youths and girls
lost their lives,[41] are at the back of the myth of
Theseus' rescue of the Athenian children from the
Labyrinth and his slaying of the Minotaur. These
reminiscences derive of course from the days of
the glory of Cnossus. They were quite naturally
attached to the hero who carried off the vegetation
goddess, because both myths were of Minoan origin;
and thus a very impressive myth was created. If it
is stripped of its characteristic detail, a tale remains
which tells that in spite of many perils a youth won
and carried off a princess. That is perhaps the most
common plot of the folk-tale and it gives the frame
into which were put the elements derived from the
Minoan world.

Quite a number of other myths in which Minos is
implicated are enacted in Attica and its neighborhood.[42] One is the story of his son Androgeos, who
went to Athens and in one way or another, for it is
differently told, met his death there. His death is
said to be the reason why King Minos went to war
against the Athenians and imposed upon them the
tribute of the seven youths and the seven girls. This
myth is a later invention made in order to rationalize

[41] I am afraid that we all are a little hypnotized by the name
Minotaur, writing it with a capital letter and taking it to be a *nomen
proprium*. If the original sense is only Μίνωος ταῦρος "a bull of Minos'"
(Pausanias, iii. 18, 11, cp. 16, says τὸν Μίνω καλούμενον ταῦρον), it may
be nothing but a bull introduced into the bull-ring on the order of King
Minos.

[42] Cp. Bethe in the paper quoted p. 169, n. 23.

and historicize the earlier myth. It has been justly observed that the name of Androgeos has a form which is special to the Attic dialect.[43]

Nor can great antiquity be accorded to the myth that Procris fled to Minos and received from him the dog which nothing was able to escape, and the never failing spear.[44] For since Minos was a chief personage of the most famous Attic myth, it was almost unavoidable that he should be introduced into other tales too. Thus arose a certain exchange between Attic and Cretan myths. For example, the builder of the Labyrinth, Daedalus, was introduced into Attic myths.

Another myth localized in the Megaris is more worthy of consideration. When Minos warred against Athens he besieged Megara also, and Scylla, the daughter of Nisus, the king of Megara, fell in love with him and cut off the purple lock from her father's head on which the luck of the city depended. The faithless daughter was thrown into the sea by Minos.[45] This myth is firmly localized. Nisus is the eponymous hero of the Megarian harbor town, Nisaia, and was annexed to the genealogy of the Athenian kings when Athens extended its political aspirations to the Megaris. Minoa is a small island

[43] L. Weber, "Androgeos," *Archiv für Religionswissenschaft*, XXIII (1925), pp. 34 *et seq.* and 229 *et seq.*, tries to show that Androgeos is an old Cretan god who was transferred to Attica and to whom the human tribute was due which, according to the common myth, was brought to the Minotaur. The testimony referred to is, however, generally derived from the Attidographers and late identifications and do not bear out so far-reaching conclusions.

[44] Apollod. iii. 15, 1; ii. 4, 7; Eratosthenes, *Catast.*, 33; Hygin, *Astron.*, ii. 35, etc. I disagree in this with Bethe, *loc. cit.*, p. 223.

[45] The myth is first found in Aeschylus, *Choeph.*, v. 613 *et seq.*

outside of this harbor, and Cape Scyllaeum is the easternmost point of the Argive peninsula. It is often to be observed that old mythical elements are rearranged in order to afford an explanation of local names, and here is probably an instance of this tendency.

The really important fact is the name of the small island, Minoa. Professor Bethe very justly called attention to the many places in very different countries with the name of Minoa. It is possible that they imply a reminiscence of the power of the most famous king of Cnossus, Minos, although we should not be deceived by the modern usage of denoting the Cretan people of the Bronze Age as Minoans. Space forbids, however, a discussion which does not immediately concern our subject.

The date of the last mentioned myths is consequently uncertain; they are corollaries to the myth of Theseus, presupposing even the war of Minos against Athens. It may be safer to take them to be post-Mycenaean. But the myth of Theseus' adventures at Cnossus, of Ariadne and the Minotaur, goes back to Mycenaean and even to Minoan days, and that suffices amply for our purpose. Twenty years ago in a paper which has often been quoted, Professor Bethe called attention to this fact and added that the great antiquity of this myth is astonishing but ought not to frighten a scientific mind, for there are many instances proving that historical reminiscences in mythical form lived and were preserved through centuries.[46] That is eminently true and agrees completely with the view which is here ad-

[46] Bethe, *loc. cit.*, p. 321.

vanced throughout in regard to Greek mythology.
The idea ought to be followed to the end consistently.

I cannot leave this subject without emphasizing
the fact that reminiscences of Minoan Crete are
found in Attic myths only. This fact is really worth
considering and an explanation is needed. Why, for
example, has Argive mythology, which is much
richer, nothing to say of Cnossus and Minos except
for the faint reminiscence of the bull-ring which may
be contained in the localization of the capturing of
the Cretan bull?[47] An evident explanation seems
to be found in the view which I have sketched elsewhere[48] as a probable hypothesis concerning the
immigration of the Greek tribes; viz., that the
Ionians came first, plundered Crete, and traded
with its people during the first and second late
Minoan periods, but were ousted from Argolis by
a new invading Greek tribe, the Achaeans, who
sacked Cnossus finally about 1400 B. C. After the
sack, and the downfall of the Minoan civilization,
there was nothing to carry off from Crete and nothing to tell about it. Consequently Argive myths
forgot the Minoans, but the Ionians who had seen
the proud palace of Cnossus in its splendor and had
learned to know the wealth and to fear the power
of the king of Cnossus kept the memory in mythical
form in that province to which they were thrown
back, Attica.

[47] See below p. 217.
[48] In my *Minoan-Mycenaean Religion*, p. 32 *et seq.*

9. Conclusion

In this chapter I have surveyed the Greek provinces; I have briefly called attention to their Mycenaean monuments and to their relative importance in the Mycenaean age; I have recapitulated the myths and discussed their probable references to that age. The following summary may be made:

Argolis is the province which far excels all others both in the number and greatness of its Mycenaean sites and monuments and in the copious richness of the finds from this age. It is also the only province of the Peloponnese in which extensive and famous cycles of myths are found; these, moreover, are attached to the Mycenaean sites, especially to the two most famous sites, which by the beginning of the historical age had become extremely unimportant. The cycles of the Perseidae and of the Atreidae belong to Mycenae; the Heracles who performed his Labors is localized at Tiryns as the vassal of the king of Mycenae, and the fable which is the introduction to the adventures of Bellerophon is enacted at the court of Tiryns—not to speak of minor myths. Other sites are far inferior to these two, and the myths attached to them are correspondingly less important. The myth of Io is connected with the Heraeum, once a Mycenaean city, and that of the culture hero Palamedes with Nauplia. The myths of Argos, the capital of the province in historical times, are also unimportant, but the tendency is marked to enhance its mythical glory by appropriating and inventing myths.

One site remains which is conspicuous for important monuments and brilliant finds but from which myths are almost absent. It is the third of the Mycenaean fortresses in Argolis, Midea, whose walls enclose a larger area than that of any other site in Argolis and whose king was buried together with a wealth of precious objects in the bee-hive tomb at Dendra near by. This is a striking exception, but it finds its natural explanation. The area within the walls is not yet excavated but the sherds picked up on the surface are Middle Helladic and Mycenaean only; later sherds are wanting. Unlike the sites of Mycenae and Tiryns, Midea was not inhabited during the Geometric period. Through the cessation of the occupation of the site the tradition was interrupted or weakened. Midea was almost forgotten in myth and in the life of the age. With this exception, there is a close correspondence between the mythical importance of the Argive towns and their importance in the Mycenaean age.

The same correspondence is evident in the other parts of the Peloponnese. None of the other provinces can in any wise be compared with Argolis in respect either to its myths or to its Mycenaean remains. But two districts have yielded more numerous and remarkable finds than others; namely, the Laconian plain and the western coast of the peninsula. In both these districts there are hardly any great mythological cycles to mention, but several myths with Mycenaean connections are localized there. In Laconia, Helen and the Dioscuri are at home and were probably pre-Greek gods metamorphosed into heroes and received into heroic mythology.

The Mycenaean settlements on the western coast of the Peloponnese are comprehended in Pylos, the Homeric dominion of Nestor. Here we may perhaps speak of a cycle of myths, that of the Neleidae; and fragments of an epos, the chief hero of which was Nestor, celebrating the struggles of the Pylians with their foes in the north and in the east, were incorporated into Homer. But this cycle is not very important and has a special character, being more, so to speak, historical than mythical, a fact which may be understood in view of its late origin.

In the remaining parts of the Peloponnese, Mycenaean remains are scarce and poor. Mythology shows the same scarcity and poverty of heroic myths. Arcadia has some myths, mostly cult myths; its heroic mythology is of late make. The same is the case with Elis. The attempts to create a mythical story of the founding of the Olympic games are evidently post-Mycenaean, nor has anything Mycenaean been discovered at Olympia. Achaea is almost devoid of myths. The close correspondence between the occurrence of heroic mythology and of Mycenaean remains is obvious.

The parts of Greece farthest toward the west are the Ionian islands. The search for the palace of Odysseus both on Ithaca and on Leucas failed, for the plot of the Odyssey is no real myth but a romance; it is not a reminiscence from Mycenaean times in mythical disguise. Mycenaean traces proving a regular occupation are found on Cephallenia only, and the tradition of the kingdom of the Cephallenes may perhaps be connected with this late and unimportant settlement, but that must be regarded as rather hypothetical.

We turn to Central Greece. Boeotia comes next to Argolis in the importance both of its Mycenaean remains and of its myths. There were two great centers of Mycenaean civilization, Thebes and Orchomenus. They are too little known, because fate destroyed the remains thoroughly and hindered their exploration, but enough is left of their past splendor and greatness to allow us to discern their importance. A third site, the fortress of Gla on an island in the lake of Copais, has an extensive palace, but almost no finds have been made there. The fortress was evidently abandoned very early and forgotten so thoroughly that not even its ancient name is known. Thus its failure to play a part in mythology is explained.

To Thebes two cycles of myths are attached which are hardly less famous than those of Mycenae, the Cadmus-Oedipus cycle and the War of the Seven against Thebes. This latter myth contains a reminiscence of a war waged by an Argive prince and his allies against Thebes in the Mycenaean age.

The situation is very different in regard to the second great site, Orchomenus. No mythical cycle is immediately attached to this city, but the celebrated tribe of the Minyans is bound up with it, and in the Homeric poems it was famous for its wealth. The Minyans are, however, related to southern Thessaly also, and this relation is proved to be old by myths and cults common to the district of Orchomenus and to southern Thessaly. The northernmost important Mycenaean site is Iolcus on the Gulf of Pagasae, whence the Argonauts started on their famous expedition. Here myths and Mycenaean remains correspond closely. The connections of the Minyans include the dominion of Pylos also. We found reasons to think that the Minyans were more a trading than a warring people. Thus they did not attain to the same mythological fame as others in heroic mythology and epics, but their wide connections and great wealth were not forgotten.

There remains another province penetrated by the Mycenaean civilization, Attica. It has numerous Mycenaean remains and finds, but none of first-rate importance. Attic heroic mythology is correspondingly poor with one exception, the Theseus cycle, the elaboration of which belongs to a great extent to historical times. But this cycle includes also famous myths of certain Mycenaean origin, the slaying of the Minotaur, the rape of Ariadne and the rape of Helen, and probably also the capturing of the bull of Marathon. It is most interesting that the first-mentioned myth goes back to the time before the final sack of Cnossus, when the palace was still standing and the Minoan culture and power still flourished. We found reasons to assume that the rape of Ariadne and the rape of Helen are secularized forms of a Minoan hieratic myth, the carrying off of the vegetation goddess, and are identical in origin with the carrying off of Kore by Pluto.

Only one important myth is left, that of the Calydonian hunt, and this may be thought to be an exception to the rule stating the correspondence of mythical fame with Mycenaean remains. There is hardly any subject of which we have such a vivid picture from Mycenaean art as the boar-hunt; I mean the well-known wall paintings from the palace of Tiryns which depict hunters and dogs charging a boar, and even ladies driving in a chariot to the hunt. As was pointed out long ago,[1] we have in these pictures, if not the actual myth, its prototype from human life. It is interesting to note also that a woman, Atalanta, plays the foremost part in this myth of the hunt of the Calydonian boar. The myth of the Calydonian hunt ought, if any, to go back to the Mycenaean age; the only objection is that Calydon was not a center of Mycenaean civilization. But probably it was. Numerous Mycenaean sherds were picked up on the surface of the acropolis and there are walls of Mycenaean date;[2] yet the excavations carried out by Dr. Poulsen and Dr. Rhomaios in the last few years uncovered only remains from historical times. There are, however, two hills at Calydon, and on the higher hill, the acropolis of Calydon, Mycenaean remains are found. They include a Mycenaean wall for fortification, and remains of two houses of which one is apsidal; also Mycenaean sherds are found in the earth.[3] This acropolis is still left unexplored. The cursory observations which as yet are at our disposal show that Calydon was inhabited in the Mycenaean age. As there was a walled city with houses this settlement cannot have been unimportant. It would be worth while to explore this Mycenaean town in order to get an idea of its importance and to see whether the regular connection between myths and Mycenaean civilization is not to be found even here.

[1] H. R. Hall, *Aegean Archaeology* (1915), p. 190.

[2] *Praktika* (1908), p. 9 *et seq.*

[3] Kindly communicated by letter by Dr. Poulsen.

CHAPTER III

HERACLES

I have tried to show that Greek epic poetry and the great mythological cycles go back into the Mycenaean age. In order not to be misunderstood I am anxious to stress the fact that the boundaries set for our knowledge in this respect are the same as those which limit the proof that historical elements are contained in heroic myths. To take the standard example, we know that Theoderic of Ravenna and Attila, the king of the Huns, are historical personages and we know their exploits. Hence it is possible to prove that they are the prototypes of Dietrich of Bern and Etzel in the Nibelungenlied. But if we did not have this historical knowledge, we should in no wise be able to prove that Dietrich and Etzel were historical personages. We should perhaps be inclined to surmise it, and we should be able to make it seem probable but never strictly to prove it. It is not possible with certainty to deduce historical facts and events from myths. Moreover, Dietrich and Etzel are represented as living in the same age, whilst their historical prototypes belonged to different generations. We ought to know and fully to realize how freely myths and epic poetry treat and recompose historical events and personages which they have taken over.

The same is true in regard to our contention that the Greek mythological cycles originate in the Myce-

naean age. A strictly logical proof cannot be deduced from the myths themselves; they have preserved few traces which can beyond dispute be
referred to Mycenaean conditions. The proof must
be deduced from the historical facts, which I have
demonstrated, the one that Greek epics originated
in the Mycenaean age, and the other that the
mythical cycles are constantly connected with
Mycenaean sites and in their importance correspond
closely to the varying importance of these sites in
the Mycenaean age. The conclusions which can
be drawn from an analysis of the myths themselves
are limited and consist chiefly in proving that the
old kernel of a myth is in agreement with our leading
principles.

In the foregoing chapter I have treated according
to these principles the great mythological cycles
and their connections with the Mycenaean sites;
in these last two chapters I propose to treat two
cycles which are not local but general in character,
that of Heracles and that of the Olympian gods.
The method must of course be different. We must
try to find out what is probable and the connection
with Mycenaean conditions in general.

The cycle of Heracles has been treated so frequently that it is almost impossible to survey the
vast number of works and papers on the subject;
moreover these myths have been judged and explained in very different fashions.[1] Heracles was
the most popular mythical hero of the Greeks and

---

[1] I mention here only some great works on Heracles: U. von Wilamowitz-Moellendorff, *Euripides' Herakles* (ed. 2, 1895); P. Friedländer,
Herakles (1907); B. Schweitzer, *Herakles* (1922); C. Robert, *Die griechische Heldensage*, II (1921) pp. 422 *et seq.*

the development of his myths has been accordingly rich and varied. His cycle is of first-rate importance and interest and in spite of its many difficulties cannot be passed over in a discussion of our present subject.

The first difficulty is the name, a much discussed problem. The name is clearly composed of Hera and -*kles*, which is a frequent compound element of Greek names, although the vowel *a* presents some difficulty to etymology.[2] The attempt to separate the name Heracles from that of the goddess Hera has been made, but such a theory is without foundation, as the eminent philologist Professor Kretschmer has proved. At the same time he has shown how the name is to be understood rightly.[3] A brief discussion of the principle according to which the heroes of myth and of folk-tale are named will be necessary for a right understanding of the name and is of importance for a right understanding of the myth, too.

There is a characteristic difference between the names of the personages of modern folk-tales and those of Greek myths, and by virtue of this difference the contrast between folk-tale and myth seems to be greater than it really is.[4] Many folk-tales, also, have been incorporated in mythology. The folk-tale gives commonly no individual name to its heroes but only one which denotes his class or social standing; e.g. "the King," "the Princess," etc. Such

[2] We should expect *o*, as e.g., in Herodotus, but see the article of P. Kretschmer quoted in the next note.

[3] P. Kretschmer in the periodical *Glotta*, viii (1917), p. 121 *et seq*.

[4] I have to thank Dr. Halliday for useful hints in regard to this subject.

names seem to be almost wanting in Greek myths, unless Creon and Creusa are of this kind, as I am inclined to believe, for they are nothing but the masculine and the feminine forms of a participle signifying "ruling."

A second group of names which occur very frequently in the folk-tales of many countries comprises those which may be called "descriptive names"; viz., names which characterize some personage according to a certain peculiarity of his, e.g. Red Riding Hood, Blue Beard, Tom Thumb, Catskin, etc. They are somewhat akin to the names of the first group. In Greek myths such names are rare. I do not of course take into account such descriptive names as were invented by a poet for secondary personages of his own; e.g. Astyanax, Telegonus, Thersites,[5] but only old mythical names. Polyneices, the man who stirred up the great strife of Thebes, is perhaps one; Daedalus, the skilled artisan, and Palamedes, the very artful culture hero, are others. I have already explained the significance of the name of Oedipus, "he with the swollen feet."

The great majority of the names occurring in Greek myths are personal names of the same kind as living men have and are formed in the same manner, according to the well-known system of Greek personal names. In historical times, however, mythical names were not given to living men; they were, so to speak, taboo. But that is a secondary phenomenon due to respect for the heroes of mythology. In the Hellenistic age this respect was no

[5] There are many such names in Homer; see P. Cauer, *Grundfragen der Homerkritik* (ed. 3, 1921), p. 543 *et seq.*

longer felt, and mythical names were freely given to men. The folk-tale also sometimes gives an individual name to its hero, but this name often receives, especially in certain countries, an addition through which it almost becomes a "descriptive" name; e.g. Jack the Giantkiller. In German folk-tales this is more common; e.g. *der dumme Hans*, *die faule Grethe*, etc.

It may perhaps be added that popular tradition of a more recent origin sometimes associates a personage with the name of the place where he lives; e.g. the Pedlar of Swaffham, the Wise Men of Gotham. That is of course something rather modern, but ought not to be overlooked, for the Greek epos has the same manner of denoting personages of secondary importance; e.g. Chryses and Chryseis, the man, the maiden of Chryse, Briseis, the maiden of Brise, etc. To the same category belong the old tribal names which are not merely eponymous, e.g. Danaüs, Danae, the Danaides.[6]

This exposition of principles will help us to discover the real nature of the name of Heracles. Because Hera plays such a prominent part in his myth, Heracles has often been thought to be a descriptive name; but if we consider the matter closely, it will be found to be a forced and improbable explanation that Heracles should have been called "the Fame of Hera" or "the Man who became famous because of Hera," while this goddess dealt the severest blows to him and imposed pain, grief, and labor upon him. The connection between the name of the hero and that of the goddess is, however,

[6] Cp. above pp. 42 and 65.

a fact and its importance for the myth is not to be
overlooked; but the name is the *prius* and is not
originally derived from the myth in order to characterize the hero. I shall recur to this topic in a later
place. The name of Heracles is nothing but a common personal name of the same kind as Diocles,
Athenocles, or Hermocles. In historical times it
could not be given to living men because of the
mythical fame and the cult of the hero—until
Alexander the Great called so his son by Barsine;
another almost identical compound name took its
place, Heracleitus. On the other hand Diocleitus
is wanting, because Diocles was used freely.[7]

Heracles is a personal name which once was in
common use, even though the man may be as
fictitious as a folk-tale hero like Jack the Giant-
killer. I think it proper to treat him as such a
fictitious personage, not because I would be reviled
for shallow Euhemerism if I asserted that once upon
a time a man called Heracles had lived around whom
the myths clustered as time went on, but because
the question is idle. If this man really existed his
existence is of as little importance for the myth as
is that of the real Dr. Faust for the Faust legend.

This fact has a certain importance for the localization of the hero. The localization of myths is
often used as a means of mythological research and
it has been used as a cornerstone in the foregoing
chapter, but I have stressed the restriction that it
ought not to be used uncritically or without due
regard to other circumstances. Heracles is localized
in various places. I shall recur to this subject

[7] The observation is due to Kretschmer *loc. cit.*

later on; here I wish to stress the fact that a mythical figure such as Heracles is not originally limited to one locality, just as e.g. Jack the Giant-killer is not limited to one locality, but that such myths may be localized secondarily. In my opinion there are myths which are not local but are the common property of a people, just as some gods are local, while others on the contrary are the common property of a people. Of these Zeus is an example. Various forms of Zeus are localized but, generally speaking, he is not local, and the same is true of the myths: some are local, others not, but they may be localized, and this is especially true of the myths that are derived from folk-tales. The propensity to localize popular myths in a certain place is too little observed and appreciated. I have already spoken of a clear instance, of Oedipus, a folk-tale hero, who as such cannot of course have had any tomb, but was credited with four. Nor has Heracles any tomb, and he could not have one, because the myth told that he vanquished Death.

Another inference has still greater importance; namely, that all cults of Heracles are added to him secondarily; this is proved if we survey them. They are numerous, but none is of first-rate importance; nor has he any great festival, except perhaps that on Mount Oeta, which is simply an old rite appropriated by Heracles.[8] No cult of Heracles has been associated with the cult of a god; elsewhere such a process is a testimony that a hero is a faded god

[8] See my papers "Der Flammentod des Herakles auf dem Oite," *Archiv für Religionswissenschaft*, XXI (1922), p. 310 *et seq.*; and "Fire-Festivals in Ancient Greece," *Journal of Hellenic Studies*, XLIII (1923), p. 144 *et seq.*

who was superseded by a great god. Heracles was
the averter of evil (ἀλεξίκακος), the strong and great
helper in all difficulties, and according to this conception his cults are to be understood, as Dr. Farnell
has shown.[9] There may have been many small
and nameless local cults for which the name of the
great hero seemed to be appropriate and which he
took over, cults both of small local gods and of heroes.
The cults of Heracles prove nothing as to the development of his myth; they show only his great
popularity.

The problem which will be treated here is whether
the Heracles myths originate in the Mycenaean age.
It cannot be attacked by the common mythographical method, which only proves that certain myths
are late inventions or modifications. Our problem
goes back into a time which mythography cannot
reach. It can be attacked only through an analysis
of the old myths. This method is of course to a
certain extent subjective and difficult, but holds a
possibility of success.

It has often been asserted that the Heracles cycle
was formed by a poet who composed an epos of
Heracles. This old epos is quite hypothetical.
I do not wish to discuss it, but wish simply to
point out that, if it existed, it did not create the
myths but only made a choice among already existing
myths, a choice which may have determined the
contents of the cycle for a later age. I cannot believe
that this hypothetical Heracles epos was earlier than
Homer. We shall see that the Heracles myths in
Homer differ in a remarkable manner from those

[9] L. R. Farnell, *Greek Hero Cults*, p. 95 *et seq.*

current later on. Furthermore, this supposed Heracles epos treated a whole cycle, it belonged to the cyclical epics; and it is obvious that this kind of epic, which collected and arranged the myths belonging to a certain cycle, is later than the Homeric epics. It came into existence because of interest in the myths as such; whilst Homeric poetry chose a single myth or an episode for the basis of the poem. According to the economy of epic poetry this is the earlier manner. All myths were not done into verses. Many of them lived in oral prose tradition and among these were probably the Heracles myths also.

As a survey of the overwhelming mass of the Heracles myths the classification of the ancient mythographers is very much to the purpose.[10] They divide the myths into three classes: 1. the Twelve Labors (*athloi* or *erga*) which Heracles performed on the injunction of Eurystheus, alone or with the aid of his charioteer and true friend Iolaus; 2. the Incidentals (*parerga*) into which he fell while performing his Labors; 3. the Deeds (*praxeis*), warlike expeditions which Heracles undertook on his own account at the head of an army, and undertakings carried out by Heracles together with a number of other heroes; e.g. the expedition of the Argonauts. Framing these exploits are the myths of his birth and of his death and apotheosis.

Professor Robert, to whom we owe the best treatment of the Heracles myths, says that this classification has no value in regard to the development of the Heracles myths. Some of the Parerga may

[10] Cp. Robert, *loc. cit.* p. 428 *et seq.*

not be later than certain of the Labors; the only
difference is that they were not received into the
cycle of the Twelve Labors. But if we take the
Praxeis into consideration, it appears immediately
that their character, generally speaking, is different
from that of the Labors. Whilst Heracles performs
his Labors relying upon his own strength and aided
only by his true friend and charioteer, without whom
a hero could not be, when performing his Praxeis,
he appears accompanied by retainers or comrades,
at the head of an army, or in the company of other
heroes. This is certainly a later class of myths than
those in which Heracles performs his valorous deeds
by his own strength. This inference, drawn from
general probability, is corroborated if the Praxeis
are considered in detail.

The expedition against Pylos is a remodeling of
an older and more serious myth to which I shall
recur below.[11] Upon this expedition the war against
the Eleans was modeled, and thus the heroic twins,
the Actorione or Molione, were joined with the
myth.[12] The expedition against Sparta and that
in which Heracles assisted Aegimius were added only
after Heracles had become the champion of the
Dorians. It would perhaps not be impossible to
unravel the threads in this development of the
myth. Furthermore, it has long been well known
that the myth of his expedition against Troy was
enlarged gradually through the accretion of other
myths. The starting point is the myth of the capture

[11] Below p. 203; cp. also above p. 89.

[12] Professor Schweitzer errs certainly in supposing that this episode
is an old element of the Heracles myth; cp. my review of his above-
mentioned book in *Deutsche Literaturzeitung*, 1922, p. 833 *et seq.*

of Laomedon's horses, but this old motif seems to
have been transferred to the Trojan king only after
the Trojan cycle had become so famous that Heracles' glory seemed not to be complete if he had not
vanquished the Trojans also. For the capture of
Laomedon's horses is only a parallel myth to the
capturing of Diomedes' horses, remodeled according
to the scheme of the Trojan cycle. I need hardly
dwell upon the fact that Heracles' part in the expedition of the Argonauts is a very late myth. The
best proof is that the myth is compelled to dismiss
him before the expedition attains its goal. This brief
survey may accordingly be sufficient so far as the
Praxeis are concerned.

In order to proceed further it will be useful to
take the testimony of the Homeric poems, although
their evidence often is put aside and the hypothesis
of a Heracles epos unduly favored. For even if such
an epos existed, the Heracles myths in Homer offer
most important and interesting variations. As some
of them were ousted by later myths or forgotten,
they are probably of ancient origin. And Homer is
the earliest testimony to which we have access.

Among the Labors Homer mentions only the bringing back of Cerberus,[13] but it appears clearly that
the Labors were well-known, although we cannot
know which exploits were reckoned among them.
For the Labors the word *athloi* is already in Homer
a fixed word, a *terminus technicus*, and this proves
the great antiquity of this cycle. Moreover the
Labors are imposed upon Heracles by an inferior
man, Eurystheus, and the humorous detail is added

---

[13] *Il.* viii. v. 368, and in the Nekyia, *Od.* xi. v. 623.

that Eurystheus dared not to impart his commands
in person to Heracles but spoke through his herald
Copreus. The name designates him the "Dung-
man."[14] The same passage shows that Eurystheus
lived at Mycenae. Athena assisted Heracles throughout and even Zeus gave him aid.

Hera instigated Eurystheus and her wrath was
the real reason why Heracles was subject to so much
pain and labor. A well-known passage[15] relates at
length that Hera induced Zeus to swear that any
male child of his kin born on a certain day should rule
over all his neighbors, and that she held back the
birth of Heracles and hurried on the birth of Eurystheus, so that Heracles became subject to the latter.
The quarrel of Zeus and his spouse in regard to
Heracles is mentioned repeatedly, e.g., in the story
that on the instigation of Hera, Hypnus, the god
of Sleep, fettered Zeus whilst Heracles on his voyage
back from Troy was driven by storm to Cos.[16]
Two myths are especially interesting, because a later
age did not receive them. One relates that Heracles
wounded Hera in the breast[17] and the other says
that Hera's wrath caused the death of Heracles.[18]

Among the Praxeis the expedition against Troy
is mentioned repeatedly. It is stated that Heracles
destroyed Troy because of Laomedon's horses,[19]
and the Hesione myth, which clearly is a later accretion, is hinted at in the mention of a wall which the

[14] *Il.* xv. v. 639.
[15] *Il.* xix. v. 98 *et seq.*
[16] *Il.* xiv. v. 649 *et seq.*, and xv. v. 25 *et seq.*
[17] *Il.* v. v. 392.
[18] *Il.* xviii. v. 117 *et seq.*
[19] *Il.* v. v. 640, and xiv. v. 250.

Trojans and Athena built as a protection against
the sea monster.[20] Further, Nestor tells of Heracles'
war against the Pylians.[21] The Rhodian hero Tlepolemus, a son of Heracles, is mentioned, and in the
Catalogue of the Ships even his mother Astyocheia.[22]

That Homer relates the myth of the birth of
Heracles has been mentioned before. Thebes is
said to be his birthplace and Alcmene his mother;[23]
he is once even said to be the son of Amphitryon.[24]
His wife Megara appears only in the Nekyia.[25] In
the end of this book we read the well-known passage
which tells that the shadow of Heracles chases wild
animals in the Underworld, whilst he himself lives
among the gods as the spouse of Hebe. It is interesting that the typical figure of Heracles here is
represented as the great hunter.

This brief survey shows that, even if the later
parts of the Homeric poems are left out of consideration, the Heracles cycle appears fully developed in
Homer; all essential parts and all three categories
of myths are present, with the exception only of his
death and apotheosis on the pyre of Mount Oeta.
It seems impossible to imagine that this development
is owed to an epos which was contemporary with
Homer or only slightly earlier. For such a development must needs require a much longer time, and
the various accretions have taken place at different
times. I hope to show this later on.

[20] *Il.* xx. v. 145.
[21] *Il.* xi. v. 690 *et seq.*
[22] *Il.* v. v. 638, and ii. v. 658 resp.
[23] *Il.* xix. v. 99, and in the interpolated passage, xiv. v. 323.
[24] *Il.* v. v. 392.
[25] *Od.*, xi. v. 269.

Very important are the myths which Homer tells about Heracles but which later are forgotten. It must be considered closely whether such myths are inventions due to the Homeric poet himself or are due to an old tradition which was obliterated in a later time.

We may commence with a passage in the Odyssey[26] in which Odysseus boasts that he surpasses all other heroes except Philoctetes in shooting with the bow, but adds that he does not wish to rival earlier heroes, neither Heracles nor Eurytus of Oichalia, whom Apollo killed in wrath because Eurytus challenged him to a competition in shooting with the bow. It follows from this passage that Eurytus had not yet been introduced into the Heracles cycle. This introduction came about because both he and Heracles were famous archers, and quite naturally the myth told at first of a competition between Eurytus and Heracles. Different versions of this competition exist.[27]

There is a passage in the Iliad[28] in which Achilles grieves over the early death which is to be his but finds a consolation in the fact that not even Heracles escaped death but was overcome by the Moira and Hera's great wrath. It would perhaps be possible to explain the reference to Heracles' death by the passage in the Nekyia where it is said that Heracles' shadow dwells in the Underworld whilst he "himself" enjoys an eternal life on Olympus, but such an explanation would be too easily reached.

[26] *Od.* viii. v. 223 *et seq.*; cp. xxi., v. 32 *et seq.*
[27] Cp. Robert, *loc. cit.*, p. 582.
[28] *Il.* xviii. v. 115 *et seq.*

To understand the passage we must have due regard
for the connection in which it appears. It is caused
by the deep grief of Achilles, a casual instance of that
humanizing of mythology which is a most prominent
feature of Homeric poetry. It seems extremely unlikely that the old myth ended with Heracles'
death, an ending which would be quite contrary to
its character.

An old trait appears, on the other hand, in the
myths that Heracles wounded Hera in her right
breast with an arrow and that "in the Gate, among
the Dead,"[29] he hit Hades with an arrow. Here
Heracles is depicted as the reckless and rough man
who relying upon his strength uses violence even
against the gods: "Rash man, worker of violence,
that recked not of his evil deeds, seeing that with
arrows he vexed the gods that hold Olympus."
One is reminded of another tale in a late passage of
the Odyssey,[30] that Heracles treacherously killed
his guest-friend Iphitus and kept his horses. Moral
considerations are wanting in this Heracles just as
they are wanting in Autolycus whom Hermes taught
to steal and to deceive with false oaths. But the
two types differ profoundly in all other respects.
This Heracles is the strong man relying solely on
his strength, whom a rough and lawless age created
and even appreciated in a certain degree, a reckless,
violent character who proceeds to extremes, even
to rivaling the gods and to raising weapons against
them. There is an echo of this type in Homer. Such
strong heroes were not yet forgotten but belonged

[29] *Il.* v. v. 319 *et seq.* The Greek words are: ἐν Πύλῳ, ἐν νεκύεσσιν.
[30] *Od.* xxi. v. 25 *et seq.*

to a bygone age, and the humanized poet disapproved of them, although he could but admire their valiant exploits. "Mightiest were these of all men reared upon earth, mightiest were they and with the mightiest they fought, with the beasts that had their lair among the mountains and in a terrible wise did they destroy them."[31] The Homeric poet is unable to understand how a mortal man can dare to raise weapons against a god. Diomedes does so, of course, but on the command of the Goddess Athena. Other examples belong to a past age and are told to warn someone against wantonness.[32]

From such a reckless and savage nature everything might be expected. If he had killed his guest-friend treacherously and violated the unwritten laws, he would be able to lay hands on his own flesh and blood also. The myth that he killed his own children by Megara may be nothing but the extreme consequence of this characterization; but that is only a suggestion of questionable value.

In this aspect of Heracles traces of a primitive savagery appear which should not be overlooked. Homer and after him the late myths have suppressed most of these features, but, remodeled so as to become burlesque, they were preserved in popular conception. The Heracles of popular tales is no late invention. He is the Heracles who is as immoderate in eating as in love, who begets fifty sons by the fifty daughters of Thespius in one night and has innumerable offspring, who takes the oxen away

---

[31] *Il.* i. v. 266.

[32] With the exception of the story of Idas related *Il.* x. v. 558 *et seq.* The instances are collected by R. Oehler, *Mythologische Exempla in der älteren griechischen Dichtung* (Dissertation, Basle, 1925).

from the ploughman in order to roast and to consume them—this last a tale of which the popularity is shown by the number of existing versions. This Heracles is the man who relies upon his own strength; but he is regarded from the comic point of view; in both respects he resembles very much certain strong men of modern folk-tales.

The Homeric myth of Heracles' combat with Hades deserves close consideration in another respect also. It took place "in the Gate, among the Dead." The Greek word is νέκυς, "corpse"; this word, however, has in Homer not merely the significance of "corpse" but is used to denote "the Dead," a survival of the old primitive belief in a bodily life of the deceased. The words translated "in the Gate" signify as they stand "at Pylos" and are taken to refer to the city of Pylos, but it has been long recognized that this Pylos is the Gate of the Underworld. This combat is the supreme deed of the strong hero. There are parallels. Sisyphus overcomes Death by ruse; and the myths that Heracles vanquished Old Age and Perdition are modeled upon the story of his victory over Death. The victory over the God of Death is the end of Heracles' career, just as the life of mortal men is ended by death. He wounded Hades and put him to flight.

Homer did not understand the real significance of this myth, for he was completely subject to the fatalistic conviction that Death is unavoidable and that not even the gods are able to protect man against it. To him and perhaps even to his predecessors it was unthinkable that a mortal should vanquish Death. Hence the sense of the myth was obliterated and

the story was remodeled. Pylos became the Peloponnesian city with that name, and through this
transference of the myth from the Nether to the
Upper World the earliest of the Praxeis, the expedition against Pylos, was created. On the other
hand, the combat with the God of Death was superseded by Heracles' overcoming of the guardian of
the Underworld; that is, by the bringing back of
Cerberus. This myth contains the same idea, the
victory over Death, in another setting. It has been
suggested that Cerberus is an image of the all-
devouring Empire of Death, for Hell is depicted in
Medieval art as a monster who swallows the dead;
but there is nothing to show that such a belief was
current in antiquity.

The significance of the old myths which let Heracles end his strenuous career by overcoming Death
was obliterated, and the necessity appeared to find
another end for his life on earth in accord with
the later conception of him. It is the apotheosis.
Heracles was a mortal man and became a god. In
Greek mythology this is in fact an exception. The
heroes are never made gods. Mortal men are carried
off to an eternal life in the Elysian fields, or beneath
the earth,[33] but not on Olympus. Eternal life but
not a place among the gods was given to Tithonus
and promised to Odysseus. The divinity of Heracles
appears to be late, perhaps post-Homeric, although
the fact that it is not mentioned by Homer is not
absolutely certain proof that it was unknown to his
age. I think that it can be assumed with certainty

[33] This point of view is especially brought forward by E. Rohde
in his famous book *Psyche*.

that the divinity of Heracles originated in the cult. Heracles was venerated both as a god and as a hero. This ambiguity is due to the fact that a series of small local cults were attached to him; some of these were cults of gods, others were hero cults. Heracles was too great and too popular to be reduced to the rank of a servant or to a hypostasis of a great god; consequently he appeared as a god in the cults, and for mythology the problem was to harmonize his divinity with his human life.

How this happened is shown by a recent find—the discovery of his cult place on the summit of Mount Oeta, where according to the myth the pyre was lit on which Heracles ended his mortal life and from which he ascended into Olympus.[34] Bonfires kindled on a certain day are a very widespread custom and on these bonfires, offerings, puppets, or even living animals are often burned. The Greek instances have attracted less attention but they are not few and are especially frequent in Central Greece. Such a bonfire was kindled on the top of Mount Oeta and the figure burned on the pyre was called Heracles. This is proved by early inscriptions and statuettes of Heracles. So the myth of Heracles' death in the flames of the pyre on Mount Oeta was created and connected with the magnificent but late myth of Deianeira. On the other hand, fire is, according to certain known myths, a means for acquiring immortality; Achilles and Demophon are purified by fire to this end. From these premisses the myth of Heracles' apotheosis was created and the definitive solution found of the problem how

[34] See p. 193, n. 8.

Heracles, born as a mortal man, had acquired divinity. This story is the only late, probably post-Homeric element in the important myths of Heracles.

The myth of Heracles' birth presents quite a different problem. Homer knows his mother Alcmene, his father Amphitryon, and Thebes, the place of his birth. The myth is in itself of no great importance for our subject and space forbids a discussion of the story; its interest for us lies in its localization, which has presented a great difficulty both to ancient and to modern mythographers.

The Heracles who performed the Twelve Labors had his home at Tiryns, where he lived as a vassal of Eurystheus. He treacherously precipitated Iphitus from the walls of this town, and according to Hesiod[35] he drove the oxen of Geryon to Tiryns. His connection with Tiryns is so firmly established that the poet forgot that Heracles, who had seized them on the command of Eurystheus, ought to drive them to Mycenae. Homer does not mention Tiryns as his city, but as he says that Zeus brought Heracles back to Argos and that Eurystheus ruled at Mycenae, Argos must denote the Province of Argolis. It follows that Heracles as early as in the Homeric poems was at home at Tiryns.

How firmly established was the localization of the Heracles of the Twelve Labors at Tiryns appears most clearly from the difficulties caused by it to the ancient mythographers in their attempts to harmonize this localization with the localization of his birth at Thebes. The manner in which Alcmene and Amphitryon were inserted into the genealogy

[35] Hesiod, *Theogony*, v. 292.

of Perseus is known. A poem attributed to Hesiod tells that Amphtryon, having killed his father-in-law, Electryon, fled from Tiryns to Thebes.[36] That is nothing but one of the usual and easily recognized means of harmonizing two contradictory localizations and is of no value. I should rather be inclined to believe that the localization of Alcmene at Midea has something to do with old tradition.[37]

Modern scholars have attacked the problem in a different way, putting the question whether Heracles is originally a Theban or a Tirynthian, and the greater number have decided in favor of Tiryns. According to my fundamental view of the problem of localization, to ask the question is in this case wrong. For Heracles is originally as little bound to any locality as, e.g., Jack the Giant-killer. But the common scheme of Greek mythology always tended toward the localization of its heroes, and when a mythical hero was notably popular it is not to be wondered at that he was localized in various places, and that the localizations disagreed but in spite of this were retained. Consequently I think that the localization of Heracles is old both at Thebes and at Tiryns. At Thebes myths were told of his birth, which was not celebrated in the myths of Tiryns, an inconsistency such as sometimes occurred in the case of other Greek heroes. So the story of Heracles was divided between Thebes, where the story of his birth was principally told, and Tiryns, where his

[36] Hesiod, *The Shield of Heracles*, v. 79, *et seq.*

[37] The tradition of the residence of her father Electryon is very varying and little to be relied upon: Midea, Theocritus, xiii. 20, and xxiv. 1; Paus. ii. 25, 9; Tiryns, Euripides, *Alc.*, 838; Mycenae, Apollod. ii. 4, 6, 1.

Labors were celebrated. There are, however, traces showing that the Theban Heracles also performed labors. It is an idle question whether the Nemean or the Cithaeronian lion is the original one, for the same deed was localized by the Tirynthians at Nemea and by the Thebans on Mount Cithaeron. The wife of Heracles is a Theban, and the myth that he killed his children, which may be old, is also localized in Thebes.

In my opinion it is an idle question whether Heracles is originally at home at Tiryns or at Thebes. For he did not come from the one place to the other but is one of those heroes of whom myths were told everywhere and who were localized in different places. Because the myths at the two different places told of different periods in the life of the hero, this difference of localization was not wiped out.

Both Thebes and Tiryns were great centers of Mycenaean civilization. Thebes was always an important town, but after the downfall of the Mycenaean civilization Tiryns was merely a poor village, even if it was called a town and at times was politically independent. The insignificant remains of the temple to which the ruins of the megaron were adapted shows graphically how really poor it was. It is quite incomprehensible how the tradition that this place was the home of the foremost Greek hero could have come into existence if this localization is ascribed to post-Mycenaean times. In the Mycenaean age, on the contrary, and, as recent research shows, especially in the very latest Mycenaean period, Tiryns was a really important town where mighty princes must have ruled, so that we can understand why Heracles was localized there. I cannot but think that the localizations of the Heracles myths both in Tiryns and in Thebes belong to the Mycenaean age.

Heracles' localization in Tiryns agrees with the well-known fact, to which I shall recur later, that the first five of his Labors were performed in its neighborhood, in the northeastern Peloponnese. Another feature of the myth is also to be considered in this connection; namely, that Heracles performed his Labors at the command of the king of Mycenae, whom he was obliged to obey. This is an echo of the political conditions of the Mycenaean age; for it is from a geographical point of view unthinkable that the rulers of the different towns or fortresses were quite independent of each other, else Mycenae would have been cut off from the sea. Mycenae was the foremost of the Mycenaean cities in Argolis and its king must have been overlord of the rulers of the other towns, at least in the period of its bloom. Archaeology corroborates the fact, the memory of which was kept by Homer, that the king of Mycenae was the suzerain. The prince of Tiryns was his vassal.

So it is explained why Heracles is the servant of Eurystheus, the king of Mycenae; and the manner in which the demeanor of Eurystheus is described may be understood, his cowardice and his harsh commands and the almost impossible tasks which he imposes upon his vassal. For it is an ever recurring feature in all epics that the suzerain is described as an incapable and imperious coward in sharp contrast to the heroic strength of some vassal.

We find this idea in the myth of Bellerophon and in the Homeric description of Agamemnon; it is carried to an extreme point in the abuse which Achilles showers upon his suzerain in the first book of the Iliad. In the *chansons de geste* it is the more graphic the later they are. Charlemagne, who in the earlier chants figures as an old and venerated emperor, is mistreated in the later chants even more badly than Agamemnon, and his vassals shower abuse upon him as Achilles does upon Agamemnon. In the Russian epics Vladimir the Great is a kind of theatrical king who gives commands to his vassals; sometimes he casts them into prison and lets them come out only to impose difficult tasks upon them. He mistreats a newly arrived hero, but the hero defends his glory by deeds and even defies the king.

These bad relations between the suzerain and his retainers are easy to understand, for their interests were opposed. The king was eager to hold sway over his vassals, and they were equally eager to assert their independence and prowess. Stories were told and epic songs chanted in the many courts of the vassals and retainers, and when the suzerainty of the overlord broke down, their hostile attitude toward the suzerain left its imprint upon the myths. The supposition that conditions in the Mycenaean age were of this kind is well founded; it explains why the better man was obliged to obey the inferior man, and why the suzerain appears in an unfavorable light as an incapable but imperious coward.

In a later age when the Mycenaean kingdom had broken down, when the kingly power had vanished, and the many cities were independent of each other, this relation of the vassal to his suzerain was no longer understood and it was felt necessary to find a reason which was comprehensible to the new age for the subjection of Heracles to Eurystheus. This reason was not difficult to find. Perhaps it had already been given in another version of the myth. For myths and, even more, folk-tales very often tell of some invidious person who imposes difficult or impossible tasks upon its heroes; the invidious stepmother is especially well-known. The name Heracles was the reason why this rôle was attributed to Hera. Hera was the chief goddess of Tiryns; moreover, she was the stepmother of Heracles, the son of Zeus, and myths had much to relate of her wrath because of the many love affairs of her husband and of her hatred of his illegitimate children. The name Heracles is the starting point for the rôle of Hera in the Heracles cycle.

So much may be said of the myth in which the cycle of the Twelve Labors is framed and which gives the reason why Heracles was obliged to perform his Labors. It must of course be later than the Labors themselves, although this statement implies no judgment concerning the antiquity of any single Labor, or concerning their number. Certain Labors may have been added at a later time. A cycle of Labors; namely, a series of great deeds which are held together by a myth giving the reason why the hero was obliged to perform them, occurs in several other Greek myths, though they all have been obliterated through the fame of the Heracles cycle. Theseus is said to be another Heracles; his cycle was famous because it was enlarged by the Athenians for patriotic purposes. The myths of Bellerophon form a similar cycle. Both have been treated in the preceding chapter.[38]

Very similar is the myth of Phylius. It is, however, related only in late authors,[39] and the reason why Phylius performed his deeds is apparently a Hellenistic invention. He was seized by love for a reluctant boy, Cycnus, who imposed upon him the following tasks: to kill a lion without iron, to capture some vultures alive and bring them to him, and to seize a bull in a herd and bring it to the altar of Zeus. There are many traces of late influence in this myth, which is localized between Calydon and Pleuron. We cannot state anything about its age.

The myth of the eponymous hero of the city of Argos is older, for it is mentioned in the Eoeae of Hesiod.[40] To this Argos the deeds belong which are ascribed to Argus with the hundred eyes in Apollodorus.[41] He killed a bull which ravaged Arcadia and put on its hide; he slew Satyrus, who robbed the herds of the Arcadians; he killed the sleeping Echidna, and he avenged the murder of Apis. The tendency appears clearly to make the eponymous hero of Argos rival Heracles, just as the Athenians created his rival in Theseus; but on the other hand these myths are clearly old, or they would not have been localized in Arcadia.

[38] Above pp. 51 *et seq.* and 163 *et seq.* resp.

[39] Ovidius, *Metamorphoses*, vii. 372 *et seq.*; Antoninus Liberalis, *Metamorphoses*, chap. 12.

[40] Hesiod, frag. 137, Rzach ed. 3, according to Paus. ii. 26, 2, where he is said to be father of Epidaurus.

[41] Apollodorus, ii, 1, 2, 2.

Fragments of similar cycles occur elsewhere. Alcathoüs is called the Megarian Heracles. He is an old and important mythical personage and had a cult at Megara. He killed a lion which had torn the son of King Megareus into pieces. Heracles' father Amphitryon killed the Teumessian fox.

It would not be impossible to collect more instances of the same kind, but those already mentioned will suffice to show that this type, a series of valorous deeds, especially the killing or capturing of wild animals, is old and widespread. Folk-tales corroborate this statement. Such a series is similar to a string of pearls. Pearls may be exchanged, taken away, or added, and that is also the case with the cycle of the Twelve Labors of Heracles. The canonical cycle of twelve may as such be rather late, but in principle it is old, and as the myth giving the reason why Heracles performed the Labors clearly is proved to belong to the Mycenaean age, the same must be true of the cycle as a whole, but not necessarily true of every Labor.

In order to test how this result attained by general reasoning is borne out by the myths of the Labors themselves, we turn to a brief analysis of these. The scene of the first five was the northeastern Peloponnese: 1. Heracles killed the Nemean lion; 2. he killed the Hydra of Lerna; 3. he caught the Erymanthian boar and brought it living to Eurystheus; 4. he captured the hind of Ceryneia; 5. he drove away the Stymphalian birds; 6. the sixth Labor, however, the cleaning of the stables of Augeias took place in Elis; 7. the seventh Labor took Heracles to Crete, where he captured the bull; 8. the eighth

took him farther abroad, to Thrace, where he killed
Diomedes and carried off his horses; 9. the ninth
Labor was the fetching of the girdle of the queen of
the Amazons; 10. in the tenth he killed Geryon in
the far west and possessed himself of his cattle;
11. the eleventh Labor was the fetching of the apples
of the Hesperides; 12. finally, the twelfth was the
bringing up of Cerberus from the Underworld.

It will be to the purpose to work backwards, com-
mencing with the last Labors. The natural end of
the hero's career is his acquiring of immortality, and
that is told in doublets. For we have seen that the
bringing back of Cerberus has this significance, and
the same is true of the fetching of the apples of the
Hesperides. The garden of the Hesperides in the
farthest west is identical with the Elysian fields
to which the favorites of the gods are carried alive
to eternal bliss. This idea is pre-Greek.[42] The
inference to be drawn from this fact is that a cycle
of Labors was already formed and provided with its
natural and logical end in the Mycenaean age. As
the Greeks had quite a different idea of the Other
World, they did not realize that both of these adventures stood for Heracles' victory over Death; and as
they wanted a natural and logical end for the cycle,
they added the victory over the realm of Death,
which we have in doublets also, of which one was
received into the cycle, the bringing up of Cerberus;
whilst the combat with the God of Death was

[42] L. Malten, "Elysion und Rhadamanthys," *Jahrbuch des deutschen
archäolog. Instituts*, XXVIII (1912), p. 35 *et seq.* See also my *Minoan-
Mycenaean Religion*, p. 542 *et seq.* For the opposite view see P. Capelle,
"Elysium und die Inseln der Seeligen," *Archiv für Religionswissenschaft*,
XXV (1927), p. 245 *et seq.*, and XXVI (1928), p. 17 *et seq.*

THE LABORS   215

almost forgotten and was remodeled so as to become
the war against Pylos.

The three Labors just mentioned take place in
far-off countries. The expedition against Geryon
and his cattle is especially rich in parerga, which for
want of space must be passed over. I observe only
that Antaeus is by his name shown to be a specter.
For the word *antaios* is used of specters meeting men,
and the goddess of specters, Hecate, is especially
surnamed *antaie*. The feature that Heracles, in
order to overcome Antaeus, must lift him up from the
ground is explained through the idea that a specter
sinks down into the ground and escapes his an-
tagonist. The myth of Geryon was gradually moved
westward; it was perhaps in early times localized
in Epirus. Some scholars think that Geryon is a
figure of the Underworld and his dog Orthrus
identical with Cerberus, but I cannot see sufficient
reason for this view, though it may be possible.

It is uncertain what real fact underlies the myth
of the race of warlike women, the Amazons. The
opinion has been brought forward that they are a
reminiscence of the Hittite empire,[43] but that cannot
be proved conclusively, though it may be possible.
If this is so, the myth originated in the Mycenaean
age. I am not able to make any decision, but I
should like to observe that this myth was so famous
that inevitably it was sooner or later applied to the
most famous hero, Heracles.

King Diomedes, the possessor of the man-eating
horses, lived in Thrace, but the opinion is well
founded that the myth was transferred thither from

[43] W. Leonhard, *Hettiter und Amazonen* (1911).

Greece. For the Thracian Diomedes is certainly identical with the Argive king of that name who has a prominent place in Homer. Diomedes was one of the heroes to whom a long series of adventures on the way back from Troy was attributed; he occurs also very often as the founder of Greek colonies. The fame of Thrace as a horse-breeding country, known as early as in the Homeric poems, may have aided the relocalization of the adventure. Professor Robert has given the opinion that this deed superseded an older one of similar character, viz., the capturing of the first horse, Arion; but he has not proved his point.[44] On the contrary, it ought to be observed that the Homeric as well as the Mycenaean knight needs not one horse but a team, for he does not ride but drives in a chariot. The myth telling how Heracles won his horses seems to me to be old, and we recognized its double in the myth of the seizing of the horses of Laomedon.[45]

If we look away from the details of the myths of Geryon and of Diomedes, their kernel is solely the capture of a famous team of horses or of a herd of cattle, a very common motif of mythology, and merely an echo of the life of a primitive people breeding cattle and horses. Such deeds are sure to be included in the career of a hero created among such a people and in such an age.

The seventh Labor, the capturing of the Cretan bull, is essentially similar to the first five, which are

[44] C. Robert, *loc. cit.*, p. 437. The argument that Heracles appears with only one horse on the metopes from the temple of Zeus at Olympia and from the so-called Theseion in Athens is not sufficient. That may be due to considerations of artistic order.

[45] Above p. 197.

simple deeds of prowess against wild animals; the difference is only that this adventure is localized in a country farther off. I have already said[46] that I cannot see the reason why the myth of the capture of a wild bull should have been transferred from Theseus to Heracles. The Cretan localization is very well understood as a reminiscence of the Cretan bull-ring, and consequently this Labor probably goes back to the Mycenaean and even to the Minoan age.

The opinion has been advanced that the cleaning of the stables of Augeias, which takes place in Elis, is a late addition, but I am not sure that this view is right, for the myth has a folk-tale motif which agrees very well with a humorous conception of Heracles. The first five Labors take place in the northeastern Peloponnese and by reason of this localization they are generally and justly considered to be the earliest of all.

It has been observed that it is difficult and often impossible to prove that a single Labor is of Mycenaean origin, but that on the other hand there are proofs showing as conclusively as is possible in such a matter that the cycle originated in this age. But even if that is true, it ought not to be forgotten that adventures may have been left out or added in later times. The canonical cycle of twelve may in its present form be late, but from the point of view of the principles underlying this discussion, that does not impair its Mycenaean origin.

To finish our exposition we turn to the character of the cycle as a whole. Six Labors are the killing or capturing of wild animals or monsters. Such

[46] Above p. 169.

exploits are really quite primitive in character, much more primitive than the fighting through which Homeric heroes gain fame and glory. Their character thus agrees in a remarkable manner with the customs of primitive peoples, of which for want of space only very few examples can be quoted. If a Wintun Indian has contrived to kill a black bear, a special dance is performed in his honor. A similar custom is found in Central Africa among the Beli when a young man has killed a lion, a leopard, a buffalo, or an elephant. A Hottentot who has killed big game alone is considered to be a hero and claims the right to be treated as such.

Representations of hunting in the art of the historical age of Greece are usually mythological, with one notable exception, the hare-hunting so frequently occurring on proto-Corinthian vases. Hunting of boar, deer, and other animals was a favorite pastime of the Greeks but was not considered heroic. It was otherwise in the Mycenaean age; the Mycenaean gems show very often a man struggling with a lion or a bull, and hunting scenes are not rare in Mycenaean art; e.g. the lion hunt on the inlaid dagger from the fourth shaft-grave at Mycenae and the boar hunt on a wall painting from Tiryns. Mycenaean art corresponds so well to the exploits of Heracles that this coincidence strongly corroborates their Mycenaean origin.

It appears that tales of cattle-lifting agree very well with the life and the customs of this time, although it occurred at other times also. Nor is the humorous myth of the cleaning of the stables filled

[47] Cp. above p. 75.

with dung inappropriate to this age, although the time of the insertion of this myth into the cycle is uncertain, as is also the time of the insertion of the myth concerning the fetching of the girdle of the queen of the Amazons. The result of this survey is the conclusion that a number of the Labors and perhaps the majority show Mycenaean connections. As the myth giving the reason why Heracles performed the Labors is of Mycenaean origin, this result is only natural.

To sum up: In Mycenaean times people told of a strong man, who was called by a common name, Heracles. Exploits which corresponded to the ideas and life of this age and were admired most highly were ascribed to him, and around him clustered many tales of the killing or seizing of wild and dangerous animals and monsters, and probably of cattle-stealing, too. The economy of the folk-tale required a reason for these exploits and a motif through which the deeds could be held together so as to form a series. This motif was found in his being a vassal of the Great King of Mycenae, and his name, Heracles, gave the reason for connecting his myths with Hera, who became his stepmother and the foe of her stepson. His career required an end, and this end was the greatest deed of all, the overcoming of Death; this was told in different versions but one of these, the fetching of the apples from the Gardens of the Hesperides, is clearly of Minoan origin.

People liked, however, to know and to tell something not only of the life and end of the hero but of his birth also. All these myths were developed in the Mycenaean age, for the myth of his birth is firmly bound up with Thebes, and the myth of his Labors with Tiryns, two of the most important centers of Mycenaean civilization. It is just as impossible to discern the reasons for these localizations as to find out why the hero was called Heracles, but they prove that the cycle of Heracles' life was already developed in the Mycenaean age. That is certain so far as the underlying principles are concerned, but details are uncertain and often dubious. In this discussion there is no reason to dwell upon the varied later development of the Heracles cycle.

Chapter IV

OLYMPUS

We are wont to think that the gods of a polytheistic religion are regularly brought into a system
similar to that which we find in the Greek mythology,
but on close consideration it soon appears that there
is nothing in all the religions of the world which
really resembles the Greek State of the Gods. I
need not dwell upon the polytheism of barbarian
peoples, for their gods have hardly been brought into
a fixed system, but I ought to say a few words of
some ancient peoples who are thought to have had
a somewhat similar systematization of their gods;
namely, the Egyptians and the Babylonians.

The systems of gods in Egyptian religion are,
however, essentially dissimilar to the Greek State of
the Gods. Their origin is theological and cosmological speculation which tried to bring the local and
nature gods into a coherent scheme in spite of their
reluctance to fit into it. This attempt was favored
by political considerations, because the independence
of the local gods involved a certain peril for the
unity of the state. The earliest system, the origins
of which probably go back into the predynastic age,
is the solar theology of Heliopolis, in which the
Sun-god was made the chief figure. When at last
Thebes became the capital of Egypt, its local god
Amon, whose origin is rather obscure, became the

chief god of the Egyptian empire and was identified with the Sun-god. His position was due to the fact that Thebes had become the capital of the empire.

In Babylonia a similar situation arose. Theological and cosmological speculation, and the systematization of religion were not wanting, but the creation of a chief god depended even more closely on political circumstances. In old Sumer the god of a city was its supreme ruler and the other gods surrounded him as his court. The god of the heavens, Anu, had the supreme place only in so far as cosmology was concerned; elsewhere Enlil was the chief god, probably owing his position to the power of his city, Nippur. When a city was subdued by another, its god became a vassal of the god of the conquering city; and this relation was expressed by a genealogy. This process appears still more clearly during the power of the Amorites. When Babylon conquered the country and became its capital, the god of Babylon, Marduk, who up to this time was very little known, became the supreme god. When the Assyrians became the dominating people, his rôle was taken up by the god Assur.

The position of Zeus, the supreme Greek god, is due neither to theological speculation nor to the fact that a local cult developed into the cult of an empire, the city of the god becoming the capital of the empire. From the beginning Zeus was venerated by all Greeks and in many places. The Greek State of the Gods was not created to correspond to political conditions, under which one city subjugated other cities and the gods of the conquered cities became subordinate to the god of the victorious city. On the contrary, the god whose character best fitted him for a supreme position became the head of the gods. While in other countries the supreme position of the chief god corresponded to well-known political circumstances, the situation was very different in Greece. In the heavens there was a monarchical rule; on the earth it vanished very early in the historical age.

Ancient writers have said that Homer created the Greek gods. There is a certain amount of truth in this contention, and it is still more true if it is applied to the Greek State of the Gods. For the form in which Homer describes this State was impressed upon the ideas of all coming ages. The problem which is to be treated in this chapter is consequently how the Homeric State of the Gods was created, and especially where its model is to be found. For it is evident and has always been recognized that this model was taken from human life.

This fact is accepted by Dr. Finsler, one of the best Homeric scholars who has treated the question, but as his view is neatly opposed to that which I think well founded, and furthermore is complicated with an analysis of the poems, I am obliged first to discuss his opinions and reasons briefly. In the Homeric poems as they are known to us Dr. Finsler sees a thorough-going remodeling of the conception of the State of the Gods; in fact, he thinks it possible to find and to demonstrate the origin of this idea in our Homeric corpus. In his exposition of the Homeric religion[1] he makes a distinction based on differing

---

[1] G. Finsler, *Homer* (ed. 3; 1924), p. 220 *et seq.*, and "Die olympischen Szenen in der Ilias," *Program*, Bern (1906).

conceptions of the gods between the earlier and later parts of Homer. Thus he detaches the battle of the gods and the scenes enacted on Olympus. Disregarding these parts, as being of later origin, he thinks that in the remaining parts of the poems the gods are far more independent of one another, although the supreme god, Zeus, controls fate. He says that divine genealogies already existed in this stage but that the family of gods was not developed fully.

Thus he gives voice to the opinion that toward the end of the eighth century B.C. a great poet arose who undertook the task of forming the great epos of our Iliad, using the epical poems which existed at that time as materials for his poem. In forming the plot he introduced the idea of a supreme guidance of events by the gods. The detailed descriptions of the family and the state of the gods are due to this poet; he introduced the Olympian scenes. Whilst in the earlier poems the idea prevailed that the gods dwell in the heavens, with which Olympus is here identical, this poet, says Dr. Finsler, recurred to an older, almost forgotten conception of Olympus on the northern confines of Thessaly, as the mountain of the gods, and pictured this dwelling place of the gods with great fantasy.

What is of importance for my purpose is not the detailed description of the life of the gods on Olympus, for this may very well be due to a later remodeling; the salient point is the assertion that the gods are more independent of one another in the earlier parts of the Homeric poems. For on this opinion the contention depends that the State of the

Gods is a poetical fiction created toward the end of the eighth century B.C.

Dr. Finsler is a pupil of Professor Wilamowitz and has in this as in some other cases taken up ideas suggested by this great scholar. Professor Wilamowitz points to the different conceptions of the gods in different parts of Homer and emphasizes the value of this difference for the analysis of the poems.[2] He says, e.g., that the poet of the first book and the parts connected with this book depicts "an ideal world of immortal men, fond of enjoyments and not troubled by moral considerations, with the magical colors of a brilliant fantasy and sensual play." As a contrast to this picture he points to the very old-fashioned manner of the fifth and even of the fourth book.

Space forbids a full discussion and I am only able to select some important and characteristic instances. Such instances are offered especially by the lay of Diomedes; i.e., the fifth book, which Professor Wilamowitz thinks to be the oldest in our Iliad.[3] Our first observation is that the Olympian scenes fill a large part of this very book. And Dr. Finsler must according to his principles detach precisely these as being due to a late poet. The fifth book begins by telling that Athena, alleging the wrath of Zeus, removes Ares from the scene.[4] When Diomedes inflicts a wound on Aphrodite, we hear that the Charites wove her mantle and that her blood is called *ichor;* and an explanation is added that

[2] Wilamowitz, *Die Ilias und Homer* (1916), p. 316, cp. p. 284.
[3] *Loc. cit.*, p. 339.
[4] *Il.* v. v. 29 *et seq.*

the gods are immortal, not eating bread and drinking
wine like mortal men.[5] Then the scene follows in
which Aphrodite asks Ares to bring her to Olympus,
the seat of the Immortal ones. Iris unharnesses the
horses and gives them ambrosia as food. Then
Dione comforts her daughter and in her speech the
most amazing details occur: Heracles once wounded
Hera with an arrow and likewise the God of the
Underworld, Hades, who had to go to Olympus in
order to be healed by the doctor of the gods, Paieon.
After this, Aphrodite is compelled to hear the deris-
ory words of Hera and Athena and the somewhat
kinder exhortations of Zeus.[6] The next Olympian
scene is that in which Iris harnesses the horses for
Hera, and Athena takes the weapons "on the
threshold of her father Zeus." The Horae open the
gates of Olympus when she drives off in her chariot.
The two goddesses first make a visit to Zeus, who
is seated on the highest peak of Olympus, in order
to ask leave to partake in the fight against Ares.[7]
At last Ares is wounded by Diomedes with the help
of Athena, and goes to "the wide heavens" or to
"the steep Olympus," and has to listen to the re-
proofs of Zeus before he is healed by Paieon. Hebe
washes him and he takes his place at the side of
Zeus. Finally Hera and Athena make their return
to the house of Zeus.[8]

There are in this book passages which seem to be
late because older conceptions are remodeled so as
to be misunderstood. Ares leans his spear against a
cloud,[9] while a cloud elsewhere appears as a means

---

[5] *Il.* v. v. 338 *et seq.*   [7] *Il.* v. v. 711 *et seq.*   [9] *Il.* v. v. 356.

[6] *Il.* v. v. 355 *et seq.*   [8] *Il.* v. v. 850 *et seq.*

of concealing gods and men; and Apollo creates an image of the wounded Aeneas around which the battle goes on while Aeneas himself is carried to Pergamon by the god.[10] But on the whole the scenes referred to above are too numerous and too extensive to be considered, generally speaking, as later additions, as Dr. Finsler thinks them. If they are taken away, not much remains. In fact, one comes near the opinion proffered by another Homeric scholar, Professor Bethe, according to whom the fifth book is not old. He thinks that the scene in which Hera and Athena take weapons is an interpolation and in conformity with his principles he is of the opinion that the old kernel is the duels between Diomedes and the two heroes Pandarus and Aeneas respectively.

Professor Wilamowitz has still another opinion.[11] He deprecates the idea that the conception of the gods conspicuous in the fifth book should be in general ascribed to Homer and explains its peculiarity as due to the national antagonism between the Ionians and the Asiatics in the eighth century B.C.; it does not appear clearly whether he is of the opinion that the Olympian scenes are due to a later remodeling. But according to him the fifth book is the oldest book of the Iliad and he thinks that it was composed in Ionia in the eighth century B. C. with the aid of a Theban epos which probably was composed on the mainland. This same book is, according to Dr. Finsler, profoundly remodeled, and according to Professor Bethe in it nothing is old except the duels between Diomedes and Aeneas and Pandarus.

[10] *Il.* v. v. 449.
[11] Wilamowitz, *loc. cit.*, p. 339.

I make no attempt at a criticism. I have reported the opinions of the most prominent adherents of the analytical school in order to emphasize the subjectiveness of this method. Their widely differing results cannot be considered reliable. I shall merely add one remark concerning Dr. Finsler's method, because it is of most importance for my purpose. His premiss is that certain descriptions of the gods are later than others and he judges the age of various passages according to this presumption. If this premiss is questionable, he is working with a *petitio principii*. I fear that for others the old-fashioned appearance of this book depends on this very point, on the manners of the gods.

Clearly no certain result will be attained in this way, and we are obliged to try to find another method. I begin with the very well-known fact that Olympus appears in Homer as the mountain of the gods and as their dwelling place. If we go through all the Homeric passages where Olympus is mentioned, we shall make the following observations. There are only two passages in which Olympus is the dwelling place of Zeus alone; in all other passages it appears that other gods also dwell there together with Zeus. In the two passages referred to[12] it is said that Zeus hurls the thunderbolt or sends a storm. The passages mentioning Olympus as the seat of the gods are, except for the scenes actually enacted on Olympus, distributed rather uniformly; they do not occur in the sixth, ninth, twelfth, seventeenth, and twenty-third books, which are not among the earliest, and their absence is of course

[12] *Il.* xiii. v. 243, and xvi. v. 364.

THE MOUNTAIN OF THE GODS 229

accidental. The conception has taken form in fixed, often repeated phrases and verses: "the seat of Olympus," "he went downward from the peaks of Olympus," "so many gods as there are on Olympus," "the gods, or the immortal ones who possess the Olympian houses."[13] Four times as introduction to an important section the verse occurs:

"Say now, ye Muses, who on Olympus dwell."

It is also to be observed that the phrase "the Olympians" occurs twice in the sense of "the gods." Somewhat more frequently the gods are called "the Heavenly ones" (Οὐρανίωνες) or the "Heavenly Gods" (θεοὶ Οὐρανίωνες). These phrases belong to the elements of Greek mythology, and on them the very common opinion is founded which distinguishes sharply between the Olympian and the Chthonian gods and forgets that in the Iliad Hades himself once is reckoned among the Olympian gods. Olympus and the Heavens appear as identical. It is, e.g., said of Athena that she arose to the great heavens and Olympus.[15] It is, however, more important that this identity appears in the cult; that is, in prayer. People pray to Zeus looking upward toward the heavens.[16] Nestor prays to the Olympian Zeus stretching his hand toward the starry heavens.[17] Of course a man who prays may also turn toward

[13] ἔδος Οὐλύμποιο; βῆ δὲ κατ' Οὐλύμποιο καρήνων; ὅσοι θεοί εἰσ' ἐν Ὀλύμπῳ; θεοί, ἀθάνατοι Ὀλύμπια δώματ' ἔχοντες.

[14] ἔσπετε νῦν μοι, Μοῦσαι Ὀλύμπια δώματ' ἔχουσαι, Il. ii. v. 484; xi. v. 218; vi. v. 218; xiv. v. 508; xvi. v. 112. ii. v. 491 in the beginning the Catalogue of the Ships, Ὀλυμπιάδες Μοῦσαι.

[15] Il. i. v. 497.

[16] Il. iii. v. 364; vii. v. 178.

[17] Il. xv. v. 371.

the place where the god invoked is venerated, but it ought to be observed that it is never said of one who prays that he turns himself toward Olympus.

We see that the gods are in general and as a collective body the Olympians or the Heavenly ones; consequently they dwell on Olympus or in the heavens, but no single god is called an Olympian except Zeus. To this rule there is only one exception; namely, that the Muses in the introduction to the Catalogue of Ships are called the Olympian Muses,[18] a condensation of the verse quoted above in which they are said to possess the Olympian houses.

This difference is not accidental. For the gods, other than Zeus, really dwell originally neither on Olympus nor in the Heavens. Poseidon dwells in the sea and in the rivers, Artemis in the dark forests and on the green meadows. Athena is of course settled on a hill, but that is the acropolis of a city on which the dwellings of men also are erected. Only Zeus dwells originally on Olympus, because he is the weather-god, the cloud-gatherer, the sender of rain and lightning. He hurls the thunderbolt from Olympus.[19] When he sends a squall, a cloud sails from Olympus, from the radiant aether upward into the heavens.[20] This concrete conception of the mountain peak surrounded by clouds from which rainstorm and thunder come shows the nature of Zeus, the weather-god, and in this quality he dwells on Mount Olympus; he is the Olympian one. This same conception of the clouded mountain peak gave also an important contribution to the picture of the City of the Gods. The gates are clouds which are

[18] *Il.* ii. v. 491.   [19] *Il.* xii. v. 240.   [20] *Il.* xvi. v. 364.

opened and shut by the Horae.[21] Hence the other
gods, as well as Zeus himself, are often concealed
beneath clouds.[22] But mountain peak and heavens
are identical because lightning and rain come down
from the heavens as well as from the mountain
peak around which the clouds gather.

Zeus dwells on the mountain peak or in the heavens
—these are the same—because he is the weather-god;
and similarly the other gods dwell wherever their
work is visible. If the other gods are Olympian or
heavenly gods, if they dwell on Olympus, this is due
to the fact that Zeus, the one who alone was originally the Olympian, has lifted them up to his dwelling
place. That the gods dwell on Olympus is so firmly
fixed and thorough-going a conception that the fact
that it is much earlier than the composition of our
Iliad cannot possibly be questioned. It follows, and
this is the salient point, that the other gods were
from of old subordinated to Zeus. Because they
were joined to him as subordinates they had to dwell
in the same place as he. It will be impossible to
find another reason why they have been separated
from their natural working and dwelling places and
lifted up to Olympus or into the Heavens. Zeus is
the Olympian, the ruler; the other gods, the Olympians, are in a certain sense his court. In this subordination of the gods under Zeus, the Olympian
State of the Gods is contained *in nuce*, and this
conception is in no wise due to the development of
epics by Ionian minstrels. It is an ill-founded hypothesis that the gods are more independent in the

[21] *Il*. v. v. 749.

[22] *Il*. xiv. v. 350; xv. v. 153; xx. v. 150, etc., etc.

earlier parts of the Iliad; Dr. Finsler himself confesses that Zeus rules events even in these parts.

We reach the same result if we turn to historical considerations. The world of the gods is subject to monarchical rule, a supreme god is at its head. In Ionia there was nothing but political lack of unity; there were quite a number of kings and princes, one in each town. The Ionians knew of course a Great King, but he was a foreigner, the Phrygian monarch. The Ionians with their lack of political unity and unified government would never have been able to conceive the idea of concentrating all the gods under a monarchical rule, under one supreme god.

It is recognized that the model of the State of the Gods is to be found in human conditions. We do not find the necessary conditions in Ionia and must turn elsewhere. The current answer is: turn to Thessaly. Mount Olympus is situated in Thessaly, and we find there in historical times an aristocratic state with one ruler, over the whole country. These facts have contributed largely to the popularity of the opinion that epical poetry originated in Thessaly and from there was carried to Asia Minor. It is impossible to discuss this extensive problem in this place; moreover the popularity of this view has vanished to a certain extent. The reasons supporting it have been proved to be more specious than founded on facts. That the chief hero of the Iliad, Achilles, is localized at Spercheus or in Phthia in no way proves that Greek epic poetry, generally speaking, originated in these districts. If the Aeolic dialect was, as seems certain, much more widely spread on the mainland in earlier than in later times, the argument that the epics were Thessalian in origin, because their language was originally Aeolic, is fallacious.

The two arguments referred to, by which the origin of the State of the Gods is explained from Thessalian conditions, have always been considered as almost self-evident, but even they ought to be subjected to an inquiry.   I commence with the political conditions of Thessaly.   Our knowledge of these is regrettably slight and opinions differ markedly.   Professor Hiller von Gaertringen published long ago a valuable paper[23] in which he proved that in the sixth and fifth centuries B.C. there were at the same time several kingly houses in Thessaly, each possessing a limited district.   This fact is recognized, but he proceeds to assume that neither a ruler of all Thessaly nor a state comprising all Thessaly existed before the year 460 B. C., that common enterprises brought about only an occasional union; and that the tradition of the overlordship, the *tageia*, goes back only to the rule of Iason of Pherae in the fourth century B.C.[24]   These conclusions are, however, hardly warranted, and the *tageia*, the overlordship over all Thessaly, is probably of older origin;[25] but it was no kingship in the real sense and has evidently nothing to do with that kingship which was inherited from olden times.   The name is not that always carried by Greek kings whose kingship was handed

[23] F. Hiller von Gaertringen, "Das Königtum bei den Thessalern" in the volume *Aus der Anomia* (1890), p. 1 *et seq.*

[24] With this view O. Kern agrees in his paper "Die Landschaft Thessalien und die griechische Geschichte," *Neue Jahrbücher für die klass. Altertumswissenschaft*, XIII (1904), p. 219 *et seq.*

[25] See Ed. Meyer, *Theopomps Hellenika* (1909), p. 12 *et seq.*

down from olden times, *basileus*,[26] but another, *tagos*. If the list of the *tagoi* is made up, we see that these rulers were taken from different families belonging to different towns.[27] Their position was not due to any hereditary principle but to election and they were elected only in case of need. A *tagos* was elected for his lifetime; although there were periods without any *tagos*.

This institution of an overlord elected occasionally resembles very little the Olympian State of the Gods ruled by Zeus. The Thessalian *tagos* had not at all the same full power as the King of the Gods, nor did he inherit his throne as did Zeus. The Thessalian states were more oligarchic than monarchical in character. Of course it may be contended that the power of the Thessalian *tagos* was once hereditary. That can neither be proved nor refuted. As far as we can see, the model of the Greek State of the Gods cannot have been the Thessalian institutions.

The most valuable and the strongest argument for its Thessalian origin is, however, the fact that the mountain of the gods, Olympus, the mightiest mountain of Greece, the peaks of which rise high into the sky, is situated on the northern boundary of that province. It is certain that Homer has the Thessalian Olympus in mind. This appears clearly in a passage[28] where Hera, in order to entice Zeus

[26] The gods are never called βασιλεύς, only ἄναξ. Βασιλεύς is probably a pre-Greek word, and this is of a certain importance in corroborating my view concerning the Mycenaean kingship. See J. Wackernagel, *Sprachliche Untersuchungen zu Homer* (1916), p. 211 *et seq.*

[27] They are registered by K. J. Beloch, *Griech. Geschichte*, (ed. 2), I: 2, p. 197.

[28] *Il.* xiv. v. 225 *et seq.*; cp. *Od.* v. v. 50.

into love, leaves Mount Olympus, enters Pieria and
the beautiful Emathia, hurries over the snow-clad
peaks of the Thracian mountains, and from Mount
Athos goes over the sea to Lemnos, where she en-
counters Hypnus. Here the poet obviously refers
to the Thessalian Olympus. But if argument on
such minute points is permissible, there is at least
one passage in which this mountain cannot be referred to, even if we except the two passages where
Olympus may be whatever mountain you like.[29] At
the beginning of the second book of the Iliad[30] we
hear that Eos ascended the great Olympus in order
to let the light appear for Zeus and the other gods.
If we in these words should recognize the concrete
view of the rosy dawn breaking forth over the peaks
of Mount Olympus, the poet's viewpoint must be
west of the mountain and that is not suitable for
the Thessalian Olympus. But I think that it would
be hasty to draw a conclusion from such a minute
point. It is certain at least in one case and perhaps
probable in more that Homer refers to the Thessalian Olympus, but the last-mentioned passage may
raise the question whether this was so always and
originally.

There exist a fair number of mountains called
Olympus.[31] Mount Lykaion in Arcadia and a hill
near Sellasia had this name; Pisa was situated
between two hills, Olympus and Ossa, and there
was another Olympus in Elis.[32] It is not clear which

[29] Above p. 218, n. 12.

[30] *Il.* ii. v. 48 *et seq.*

[31] They are enumerated in Roscher's *Lexikon der Mythologie*, s. v.
Olympus; and in A. B. Cook, *Zeus*, I, p. 100.

[32] *Schol. Apollon. Rhod.* i. v. 599.

Olympus Diodor has in mind.[33] I pass over the mountains which in modern times have this name, on Euboea, near Laurium, and on the island of Scyros. The name is still more frequent in Asia Minor, where Mount Olympus is found in Lydia, Mysia, Bithynia, Galatia, Lycia, and on Cyprus. In view of the fame of the Thessalian Olympus it may perhaps be contended and believed that all these mountains are named after that celebrated mountain. A borrowing took place, it seems to be certain, when the two hills between which Pisa was situated were called Olympus and Ossa, but borrowing cannot be the general rule. For the name of the famous sanctuary in Elis, Olympia, is of course old and cannot etymologically be separated from the name of the mountain. If a borrowing were supposed in this case, it would involve us in unsurmountable difficulties, and these are complicated by the fact that Hera seems to be older in this place than Zeus.

The name Olympus is certainly one of the many pre-Greek words which the Greek language took over from the earlier inhabitants of the country.[34] All attempts to find a probable etymology in connection with Greek words or stems have been vain. Its very form seems to make its pre-Greek origin probable and its widespread occurrence in western Asia Minor fits in admirably with this opinion. The conclusion is warranted that Olympus is a pre-Greek word signifying "mountain," just as Ida, another mountain name occurring in Asia Minor and on Crete, has the significance of a forest-clad mountain.

[33] Diodorus, v. 80.

[34] C. Theander in the periodical *Eranos*, XV (1916), p. 127 *et seq.*

Both words were taken over by the Greeks who took possession of the country and were used by them as names of various mountains.

If this is so, it coincides perfectly with the original character of Zeus who, being the weather-god, the cloud-gatherer, the rain-giver, and the thrower of the thunderbolt, always dwells on the loftiest mountain peak in the neighborhood, around which the clouds gather and from which rain and thunder break forth. Consequently it is to be assumed that there existed several mountains with the name of Olympus in Greece, and thus Zeus was called the Olympian. At last this name was given principally to the mightiest and loftiest of all, the Thessalian Olympus, and Homer completed its fame, to the exclusion of others.

Thus we are not compelled to ascribe the origin of the conception of the mountain of the gods to Thessaly. I cannot but think it to be extremely improbable that two creations of such a thorough-going importance for Greek literature and religion as the Homeric epics and the Olympian State of the Gods should have originated in a province which never had the least importance in the spiritual life of the Greeks nor was penetrated by either the Mycenaean or the the historical Greek culture except at a late date and superficially. It seems to be much more likely on general grounds, and I have tried to prove it with specific arguments, that the conception of the mountain of the gods and of the subordination of the other gods under Zeus is an idea common to all Greeks, just as was the idea of the weather-god dwelling on a mountain in the neighborhood. From this new starting point we recur to the question of the origin of this conception. For it is impossible to doubt that the subordination of the other gods under Zeus was modeled upon the social and historical conditions of a certain age. We must try to find out which age this is. Cosmological ideas can have contributed but slightly to its origin.

We have seen that the conception of Olympus, the mountain where the gods dwell, subject to Zeus, and to which, because of this subordination, they were lifted up from their natural working and dwelling places, is pre-Homeric. Thus it is very probable that the model ought to be sought in the Mycenaean age. Our knowledge of the dark age between the downfall of the Mycenaean civilization and the new rise of civilization in the developed Geometric period is very meager, but the poor quality and the scarcity of archaeological materials from this intermediate age make it extremely improbable that such a great conception as the coordination of the gods under a monarchical rule originated in this age.

In the Mycenaean age conditions were different. The great architectural monuments and the precious works of art testify to the power and the wealth of the princes of this age. In view of the stately bee-hive tombs of Mycenae a pharaonic power has been ascribed to the kings of Mycenae. This opinion is understandable but it is not correct. With the aid of Homer it is possible to get at a closer and better understanding of the Mycenaean kingship. I have tried to do that in another place.[35] It ought, how-

[35] In my paper "Das homerische Königtum," *Sitzungsberichte der preuss. Akademie der Wissenschaften*, 1927, p. 23 *et seq.*

ever, be observed that here we meet the difficulty which we always meet when we try to conceive a historical idea of the prehistoric age of Greece: arguments are not logically binding in the strict sense, we are always compelled to be content with probabilities and analogies. Whosoever refuses to believe in them is of course justified: but it is not justifiable to take up a negative standpoint only. A really historical mind cannot give up the attempt to form an idea of the social and political conditions of this age of the greatness of which the monuments give such an impressive and concrete picture.

I must explain my opinion briefly. The fundamental fact is that the Mycenaean age was a period of very extensive movements and migrations of the Greek tribes. Opinions differ as to the time when the Greeks first invaded Greece. At all events a long time must have elapsed before they completely possessed themselves of the country. The wandering tribes went still farther, following the old highway which, along the southern coast of Asia Minor, led toward the old civilized countries of the Near East. They colonized the island of Cyprus and appeared in the Delta of the Nile about 1200 B. C. With this series of events the great Achaean kingdom, comprising Greece and parts of Asia Minor, would fit in admirably. Although its existence, which Dr. Forrer believed he had discovered, is denied, it is but what we should expect under the given conditions.[36]

Many scholars are inclined to think that these migrations were disconnected raids of small bands of

[36] Cp. above p. 60.

freebooters and adventurers,[37] but that is an idea in which I cannot possibly concur. Such disconnected raids and small bands would have been dissolved and have vanished without having such immense consequences as resulted, history proves, e.g. from the Greek colonization of Pamphylia and Cyprus. If an organization was wanting, the conditions of these migrations made it necessary to build one up. A comparison with the migrations of the Teutonic tribes at the end of the classical period and the beginning of the Middle Ages and with the expeditions of the Vikings is very valuable and illuminating. Even the expeditions of the Vikings were not merely disconnected raids; behind them was the well developed military organization of the Scandinavian kingdoms, an organization which has been for the most part unnoticed. The Danish king, Canute the Great, conquered England, and Swedish chiefs founded the Russian empire of Kieff. The eastern Teutonic tribes which undertook the most extensive wanderings developed a much stronger organization of the kingship than the tribes of western Germany which were more sedentary.

The Teutonic kingship offers a precious analogy to the Greek kingship. It was hereditary in a certain family. It preserved so much of its religious origin that the king was held responsible for the luck and good fortune of his people. (There is a trace of this same idea in Homer.[38]) The king was in the first place a war-king, leader of the military expeditions; he had at his side a council of chiefs and the

[37] E.g. G. Murray, *The Rise of the Greek Epics* (ed. 3), p. 127 *et seq.*
[38] *Od.* xix. v. 109 *et seq.*

assembly of the army, the earliest form of the popular assembly. The power of the king was small during peace but waxed greatly in war. The old hereditary Greek kingship is precisely of the same kind, as is proved by the institutions of Macedonia and Sparta, where it was preserved.

The Homeric kingship is of the same kind also. Agamemnon is in the first place a war-king; moreover, his kingship is hereditary and invested with a rather full power. We see that especially in the famous passage in the second book which is generally recognized as reflecting early conditions.[39] The king appears in the popular assembly carrying the scepter which Zeus gave to his ancestor Pelops and which had been handed down through the generations of the kingly family until Thyestes gave it to Agamemnon to rule over all Argos and many islands. In view of this passage many scholars have recognized that Agamemnon was a Great King who held sway over many vassals. Although the vassals are very obstinate and inclined to quarrel and to extend their independence, this respect for the king is ingrained. Old Nestor gives the good counsel to avoid strife with the king who carries the scepter.[40]

At the side of the king we find the assembly of the army, which is convoked to discuss important matters. The members give voice to their opinions in speeches or acclamations, but the decision depends on the king alone; he is able to make a decision which runs counter to the opinion of the assembly, as

[39] *Il.* ii. v. 100 *et seq.*; cp. above p. 43 *et seq.*

[40] *Il.* i. v. 277 *et seq.*; ix. v. 37 *et seq.*; cp. iv. v. 402.

Agamemnon does in refusing to let Chryses ransom his daughter in spite of the Achaeans' approval of Chryses' request.[41]

The chiefs appear throughout as the king's vassals, although their stubbornness and endeavors to guard and to extend their independence are very prominent. How this state of affairs was fostered and promoted is shown by another consideration. The aim and at the same time the reward of the war was booty. The king received the lion's share; large parts were selected for the chiefs; and the men of the people were content to divide what remained. It is to be observed that in the period during which the Greeks were taking possession of the country, the booty consisted not only of implements, cattle, slaves, and so forth, but also of land and towns. The territory was divided; selected parts were given to the gods and to the king (they were called *temenos*), and parcels were divided among the men of the people by allotment; hence they were called lots (*kleroi*). Certain passages of the Iliad prove that the king possessed towns which he was able to give over to others.[42] These towns belonged of course to his part of the booty and he could dispose of them only by giving them to men whom he trusted and who possessed them as his vassals. The vassals strove to guard their interests and to enlarge their independence. The power of the king depended

[41] *Il.* i. v. 22 *et seq.*

[42] Agamemnon promises to give seven towns in Messenia to Achilles *Il.* ix. v. 144 *et seq.* (cp. above p. 84 *et seq.*). Menelaus expresses the wish to evacuate a town in order to settle Odysseus there with his people, *Od.* iv. v. 174 *et seq.* Peleus settles the fugitive Phoenix in the extremity of Phthia as ruler of the Dolopes, *Il.* ix. v. 480 *et seq.*

on his energy, and its basis was his retainers, his personal followers.

As long as the wars and military expeditions went on, the duty of the vassals to follow the king was effective and they were obliged to obey him. The power of the king was correspondingly great. But when the military expeditions ceased and people stayed at home each in his town, the subordination of the vassals to the king was weakened and vanished; for the organization just sketched was good for war only. The king had no means of checking the striving of his vassals to assert their independence. The decay of the kingly power has progressed far in some parts of the Iliad and still farther in the Odyssey, but we recognize that this power was once very full.

The Mycenaean monuments teach us in what age kings with such power existed; witness the stately bee-hive tombs, especially those of Mycenae which are both imposing and well built; and the wealth of precious objects in the shaft-graves of Mycenae and in the recently discovered bee-hive tomb at Dendra near Midea. The large and stately halls of the palaces are illuminating in regard to daily life. On the floor of the hall in the palace at Tiryns a separate section is marked off by the floor painting; it cannot but be the place set apart for the throne of the king. Each of these princes governed his people but was subject to the Great King, with whom of course each strove to compete in splendor. The full power of the Great King of the Mycenaean age, which we recognize from a comparison between the traces of it left in Homer and the Mycenaean monuments, supplies precisely the wanted model, which is sought in vain elsewhere, of the power of the King of the Gods.

We return to the State of the Gods. In regard to the Olympian scenes attention has been especially and unduly directed toward the strife between the gods, their refractoriness and stubbornness, their attempts to delude Zeus by ruse, the pride of Zeus in his strength, and the threats which he showers upon his adversaries. These descriptions are sometimes tainted with burlesque, a tone due to the Ionian minstrels, who were fundamentally irreligious. They remodeled earlier myths according to their taste; e.g. the holy wedding of Zeus and Hera is made a rather sensual love affair.

Much less has it been noticed that the gods many times show a very great veneration and respect for their king, and monarchical rule is an exception in Greece. Due regard ought to be given to these features also; they are earlier and were partly obliterated by later ideas. When Zeus enters among the gods gathered on Olympus, nobody dares to remain on his seat; but they all rise to greet him.[43] They recognize his rule as a self-evident fact, saying: "Thou rulest among the Immortal ones."[44] There are occasions where the gods obey his orders without any idea of opposition. Thetis does so when Zeus bids her go to Achilles and tell him to give over the corpse of Hector to Priam,[45] and Hera when she brings to Poseidon the order of Zeus to desist from fighting; that, however, was after she had enticed Zeus into love in order to divert his attention from

[43] *Il.* i. v. 534.
[44] *Il.* xviii. v. 366.
[45] *Il.* xxiv. v. 90 *et seq.*

the battle.[46]   Once when Athena and Hera are on
their way to the battle they go back at the command
of Zeus;[47] in another chant they make a visit to
Zeus in order to gain permission to take the field
against Ares;[48] and later they hold Ares back from
throwing himself into the fight.[49]   We hear often
how highly the gods fear and respect Zeus.

It is frequently stated that the reason for this
overwhelming power is the strength of Zeus, and
Zeus himself illustrates this by coarse instances, e.g.
the punishment of Hera[50] and the tug of war.[51]
Poseidon tells in plain words why he obeys: Zeus is
much stronger than he.[52]   But this superior strength
is not the only reason.   When Zeus sends the command to Poseidon to desist from helping the Greeks,
he claims not only superior strength but also his
right as the elder brother.[53]

The following passage is illuminating.   We hear
that the sons of Cronus took possession of their inheritance and divided it; each got his part, but the
earth and Olympus remained, being common property.   They were selected in the same way as was a
temenos.   Poseidon says, just as an obstinate vassal
would, that Zeus ought to be content with the third
part allotted to him; he is of the opinion that Zeus
ought to allow the other gods to act as they please.
But Iris reminds him that the Erinyes always follow

[46] *Il.* xv. v. 78.
[47] *Il.* viii. v. 432.
[48] *Il.* v. v. 753 *et seq.*
[49] *Il.* xvi. v. 21.
[50] *Il.* xv. v. 127.
[51] *Il.* viii. v. 19 *et seq.*
[52] *Il* viii. v. 209: ἐπεὶ ἦ πολὺ φέρτερός ἐστι; cp. xv. v. 108.
[53] *Il.* xv. v. 165: εὖ φημι βίῃ πολὺ φέρτερος καὶ γενεῇ πρότερος.

the eldest brother—and Poseidon obeys. Zeus has inherited the kingdom by virtue of his being the eldest brother; this is the moral ground of his position as ruler.

Close scrutiny shows that the power of Zeus is much greater than that of Agamemnon, not to speak of the historical Greek kings. He is much more impatient of opposition, and more veneration is shown to him. How came Zeus into possession of this full power which of course did not originally belong to the weather-god? Everyone repeats the phrase that the model must be sought in human conditions, but nobody has followed the idea to its logical conclusion. As attention was directed to the strife of the gods, the fundamental question was forgotten. Why was the supreme rule attributed to Zeus and why was he invested with such full kingly power?

This conception lent to the Greek, or more justly to the Homeric, World of Gods a strictly monarchical constitution, which became later even the starting point of a kind of monotheism. Nothing similar is found elsewhere among polytheistic peoples. It is a necessary assumption that a historical development is behind this conception; i.e., Zeus was not the supreme god in the beginning; and that he was not is corroborated by the fact that he does not possess a like supreme position in the Greek cult and popular belief of a later age. The monarchical constitution of the State of the Gods is specifically Homeric, and Homer impressed it upon later generations. These took over the idea but had not the right appreciation of it. The real ground of the supremacy of Zeus, the right of the eldest brother, was superseded by a current folk-tale motif, which made Zeus the youngest son of Cronus, and Hesiod had already made the gods elect Zeus their king after the victory over the Titans.[54] The forms of Greek political life diverged ever more from those of the State of the Gods. In the Heavens monarchy prevailed, on the earth the republic. The attempt of Hesiod to make the State of the Gods follow the development of earthly politics failed.

The supreme rule of Zeus is due to a historical development for which human life presented the model. We do not find the model in Ionia, which was not united by a monarch but split up into a number of petty cities ruled by the aristocracy. Nor do we find it in Thessaly, for the power of the *tagos* is a rather poor and late image of kingly power. Nothing remains but the mighty war-kings of the age of the great migrations of the Greek tribes, the Mycenaean age. Only here can such a full kingly power be presupposed as to correspond to the power of the King of the Heavens.

The partition of the world by the three sons of Cronus is thought to be an old cosmogonic myth. This may be true to a certain extent, but cosmogonic speculations do not explain the manner of the partition. The sons of Cronus divide the world among themselves in the same manner as the sons of Aristomachus divided the Peloponnese. It is characteristic that both the conquered country and the world are considered to be possessions of the ruling family and are divided among the heirs of the ruler. As far as we know Greek conditions, this is unthink-

[54] Hesiod, *Theogony*, v. 881.

able, but in the Mycenaean age, in which the king gave away towns at his pleasure, it is quite natural.

Other features of the myth will be better understood from this point of view, if the myth is taken not as free poetical fiction but as a reflection of life; it is so certainly to a great extent. In the stormy age of the great migrations of the peoples, there must have occurred frequently, in the ruling families, strife and contentions which often had a tragic and gloomy issue; heroic mythology is crowded with such tales. Zeus possessed himself of his kingship by an act of violence against his father, and other gods made the attempt to deprive him of it. The myth that Hera, Poseidon, and Athena tried to fetter him but that Thetis injected fear into them, fetching the hundred-armed Briareos,[55] resembles strikingly, if the mythical color is disregarded, a story telling of an attempted revolt in a kingly family, which was quelled by calling upon foreign aid.

The other gods appear as the retainers of Zeus whom he summons to counsel or to meals just as Agamemnon summons the elders. Just as the war-king summons the army assembly, Zeus summons twice an assembly of the gods in which even the lesser gods take part.[56] The rivers, and the nymphs of the springs and of the meadows are mentioned especially. This may be thought to be a later invention, but it is very noticeable that Poseidon once does his brother the service of unharnessing his horses;[57] i.e., his relation to Zeus is that of a "friend"

[55] *Il.* i. v. 400 *et seq.*

[56] In the beginning of the eighth and the twentieth books.

[57] *Il.* viii. v. 440.

or "servant," as the Iliad calls the retainers of the king. On the other hand there are of course heralds and servants on Olympus also. The Horae harness and unharness the horses and give them food and open and shut the gates of Olympus.

The gods could be conceived as vassals of the supreme god, since they ruled each over his domain; this conception got the upper hand, since it corresponded to the subject of the Iliad, the war about Troy, in which the gods also took part. This conception agreed also with the inclination of epic poetry to favor the vassals in opposition to their suzerain. A very common motif of epic poetry is wrath or strife between two heroes.[58] The famous Olympian scenes are due to this predilection of the minstrels.

The Olympian scenes as they are depicted in detail wear of course partly the stamp of a later age, that in which nobility ruled the state, but it is doubtful if the conditions of this period were the model of the description of Olympus in its essential outlines. Zeus is seated on the highest peak when he desires to be alone. He has there a magnificent palace in which the gods assemble for meals and for taking counsel. It is surrounded by the dwellings of the other gods. The City of the Gods is surrounded by a wall the gates of which are watched by the Horae. This picture corresponds of course to the conditions at the beginning of the historical age of Greece, in which every city had a king whose house was situated on the acropolis, surrounded by the dwell-

[58] Cp. my paper "Götter und Psychologie bei Homer," *Archiv fur Religionswissenschaft*, XXII (1923–24), p. 364.

ings of the noblemen; but it corresponds also to the
conditions of the Mycenaean age, in which the
stately palace of the king was also situated on
an acropolis and was surrounded by the dwellings
of his retainers. There are other houses than the
palace on the acropolis at Mycenae and at Tiryns.
The great number of graves with rich and precious
funeral furniture is a proof of a numerous and
well-to-do or even wealthy population. The picture
of the City of the Gods on Olympus may go back
into the Mycenaean age. The idea arose spon-
taneously as soon as the gods were transferred to
Olympus as subjects of Zeus. A later age took the
picture to be natural and embellished it further. In
a well-known passage of the Odyssey the features of
the description are taken from the Minoan idea of
the fields of the Blest.[59]

Opinions may differ in regard to this and other
details, but that is unimportant if only the chief
outlines are recognized. I conclude my argument
by summarizing these outlines:

That a monarch was put at the head of the gods is
in Greece as well as in other countries due to political
conditions. This idea did not originate in Greece,
as it did in other countries, from the fact that a city
made other cities and their gods subject to its god.
In Greece that god became supreme god who was
fittest by virtue of his nature—the weather-god, the
cloud-gatherer and sender of rain and thunder, who
dwelt upon the mountain peaks; that is, upon
Olympus. As the other gods were made his subjects,
they were transferred to his dwelling place, Olympus

[59] *Od.* vi. v. 42 *et seq.*

or the Heavens, from their natural working and dwelling places. The conception of Olympus as the common dwelling place of the gods originated in the pre-Homeric age and by the time of the Homeric poetry had been long established. The model of the monarchical institutions of the State of the Gods is not to be found in the social and political institutions of the historical age of Greece, which deviated ever more from this pattern. Such a full kingly power as that of the supreme god can be ascribed only to the mighty kings of the Mycenaean age who built stately palaces and imposing tombs for themselves, were surrounded by a retinue, and exercised their sovereignty over a number of vassals. In such conditions the models of the strife and the contentions between the gods are also to be found. On the whole the monarchical power of Zeus is such as is found in no other time than the Mycenaean age. The idea of Olympus and the State of the Gods under a strong monarchical rule originates in the Mycenaean age.

INDEX

INDEX